W9-BHZ-360

CROSS-COUNTRY SKIING GUIDE

CROSS-COUNTRY SKIING GUIDE

Edited by John Hamburger

World Publications, Inc.
Mountain View, California

Recommended Reading:
Nordic World Magazine, Box 366,
Mountain View, CA 94042; $6.50/year
Write for a free catalog of publications.

Library of Congress Cataloging in Publication Data

Cross-country skiing guide.

    Includes index.
    1. Cross-country skiing—Addresses, essays, lectures.
2. Cross-country skiing—United States—Guide-books.
3. United States—Description and travel—1960-
Guide-books.   I.   Hamburger, John, 1948-
GV854.9.C7C76   917.3   78-55791
ISBN 0-89037-131-8

©1978 by
World Publications
P.O. Box 366
Mountain View, CA 94042

Library of Congress Number 78-55791
ISBN 0-89037-131-8

CONTENTS

Foreword

It was very cold with a rising wind. The summit of Mt. McKinley still was clear above, but the lower ridges were dams over which the deteriorating weather spilled. I sat wedged into a crevasse, the tips of my boots and crampons hanging over the blue depth below. My hands were clumsy in heavy mittens, making difficult the rope belaying of my partners up the steep slope. This trip was ski touring in the extreme. We were midway through the first ski circuit of McKinley within the limits of its glacial system. For one of the first times light touring skis (47-mm waist width) and specially designed 50-mm racing boots were used for transportation in the high mountains. We were pushing the limits of our abilities and our equipment, just as racers do on their prepared competition tracks. But our skis were performing in a very different arena from that of the racer.

The McKinley Expedition was my fourth of a series of long ski treks in North America. A couple of years ago I realized that skiing was extremely important to me. It was, really, my life. Everything I did as an occupation—writing, photography, teaching, adventuring, lecturing, and consulting—was somehow rooted in skiing.

Recently, I also discovered the joys of racing. Although racing lies at the other end of the ski touring spectrum from expeditions, it has been equally important to me. Last year, in an obvious lapse of sanity, I found myself once again lined up on the starting line. The gun sent me off with a few others in local races, with a thousand in the 60-kilometer Vermont Marathon, and with 2,500 in the American Birkebeiner. (There racers pay good money as an entry fee to leave a nice warm bed at 5 a.m., attempt to force a predawn breakfast down into a butterfly-infested stomach, and hurl themselves against that first horrible hill of 400 vertical feet. That inevitably entails herringboning on each other's skis at the top.)

I had hardly raced since leaving "serious" competition in 1969. The years away from high-pressure racing had mellowed my outlook on racing, as had seven years skiing in the western mountains of the U.S. Now as I race I talk to other competitors as we cruise through the course. I encourage those I pass, and especially those that pass me. It is fun now. I think the reason that I can occasionally place respectably with minimum training is because my mind works differently than it did when I was on the national team. Enjoyment produces results.

John Caldwell, who gets around pretty well for a Vermonter, used to be a coach of the national team. He is a man who leads his life on the premise of serious enjoyment. At the time that I was an uptight racer, I never understood what he was trying to do for us. One cannot race effectively with a knotted mind. Only now do I understand the importance of his attempts at making training fun.

Cross-country skiing should be nothing but pure enjoyment. It can be enjoyed on various levels: the races are fun, the overnight trips are challenging, the teaching and learning are rewarding, and the off-trail tours are relaxing.

Cross-country should be enjoyed on your own terms, in your own way. It is true, as Peter Davis writes, "Improving your skiing technique is probably the most significant single factor linked to continued enjoyment of the sport." Bob Woodward is right when he keeps you on the straight and narrow with quality equipment advice. Wayne Merry explains the joys and realities of true wilderness skiing that you will discover if you are totally committed. These people write from extensive experience. You'll enjoy skiing more if you follow their advice.

No matter how fast, how far, or how hard you ski, a relaxed fun style of skiing is the key. In a world that speeds on at an ever-accelerating rate, we all need the relaxation of the woods and meadows; of jogging, laughing, and learning simple transportation; of adventures; of low-key competition; of freedom of cross-country skiing.

Cross-country is a multifaceted adventure. The shufflers can go a flat, slow kilometer. The daredevils can fly down a tree-speckled, powder-laden slope. The racer-scientists can wax skis to perfection. The nonchalants can hitch on a pair of waxless boards. There is something here for all of us—a truly remarkable sport.

There is something in the *Cross-Country Skiing Guide* for all of us regardless of skiing ability. This is the way a book on the sport ought to be written. John Hamburger has gone out and found those who are experts in particular fields. In this way not only has he obtained the best information, but he has also included different authors' opinions, feelings, and sensitivities.

People write poorly about subjects in which they have little interest. I love skiing, but dislike writing about equipment; this comes through in the overall feeling of my equipment writing. But Bob Woodward has fun with his equipment articles. He somehow brings life to those inanimate pieces of fiberglass, wood, metal, and leather. And he concentrates on the essential in equipment purchase—quality.

The book provides an overall view of cross-country as it is in the U.S. today. Many authors supply the objectivity that is so hard to obtain from one author. You'll get to know lots of new people as you tour through the *Guide.*

One of the most intriguing authors is Lito Tejada-Flores. Don't miss him. Lito is definitely on my list of the ten most perceptive lads involved in skiing. In his chapter on winter safety, he asks some broad questions, especially concerning responsibility.

The chapters on training and conditioning are reasonably sophisticated, but still applicable to the layman interested in discovering how one's body operates and how to lead a healthy life. Trina Hosmer follows with realistic and practical advice on how to fit a bit of physical fitness into the hectic lives most of us lead.

When we had skied about 52 kilometers into the Vermont Marathon last year, Bob Gray said to me, "Keeps you honest, doesn't it!" As I was contemplating this, he coolly double-poled away out of sight. Quite rude I thought. In his chapter on training Bob makes another statement that is the key to it all: "Still, I haven't found that my ideas have changed much [over the years]."

If you finish this book with no other realization, remember this: the values one seeks in skiing across the countryside are the same as they have always been. They are unchanged by the new materials that are used in equipment, the new techniques of hot racers, the waxing fads, clothing fashions, advertising, ski cosmetics, and publicity. You still look for equipment that performs for your ability and use, technique that is efficient and effective, and clothing that protects while allowing free movement. With the entry of popularity and pressure sales into the cross-country scene, keep a level head even though those about you may be losing theirs.

In the end we are all looking for a pastime that is fun and rewarding. Gather information from books such as the *Guide* and from people with experience. Discover the traditional values; they will serve you well during your cross-country career. The most important thing is to be out there skiing and having fun, not worrying about what brand of ski you are using. It is the skiing that I love, not the frills.

If I were to reread the *Guide*, I would read David Brower's chapter first, then Bob Gray's. Why? They truly love skiing, but from very different sides: Brower via wilderness and Gray via racing. It will set you off on the right track.

—Ned Gillette

Introduction

In the past decade, there has been a revolution in the sport of skiing. Today, many people are seeking a sport that combines the thrills of speeding down an open slope, the beauty of weaving through a forest in winter, and the peace of skiing off the well-tracked path, away from the hordes. Cross-country skiing offers all of these—in wilderness settings, each with its unique challenges. Anyone, no matter what level of skill, can take part in cross-country skiing.

Whether you approach cross-country (or Nordic) skiing as a novice or as an experienced downhiller, you will find the sport exhilarating and challenging. Approach it on your own terms. Appraise your own capabilities and physical condition, and begin with a program that is reasonable for yourself. That is what the *Cross-Country Skiing Guide* is all about. I have compiled a book that includes vital information to prepare beginning- to intermediate-level skiers to embark on the trails. This book can help you at the early stages, when you are wondering what equipment you will need, and how to plan your first ski tour. It can also give you direction in training to improve your speed and endurance, so you can extend your tours or enter your first citizen race. And if you are interested in braving the cold for the beauty of snow camping, the *Guide* will help prepare you for that, so you can approach it safely and with minimum hassle.

Beginning with a brief history of the sport, the *Guide* moves directly to a discussion of the equipment you will need for your first day tour. This is not a brand guide, but rather a consumer's guide that discusses the most important factors to consider when choosing boots, skis, poles, and clothing. The equipment section will help you decide between waxable and waxless skis, and offers guidelines for waxing.

The training section discusses the physiological basis of cross-country skiing, so you will understand the physical demands of the sport. There is a discussion of injury prevention and cure. The psychological demands of cross-country training and racing are also covered—including the psychological aspects of high-level competition.

Preseason and on-snow training techniques are presented in a progressive format, so that you can tailor the training program to your own fitness (and interest) level. The training program is similar to the one used by the U.S. Nordic Ski Team, except that it begins at a more basic level. Two of the top cross-country competitors of the past few years offer sound training advice. Trina Hosmer (U.S. team, 1970-74) offers realistic training advice from one who is a serious competitor, but must squeeze training into a busy work schedule. And Bill Koch, who at the 1976 Olympics became the first American to win a medal in cross-country, offers his unique perspective on the sport.

The technique section brings together several different, but complementary, styles of skiing. One article deals with techniques designed for prepared tracks, and addresses specific problems of the beginning- to intermediate-level skier. Another article discusses the technique for skiing off the trail and into deeper powder, using the beautiful telemark turn. Finally, a piece on one of the most exciting and new aspects of cross-country technique—parallel turning on downhill runs—is included. The reader is encouraged to take the *Guide* out to the slopes and trails to practice these techniques. This section is carefully illustrated, so the skier can easily follow the descriptions.

Next, the skier is ready to consider planning ski tours—day tours, as well as snow-camping overnights—in wilderness areas. This section offers basic advice on equipment, preparing shelters, and food for the trip. As long as you are prepared with the essentials and know how to use them, you can plan treks that may now seem beyond your capabilities. This section is oriented toward getting you out on the trail, so you will not become bogged down in preparation.

If you take tours in the backcountry, it is essential that you have a good understanding of winter safety. When you travel to high-mountain areas in the winter, you become vulnerable to such problems as frostbite, avalanches, whiteouts, and getting lost. This section will help you learn not only how to avoid such difficulties, but to know what to do in the event you are faced with them. This kind of preparation will help you appreciate the power of nature, while encouraging you to understand and work with it.

Ski touring varies markedly in different parts of the country. So writers from six regions were assigned to explore the special character, climate, and snow conditions of their areas. These include: Sierra Nevada, Pacific Northwest, Rockies, Midwest, New England, and Alaska. These writers do not attempt to present a place-by-place guide to ski tours in each region. Rather, they give you a flavor for the areas, discuss appropriate ski techniques and waxing, and give you a feeling for the way the winter season evolves.

Citizen racing offers intermediate-level skiers an opportunity to compete in cross-country skiing. The section on racing details prerace preparation, training for races, and racing technique. There is also information on how you can become involved in racing at this most basic level—a level at which having a good time is more important than a good racing time.

Often, in our enthusiasm about this wilderness sport, we forget that the wilderness will not be preserved unless we take steps to protect it. In this age of urban growth and development, it is increasingly important that we set aside extensive land areas as wilderness, inviolate and protected. The beauty of cross-country skiing is that we can ski in wild and remote places, treading the terrain lightly, and leaving behind only our ski tracks. In our time, this is a rare and exquisite experience— one to be savored. The chapter on skiing and the winter wilderness develops an appreciation for preserving the wilds.

I hope that this book conveys some of Bill Koch's feeling, when he said, "There is something very spiritual about cross-country. . . . Sometimes I see it as an art form."

—John Hamburger

Part I

BEGINNINGS

1

History of Skiing

by John Hamburger

Understanding the history of cross-country skiing requires peering back through the mists of time, long before man had any notion of the now-ubiquitous automobile, long before the machine age, to a time when man's needs were far more direct. In those days—about 2500 B.C.—man's game was survival. His days were filled with hunting, keeping warm, and eating.

In the northern parts of Asia human beings were skiing. These ancestral athletes were engaged in a grueling competition —not with each other, but with the caprices of nature. It was a fiercely competitive struggle in these northern climes, particularly in the dark of winter when the ground became blanketed with snow and ice. Winter hunting trips were more complicated and dangerous. These early men found it difficult to slog through the powdery snow, with wind screaming into their faces and their flimsy foot-coverings sinking knee-deep.

So it was that some precocious inventor tied a primitive ancestor of skis onto his feet and clomped proudly out of his shelter. For this proto-sportsman, skiing was not yet a sport; it was a means of transportation over cold and forbidding terrain. It afforded him the capability of covering far more distance with considerably less effort. No doubt, his hunting catch multiplied many times, and we can surmise that even his social relationships improved as well.

Early skiing was most common in those parts of the world that were landlocked and snow-covered for much of the year. In such places, man's ingenuity inspired him to seek a better means of crossing snowy plains and mountain passes. During the long northern winters people in various primitive societies found that skis (or snowshoes) offered ways to venture out of

2

their small shelters and to traverse the snow. "Sport" in those days was nothing less than the art of survival.

ARCHEOLOGICAL EVIDENCE

The earliest "skis," found in the Altai Mountains of Siberia in Central Asia, date back to 2500 B.C. These early skis, which were more akin to present-day snowshoes, were made of grass reeds sewn together. Other primitive skis, also resembling snowshoes, were made of animal bones strapped to the feet with thongs of animal hide. Each settlement used materials that were available. So, of necessity, a wide variety of snowshoes developed. Skiing, as it was known then, developed independently in several parts of Asia, and then spread to the Scandinavian peninsula.

A ski, dated to 2500 B.C., was discovered in a Swedish peat bog, and a pair found in Finland is said to go back to 2000 B.C. Of this latter pair, one ski was long and narrow, with no fur on the bottom, while the other one was short and wide, with a fur sole. It is presumed that the short ski was used to provide a kick for propelling the skier forward, while the longer ski facilitated glide. It is interesting to note that years later, in the eighteenth century, when skiing became popular in Norwegian towns, most people still skied on one short and one long ski. Considering the spills and pratfalls of most first-time skiers, it is amusing to imagine the generations of skiers cursing their mismatched skis, one 4 to 6 feet and the other 8 to 10 feet long. Imagine how much more difficult it must have been to become accustomed to those awkward slats.

A 4,000-year-old drawing on a rock wall on the island of Rodoy off the coast of Norway depicts a man on skis. This primitive stick figure shows our ancestor engaged in an activity not too different than the sport we are likely to pursue over a holiday weekend. Rock carvings, or *petroglyphs*, showing skiers hunting or at war have been discovered in Siberia and Norway. These date back to about 1000 B.C.

The early skis can be subdivided into three categories:

1. *Arctic skis:* These were short, wide, and fur-clad on the running surface. They were used from northern Russia eastward, through Siberia to the Pacific coast.

2. *Southern skis:* These were longer, but were without the fur bottom. On top, toward the front of the ski, was a steering rope held by the skier. These were used primarily in Scandinavia.

3. *Scandic skis:* These evolved as a combination of the other two types of skis. The two skis were of unequal lengths: one short and fur-clad; the other longer, with a steering groove on the running surface. These were used primarily on the wide, gently sloping plateaus of central Scandinavia.

Early bindings usually consisted of simple toe straps made from leather or ropes constructed from the twisted bark of a tree. Most Scandinavians wore reindeer-skin moccasins.

SKIS IN LITERATURE

Many early records of skiing have come down to us through literature. References to skiing and snowshoeing appear in unexpected places in various written records. But even before man began to record his thoughts on paper (or stone), his ideas and dreams were communicated through myths and legends. These early folktales, many of a spiritual nature, give us the first inkling that man and his gods were already on skis. The Vikings in Norway had gods and goddesses to represent their hopes and fears related to snow and winter. Uller, the god of winter, was so huge that he traveled on skis the size of boats. Skade, the goddess of winter, had snow in her hair and clothing. She was imbued with the strength of womanhood and had the ability to hunt and provide.

The earliest known written account of skiing was made by the Greek historian Xenophon (430-355 B.C.) who wrote of "Armenians who were wont to put enlarged shoes on the horses while traversing the mountain passes."* Skiing was also mentioned by the Byzantine historian Procopius, who wrote in the sixth century A.D.

The *Sagas,* the classic literature of the Viking period, also offer vivid accounts of skiing. These tales, written around 1000

---

*Charles M. Dudley, *60 Centuries of Skiing* (Brattleboro, Vt.: Stephen Dayes Press, 1935), p. 31.

A.D., describe the superb Viking skiers. Skiers became so proficient in this part of the world that in 1200 King Sverre of Norway equipped his scouts with skis during the Battle of Oslo. The Norwegian scouts were able to surreptitiously reconnoiter the Swedish enemy, camped in deep snow.

Later, during the Norwegian Civil War, the king sent two scouts over the mountains on skis. This event is commemorated to this day by the annual Birkebeinerrennet cross-country ski race, which follows the 35-mile route the king's scouts took many years before.

Skiing was clearly born out of practical necessity. The earliest nomadic tribes skied for self-preservation: in search of food, as well as to escape enemies. Skiing later evolved in the Scandinavian countries to provide strategic advantage in war. By the twelfth century, skiing had become a royal pastime in Scandinavia. Only later did the sport filter down to the common people.

Skiing also appears in historical literature that grew out of the area around Tibet. Milarepa, an itinerant Tibetan-Buddist poet, visited the remote region of Lashi Snow Mountain. Milarepa's disciples felt they had so much power with his guidance that they could "conquer the snow without snowshoes."*

HISTORY OF NORWEGIAN SKIING

Because of its long, northern winters, Norway inevitably evolved as a skiing center. In 1721, a ski company was organized in the Norwegian army. The soldiers used a single, solid pole as a brake when skiing downhill, and as a pusher to increase speed on flat surfaces. This same system carried on into the mid-1800s in the mining towns of the United States. By the late-eighteenth century, each town in Norway had developed its own unique type of ski. The most common variety was the long/short combination previously described.

In the 1830s, a man named Sondre Norheim, from Telemark, Norway, developed a turn that later was named for his hometown. The telemark turn proved particularly effective in the

*Garma C.C. Chang, trans. and annotated, *The Hundred Thousand Songs of Milarepa* (Boulder, Colo.: Shambhala, 1962), p. 26.

A motley crew of skiers displaying their skis in La Porte, California.
(Photo courtesy of the California State Library)

deep powder conditions that prevailed in much of Norway. Norheim's major rivals in ski-jumping events hailed from the town of Christiana (the former name of Oslo). Skiers in Christiana developed a turn (known as the christiana) that was done with the skis wide apart and parallel. Devotees of these two schools of skiing met head-on in early ski competitions.

By the 1870s, ski carnivals had become common in Norwegian towns. These included both cross-country skiing races and jumping events. At the outset of the international skiing championships, Norway ran off with the bulk of the medals. Their centuries of preparation paid off, as Norway dominated the first seven Olympiads.

SKIING COMES TO THE UNITED STATES

Skiing was introduced in the mining towns of the West in the early 1850s, when Norwegian sailors jumped ship in San Francisco and headed for the goldfields. With them, they brought along their skiing heritage. There, with nothing but long winters and plenty of imagination, the miners organized the first recorded ski races in the Western Hemisphere. These were wild events, prodded on by the dares and bets of the restless, hard-living miners.

Photographs of early ski competitions in the Sierra show the frighteningly long racing skis that ranged from 10 to 25 feet in length. The skiers' boots were held in place by crude leather straps. Like their Norwegian forbears, these skiing miners used a 6-foot pole, or *stav*, to aid control.

Racing clubs were started to take the boredom out of the cold winter days. Races gave the miners something to occupy their time, as well as further excuse to drink and gamble. The Sierra gold camps of LaPorte, Alturas, Poker Flat, Port Wine, Murphys, and Onion Valley became the focus of these early ski competitions. The races were colorful events, as the following description testifies:

> Here for a bucket of lager beer, a hundred silver dollars, or a gold-mine claim, bearded and crusty miners poured out of their glory holes, strapped on their 12-foot skis (some were made out of solid oak and weighed 25 pounds), and went hell-for-leather down the Sierra race courses at speeds up to 80-plus miles an hour, riding a long pole that looked like a cross between a barber pole and a plumber's helper. Everyone from the Chinese to the Scandinavians was either racing or out there to cheer them on. Even the horses clumped around on foot-long snow-shoes with leather bindings. There were portable bars at the "finish" gates to provide the cup-thumping along with an occasional fistfight. The side bets went into the thousands.*

In efforts to ski faster than the next man, and thus to win more cold cash, ski racers began to experiment with precursors to waxes that would help increase their speed. These concoctions, known in the trade as *dope*, were avidly researched by many a high-country wheeler-dealer. The secrets of the dope formulas were closely guarded, and their inventors became as popular as the star racers themselves. A typical dope mixture

---

*Robert Scharff and the Editors of *Ski Magazine*, eds., *Ski Magazine's Encyclopedia of Skiing* (New York: Harper & Row, Publishers, 1970).

included such substances as spermacetti, burgundy pitch, venice turpentine, oil of cedar, tar, camphor, and castor oil.

"SNOWSHOE" THOMPSON

In those days, skis were referred to as "Norwegian snowshoes," an obvious tribute to the rugged immigrants who had introduced skiing in this country. One of those early immigrants, known far and wide as "Snowshoe" Thompson, was a spirited competitor in the early races, besides having achieved fame as a mountain mail-carrier. In 1869, Thompson was compelled to compete in one of the most intense competitions of those early years of skiing. "Snowshoe" traveled a full 200 miles to vie with Frank Stewart in the 1869 Alturas Club races. "Snowshoe," who had practically been born on skis, felt he had the upper hand on Stewart. But "Snowshoe" underestimated Stewart, the man credited with inventing "dope," and no doubt an experimental scientist of the sport. By making use of his "dope" and his lighter skis, Stewart was able to defeat "Snowshoe," and strut off proudly carrying the $500 gold-dust purse. "Snowshoe" skied home, both shamed and mystified by his defeat in that race and one other. But the race between Stewart and Thompson was no mystery to the president of the Alturas Snowshoe Club, who said in the *Sacramento Union:*

> Why, Doc Brewster has a mule that has been practiced on snowshoes this winter that can beat [Thompson]. You may think I am a bit rough on this man Thompson. It might not have been so, had he gone back to his friends and frankly acknowledged what he then knew to be true— that to be a good traveller on snowshoes is one thing, but to be a scientific racer is another.

"Snowshoe" Thompson was a significant figure in the history of skiing in the United States, so his story does not stop here. His feats on his heavy oak skis made him a mythic figure in western U.S. history. "Snowshoe" may have been shamed on the downhill slopes before the catcalls of inebriated miners, but his long-distance endurance on skis represents the heritage of cross-country skiing in this country.

Early ski racers in California. Note the long poles used for control, and the race starter with his gong. (Photo courtesy of the California State Library)

"Snowshoe" Thompson came to the United States from Telemark, Norway, when he was ten. For a time, he was a rancher in the Sacramento Valley in California. But then a great restlessness set in. Thompson heard about the problems of winter mail delivery in the Sierra, and was spurred on by the challenge. After constructing a pair of weighty 25-pound slats, Thompson applied for the job of carrying the mail over the mountains in the winter. The trek was a cold, grueling 90 miles from Placerville to Carson Valley, tracing the route of Kit Carson and John Fremont.

Thompson began this job in January 1856, and continued for twenty years. At the time, this was the only winter land communication between the Atlantic states and California. "Snowshoe" skied at times over snowdrifts 30 to 50 feet high, carrying up to 120 pounds of mail (at $2.00 a letter for the federal government). For those winters of 1856-76, "Snowshoe" skied through fierce mountain storms, bringing mail, news, and even supplies to mountain communities otherwise cut off from the outside world for months at a time. To make these runs in the dead of winter, he must have had awesome endurance, sense of direction, and mountaineering skill. Many stories are told of Thompson coming across snowbound or wounded miners and trappers. Invariably, he helped them to safety.

CROSS-COUNTRY SKIING COMES OF AGE

After the years of the gold rush, interest in ski competition declined considerably. Miners who had been holed up for winters in camps began to disperse to areas offering better opportunities. With fewer people stranded in these mountain communities for the long winter months, interest in ski competition became less pronounced.

Similarly, Sondre Norheim's famed *telemark turn*, which he had developed for skiing the deep powder near his hometown in Norway, fell into relative obscurity for a time. But today, this unique turn has resurfaced—on high Sierra meadows, in the wetter snow of the Pacific Northwest, and most appropriately of all in the dry powder of the Rockies. The telemark is a turn perfectly suited to skinny skis and flexible toe bindings, and brings the cross-country skier closer to the terrain he is covering; he must be aware of its every undulation. Today, the telemark turn—long hidden in the Norwegian outback—is returning to give the cross-country skier a grace of movement, and a maneuver truly his own.

In the Colorado Rockies skiing was more than just a sport in the mid-to-late 1800s. According to historian Jack A. Benson skiing was the major means of transportation into mountain communities in the winter.* Most mountain towns lay beyond the reach of the railroad, so skis were the primary means of transportation. Prospective travelers had to construct their own skis, which were usually 8 to 12 feet in length. These skiers used a single 8-foot pole for balancing and turning, as had been used earlier in Norway and elsewhere in the West. It was not until the early twentieth century that skiers began to use a pair of ski poles for improved control.

The Colorado skiers used a technique they called "the early American ski technique." Benson interpreted this to mean that our pioneer skiers "stand up and pray the snowshoes will

---

*Jack A. Benson, "Before Skiing was Fun," *Western Historical Quarterly* 8 (1977): 431-41.

go straight." Skiers attempted to change direction only to avoid trees, rocks, ledges, and other minor obstructions in their paths. But nineteenth century skiers were able to move in a fashion similar to present-day cross-country skiers, since their boot heels were not attached to the skis. The major impediments to mobility were that the skis in those days were longer, wider, and heavier than today's svelte versions, and poling was more difficult with one long, clumsy pole than with the modern bamboo or fiberglass models. When climbing hills, these pioneers attached skins to the bottoms of their skis for added friction; these were later removed for the downhill schusses.

After a lull of several decades, skiing began to flourish again in the western United States in the 1920s and 1930s. During this time, a hut system was developed in the area of Yosemite National Park. The Sierra Club's four-day winter ascent of Mount Lyell in Yosemite in 1936 initiated more extensive ski mountaineering.

The first Winter Olympic Games were held in Chamonix, France, in 1924. These included cross-country skiing events, which were largely dominated by Norway. Along with competition came experimentation with waxes. The earliest of these included tar, fat, and candle wax.

From there, cross-country skiing began to develop faster and more extensively. Competition sharpened as skiers and coaches developed more refined techniques, both for training and for actual skiing.

While cross-country skiing has been around in one form or another for thousands of years, the past decade has seen unprecedented growth in the sport in America. For example, in 1967, 12,000 pairs of cross-country skis were sold in the U.S.; by 1976, the annual figure had snowballed to 415,000.* New ski-touring centers, now about 400, are popping up everywhere there is snow. They feature such amenities as machine-made ski tracks, ski instruction and rentals, and even saunas and moonlight sleigh rides. At the same time, citizen races, such as the American Birkebeiner at Wisconsin's Telemark Ski Area, are drawing more entrants than ever before.

---

*Peter Wood, "The Unloneliness of the Long-Distance Skier," *New York Times Magazine*, December 18, 1977, pp. 19-40.

Innovations in equipment have kept pace with this increased interest in Nordic skiing. Manufacturers are competing to produce the most dependable and responsive skis. Improvements in the efficiency of other Nordic equipment have kept pace as well. (See chapter 2.)

To elaborate further on the modern history of cross-country—the races, the Olympic results, and the extensive skiing done at private ski areas and on public lands—would take volumes. Any interest you had would become dormant and likely cause you to hibernate for the rest of the winter. So let's ready those skis before you get too comfortable in your slippers and your easy chair. The trails await you.

2

Equipment
by Bob Woodward

The first thing a prospective equipment buyer usually thinks about is buying skis. But this is the wrong thing to concentrate on. The main concern should be boots, because if the boots don't fit, don't break well over the toes, tend to rub at the heels, and are generally inadequate in construction, you're in for some serious misfortune.

The second concern of the new buyer is getting into the sport relatively inexpensively. This is the next biggest error, for out in retail-land, ski package deals are designed to give you a great deal—at the sacrifice of the most important part of the equipment, the boots. Even when the boots are top quality, many packages keep the price down by substituting a ski made in a mysterious land by a factory that makes sail battens for the Greek navy. Caution is required when approaching packages; like wild animals, they are best observed from a distance.

The third concern is durability. Durable equipment means a great deal: (1) if you ski often and want tough gear to handle your constant demands; (2) if you are a once-in-a-blue-moon skier who needs equipment that can take a beating every time you go out skiing; or (3) if you're a family person buying for several people, and the economics of buying new gear after equipment breaks down is unreasonable.

SOME BACKGROUND

Starting with boots as our focal point, it is necessary to explore a bit of history before embarking on some selection criteria. Until the early seventies, people could buy either a high-topped touring boot with a notched heel to accommodate

13

cable bindings, or several versions of high-, mid-, and low-cut boots for three-pin bindings. The Alpine skiing orientation had many off-track skiers using cable bindings for touring. The cable was unhitched so your heel could ride up during touring, and clipped down only for downhill runs.

The advent of more prepared tracks in Scandinavia and Europe made the three-pin rat-trap binding more popular. This binding held the foot securely in place, with a metal bail over the toe piece, and the three pins sticking up into the sole of the boot toe for additional anchoring. By 1973, three-pin bindings had pushed the cable binding into retirement, and touring boots designed for three-pin shoes took over.

About the same time, boot manufacturers began to experiment with changes in construction. For years touring boots had been stitched, so that the leather uppers were stitched to a mid-sole and an outer sole. Not only was stitching labor intensive and costly, but it also resulted in a nonwaterproof seam between the upper and the sole. But the stitched boots were rigid where it counted. Searching for a better method of manufacture, to keep prices in line and get a better waterproofed seam, companies explored cementing and vulcanizing processes. Both processes bonded the uppers to the soles under pressure. These processes worked, and the newer cemented and vulcanized boots of the mid-seventies were more waterproof, but not quite as rigid as their stitched counterparts.

Then, in a cooperative effort, binding manufacturers and boot-makers introduced standards for all cross-country boots and bindings. The idea was that all toe pieces on boots, as well as all bindings, should be a certain width. This would ensure that people could interchange boots and bindings with regularity, without worrying whether a particular boot would be compatible with a certain binding. This "Nordic norm" came to pass, and all boots and bindings then fell into three categories— 71 mm, 75 mm, and 79 mm, measured across the binding pin area and across the boot toe piece.

Everything was set for the cross-country consumer to ski off into the sunset without having to worry about compatibility. Then something happened. Adidas tried a new boot and binding combination on the Russian racers at the 1976 Olympics.

There, the world saw the bindings fail, then work, and then fail on the feet of the Russians. The boot and binding combination was unique in that the boot had a plastic sole, with a long, narrow toe fitted into a narrow binding. The toe was secured by a pin running through both the boot toe and the binding. The pundits declared the bindings to be pure hogwash not worth serious consideration. But, lo and behold, Rottefella, the major binding producer, soon introduced a slightly wider binding for boots with plastic soles and long toe pieces. The only differences were that the Rottefella concept called for the

Boots with four major types of bindings (left to right): 50-mm racing norm, 38-mm Adidas norm, three-pin Nordic norm, and cable.

boot toe to be 50 mm wide, versus the Adidas 38 mm, and to be secured to the binding by a *bail* like all standard three-pin models.*

So, the game changed again, and despite statements that the new types of boots and bindings would never be used for touring, they are being used for everything from ski touring in the backyard to month-long mountaineering expeditions. The consumer is now faced with a choice between traditional three-pin boots and the new 38-mm and 50-mm systems.

BOOTS

Several factors are important in boot selection:

- *Torsional rigidity.* This involves holding a boot by its heel with one hand and under the sole with the other, then twisting it to make sure of its rigidity. A torsionally rigid boot supports the skier so he doesn't twist sideways off the ski. It is essential in making turns and on downhills.

- *Forward flex.* The boot must flex forward with ease so your kick and glide technique will not be hampered. The boot must break nicely over the toes, so it does not cause blisters or constant pain.

- *Fit.* A cross-country boot should fit like a running shoe, with about ¼ inch of room in the front. Try the boots on with the type of socks you plan to wear, and walk around the shop flexing the boot forward to check the fit. Make sure your heel does not lift up excessively. Many people wear boots that are right in between two sizes. Take the snugger ones and have them stretched out a bit, if this is feasible; if not, choose the large ones and take up the excess space with insoles.

In choosing boots, you need to be concerned with warmth, boot height, and waterproofness. Boot height depends on the type of touring you plan to do. Boots for off-track or un-tracked touring are usually higher cut or mid-cut. This is for snow protection, not for ankle support. Ankle support is best

---

*The *bail* is the wire piece that snaps into place over the boot toe to secure the boot in the binding.

gained by exercise. For added snow protection, a low *gaiter* is a good thing to wear around the ankle.*

Low-cut boots are designed for active tourers and racers who want the lightest, most flexible uppers. Lightness is part of the thrill of advanced technique. It allows you to fly along a track or on untracked snow with a minimum of weight on your feet.

Boots are made from a variety of leathers and synthetics. The most popular boots are made of top-grain leather (full grain), split leather, and nylon (textile). The better the leather, the better the durability, warmth, and waterproofness. Nylon is excellent for the light tourer and racer, but it leaves a lot to be desired for warmth and waterproofness. Some split-leather boots are impregnated with silicone or some other chemical to make them more water-resistant, but generally they are not as good for keeping your feet dry.

Warmth and waterproofness can be enhanced in any boot by several techniques:

- An insole can be inserted in a boot for added insulation against the cold.
- Most boots, nylon excluded, can be coated with a water-sealing agent for added waterproofing protection.
- In wet snow use a rubber overboot for added warmth and waterproofness. If the snow is more dry, use either a combination nylon/rubber overboot or an oversized athletic sock over the boot. This technique is the most effective of the three.

Lined boots are wonderful for inactive tourers, but more active skiers need unlined boots, which will pass off moisture from perspiration through the leather. An active skier will get cold feet from the moisture locked in a lined boot. After skiing many kilometers the lining will wear down, so the boots become a size larger than when they were purchased.

Traditional 71-mm, 75-mm, and 79-mm Nordic boots are compatible with the bulk of the bindings now available. The 71-mm size fits children's boots, the 75-mm boots include most adult sizes, and the 79-mm boots fit especially big people.

---

*A *gaiter* is a cloth leg covering, reaching from the instep of the foot to the ankle, mid-calf, or knee.

Be sure your boots have built-in toe reinforcement to protect the pin holes from being ripped out.

The new 50-mm and 38-mm boots are better for skiers who want the absolute in forward flex, lateral stability, torsional rigidity, and better downhill control. The 50-mm and the 38-mm boots offer the best control for turns and downhill skiing. This is because they have either wedge-shaped heel pieces that fit into grooves on the boot heel, or else soft rubber heels into which conical heel pieces fit snugly.

No matter which type of boots you choose, fit should be your final selection criterion.

BINDINGS

Since bindings are closely related to particular boots, it would be helpful for you to try all three types of boots and bindings before buying. A three-pin boot won't fit into the newer narrow bindings, and vice versa. If, however, you decide to change binding systems midway through a season, the screw holes on most of the bindings are positioned in the same place. This precludes having to fill old screw holes and drill new ones, a process that can affect the strength of the skis.

In selecting a traditional three-pin binding, there are several types to choose from. The major differences are: construction material, weight, type of bail, and manner of entry and exit.

The majority of three-pin bindings are made of aluminum alloys with steel pins. Lighter models for light touring and racing consist of a thinner metal, while the touring models use a thicker metal. All-plastic three-pin bindings weigh midway between the others.

It's from the construction of the bail that the three-pin binding got the name "rat trap." A flat bail is the more popular type. It is a few millimeters wide so that pressure is applied evenly on the boot toe piece. Thinner, rounded steel wire bails are used extensively on lighter touring and racing models. These generally do not exert as even a pressure across the boot toe, sometimes resulting in toe pieces that bend upward in the middle.

For the lazier skier, modern three-pin bindings come equipped with pieces attached to the bails, so they can be snapped in place over the boot toe, and released by simply pressing on the binding with a ski pole tip. This type of binding is called a "step-in" model. "Non-step-in" bindings require that the skier bend over to engage and release the bail.

All types of three-pin bindings come in the standard sizes of 71-mm, 75-mm, and 79-mm-wide toe pieces.

Each binding has an accompanying heel piece that should be tacked or screwed in place directly under the heel. The heel piece serves as a platform for holding the skier's heel onto the ski during downhills and turns. Some heel pieces are conically shaped to stick into the boot heel. Others have sharp serrated edges to dig into the heel. All have plastic backing pieces to keep snow from gathering and icing on the heel device. Although heel devices work quite well, wet snow has a natural tendency to ice up. All sorts of tricks have been tried, from melting paraffin onto the heel piece to trying rubber substitutes.

The heel pieces are not as susceptible to icing as the area just behind the toe piece. If ice does build up on the angled surfaces, it is easily broken off by the action of the boot coming down on the heel piece. Plastic soles also seem less conducive to snow buildup on the skis, since plastic breaks up wet snow as it forms, rather than compacting it as rubber and composition heels might.

A worse problem in wet snow is the ice buildup just in back of the binding under the ball of the boot. As the skier raises up for a kick in his diagonal stride, snow gathers under the ball of the foot. It can be bothersome and cause problems in ski technique. One way of preventing this is to cut pieces of plastic out of coffee can lids and then to apply duct tape. It's best to experiment with remedies and consult local touring luminaries for their ideas.

The new binding sizes don't seem to induce the same icing problems, mainly due to the use of different-shaped heel pieces and plastic soles. But some of the 38-mm and 50-mm bindings produce snow buildup on the binding, under the bail, a problem that can cause the bail to pop open while in use.

Like their 71-mm, 75-mm, and 79-mm predecessors, 50-mm bindings use a bail and have two or three pins. Bails are usually made of sturdy wire, but there are new flat-bail models coming into the market now. "Step in" models are not as popular as the bend-down, do-it-yourself types. Remember that while the traditional three-pin bindings have a left and a right foot binding, 38-mm and 50-mm bindings are symmetrical, so that either foot will fit into either binding.

The 38-mm bindings come in a wide variety of choices, from the original Adidas light aluminum model to bail-operated light plastic models. In between, there are several metal bindings with metal bails. The 38-mm toe piece differs from the 50-mm one not only in width, but in the ways in which it is secured to the binding. Thirty-eight-millimeter boot toes have a hole running through the toe end and a raised lip on the top near the end of each toe piece.

In the original Adidas binding, still very popular, a long needle is inserted through holes in the binding sidewalls and the hole in the boot toe to secure the boot to the binding. Later bail models clip over the lip on the boot tongue to harness the skier in.

We should not leave bindings without a word on children. For very small children (three to six years old) use a Balata binding and a hiking or work boot or galosh. The Balata has two simple stirrups, which will accommodate all the above boots. After age seven, children should use the three-pin boots and bindings. There are plenty of children's boots in a variety of price categories. And there are plenty of rental sales annually for the real bargain hunters. A good three-pin combination gets the child off on the right foot (ski) in learning good technique.

You may wonder why I don't recommend the venerable cable binding. Well, like most parents, I have banged, beaten, and adjusted junior cable bindings to make them work for two frustrated boys. My frustration grew to equal theirs and three-pin bindings were installed on their skis, much to their delight. They suddenly had no mechanical problems and felt very independent, being able to climb in and out of their "rat traps" at will.

SKIS

This brings us to wood skis. They look great, but are not as durable as synthetic (fiberglass) skis, and are fast fading from the marketplace. This is not a condemnation of wood or its skiability. But an average fiberglass ski will be five to seven times stronger than wood. The major ski manufacturers are making fiberglass skis because the technology is better suited to modern manufacturing techniques. For this reason we will discuss fiberglass skis and leave wood at this point, with a wistful look and a thank you for many hours of fine skiing.

Leaping directly into the fray, we attack the question, "Which are better, waxless or waxable skis?" For the beginner who wants a minimum of problems starting out, waxless skis are a real boon. For the person who only skis once or twice a year, a waxless ski is better because you don't have to waste time waxing. Kids are independent of Mom and Dad, if they have waxless skis.

Waxable skis are better for active skiers who get out many times during the year and want to get the best performance out of their skis each trip. Most advanced skiers have an obsession with waxing perfectly for each snow condition, and so are particular fanciers of waxable skis. Any time you want the best grip and glide on snow, a waxable ski is best to have.

Cold, dry snow is very easy to wax for; transitional snow is very difficult; and wet snow can be a pain. So the optimal situation would be to have waxable skis for cold snow, and waxless for wet and transitional conditions. Check the general snow conditions of your local area. Match these with the frequency and type of skiing you plan to do, and base your choice of waxless or waxable on these criteria.

Several simplified wax systems have been developed. Many of these two-wax systems (one for wet, one for dry snow) help people who seek the joys of waxable skis, with the ease of waxless. The different systems vary in cold and wet snow in various geographical areas. Seek the recommendation of a reputable touring center or teacher in your area.

Among the waxless skis, there are patterned bases (steps,

diamonds, radial, and bell cuts), mohair strips, mica, and fish-scale. One company produces a ski with removable strips, so you can insert a step pattern, a mohair pattern, or a waxable pattern depending on the day's conditions. The patterned bases are the most popular. There are two types: those that have indentures (cut into the base) and those that have the patterns added on.

Various cross-country ski bottoms (left to right): step pattern, mohair strip pattern, fishscale pattern, waxable fiberglass, and wood.

All the patterns are located in the ski base from just in back of the binding area to a point further forward on the ski. This area, called the *kicker* area, can range from 90 to 150 centimeters in length. The idea of every ski, waxless or waxable, is to enable the skier to be able to depress the kicker area so that the ski grips.

Fishscale skis have been the leaders in waxless ski patterns since 1970. With the advent of the fishscale pattern, the waxless revolution started. The pattern consists of a series of small, scale-like protuberances heat-molded onto the ski base. The scales, of varying depth, grip the snow and do not inhibit forward glide.

In the case of the step pattern—the most popular in use—the slightly slanted cuts look like a staircase. The object is for the rearward slanted cuts to grip the snow with the skier's weight on the ski, but slide easily forward on the glide, because of their slant. There are raised steps, which are replaceable, but most are cut into the ski base. The other patterned bases are named for the way their respective cuts appear to the eye.

Mohair strip patterns are related to the skins used by skiers centuries ago for grip. A long strip of mohair is inserted into a groove on either side of the bottom groove, just under the foot area. When kicked for grip, the hairs bristle upward, thus gripping the snow. As the ski glides forward, the hairs flatten out, leaving the glide unaffected.

Mica-based skis are new to the market, having been recently introduced by the Norwegian ski industry. Flecks of mica are imbedded in the ski's running surface. The flecks or chips are slanted backward for grip. This backward slant does not interfere with forward glide.

All waxless skis will ice up under certain conditions, particularly in wetter snow. This can be avoided by spraying the pattern with a silicone spray before each outing.

In both categories of ski, waxable and waxless, there are three types of fiberglass ski constructions: *fiberglass sandwich, injection molded,* and *torsion box.*

A fiberglass sandwich ski is constructed in several layers, with the final product resembling a sandwich. The top layer consists of a sheet of hard plastic, followed by one or more layers of reinforcing fiberglass, a core of wood or foam, another fiberglass layer, and the base. This is the most popular type of synthetic ski construction.

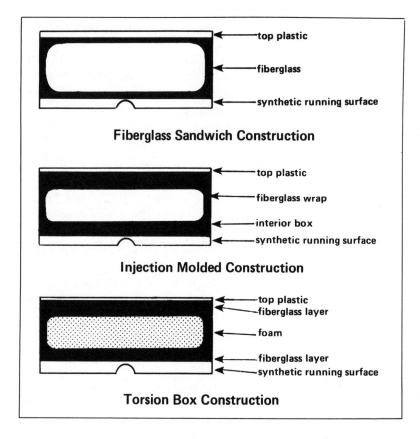

Fiberglass Sandwich Construction

Injection Molded Construction

Torsion Box Construction

The next most popular type of ski is made by the injection molded construction process. Here, the ski's topsheet, sidewalls, base, and reinforcement layers are preassembled and a foam core is injected. This is a very cost-effective method of producing skis.

The torsion box method is used by few companies because of its inherent high cost. It is said to produce the most durable skis. A core of wood or foam is wrapped completely in fiberglass, layers of reinforcing fiberglass are added, and finally the topsheet and base are adhered.

In all the ski constructions the topsheets are made of hard plastic to protect the ski. This hard plastic is generally acrylonitrile-butadiene-styrene (ABS). Sidewalls vary in thickness and in materials; many are ABS, while others are made of lighter foam materials. Base materials of fiberglass skis are all plastics of one variety or another. The most popular base material is polyethylene, which comes on skis under such brand names as P-Tex and Kofix. No matter what base material is used, the criteria for choosing a base are that it holds wax well and stands up to rough skiing.

All the above construction types are used for making each category of skis. There are four types of skis for cross-country skiing: touring, light touring, mountaineering, and racing. Within each category there are many different subtypes to choose from.

Touring Skis

Touring skis are generally wider and have some *side-cut*. Side-cut means that the tip and tail of the ski are wider than the middle (the *waist*). This feature gives the skis greater stability in untracked snow, and is helpful in turning. Many companies disagree with the side-cut theory, and make their touring skis with parallel cuts (the same width throughout). They argue that a turn can be generated more rapidly and at lower speed with a parallel cut ski.

The tip and tail on a touring ski will flex fairly stiffly; if you pull the tip of a touring ski toward you, it will give slightly. Twist the tip and it will give some. Torsional flex is necessary to ride through bumps and other changes in terrain, and is an aid in turning. The stiff tail supports the skier during downhills and turns when the weight is back of the heels.

It's time now to mention *camber*, for this one aspect is the most important in any ski. Camber is the curvature of the ski along its running surface. Put two skis base to base and you'll notice how they bow: this is the camber. In order to grip the snow, the camber is designed to be depressed by the skier's weight during the kick phase of the kick and glide technique. When the skier's weight is off the ski, the camber rides off the snow, giving the skier glide.

Camber is soft on most touring skis because beginners and off-track ski tourers need soft camber. If the beginner cannot get the mid-section of the ski down for grip, the skis will slip and slide miserably. The off-track skier needs a soft cambered ski so he does not have to push down excessively in soft, loose snow for good grip. The combination of soft camber and stiff flex aid both the off-track snow skier and the wobbly beginner.

Light Touring Skis

Light touring skis are more narrow at the waist than touring skis (49 mm versus 55 mm). Due to variations in construction, they are lighter and are much more lively in their flexes. Flexes are designed for skiers who want a responsive tip for turns and skis that jet through terrain changes.

The light touring ski is recommended for intermediate and advanced skiers who appreciate good skis. They are also for beginners and intermediates who ski on prepared tracks most of the time. In a track, side-cut can be a hindrance, since the skis tend to ski out of the track and turn. As a result, many light touring skis have marginal side-cuts or are parallel cut.

Because they are usually used in hard, prepared tracks or by knowledgeable, technically skilled skiers, light touring skis have slightly stiffer camber. This allows the skier to get a fast kick for grip, while having the ski glide on very little of the base.

Mountaineering Skis

Most mountaineering skis are compromises between Alpine and touring skis. They are wider than normal touring skis and have some sort of edge (steel or aluminum). Most have a pronounced side-cut for support and turning ease in untracked conditions. They are heavier, and should be used with a heavier-weight touring boot and a sturdy three-pin binding, or with mountaineering boots and a specialized quasi-Alpine ski binding.

The cambers of mountaineering skis are soft because it is difficult to kick a big camber down with a 40-pound pack on the back. The flexes are stiff, because the added weight of the skier and pack would overwhelm a softer flexing ski, making it hard to ski on.

Racing Skis

Racing skis are the lightest skis made. There are two kinds of racing skis: *competition* and *training*. Competition skis are designed by and for the top international racers. They are made of exotic materials that ensure lightness. The flexes vary, depending on the advice of particular companies.

Training skis, which are slightly heavier, are designed for citizen racers and super-light tourers. Their flexes and responsiveness are more like light touring skis than competition racing skis.

All competition skis have *double cambers*. A double camber is a second camber that requires a highly developed kick to get the ski down onto the snow. The reason for the second camber is to make the ski ride only on its tips and tails during the glide phase, to cut seconds off race times. Training skis, while stiffer than touring skis, do not, as a rule, have double cambers.

Double-cambered skis work well in wet snow, where you want as much of the ski out of the snow as possible, when gliding. Such skis do not, however, work as well on cold snow, where more ski surface on the snow is helpful for increased grip. With this in mind, most racing ski manufacturers offer soft, medium, and stiff cambers for discerning skiers.

With few exceptions, racing skis are parallel cut, and very narrow (around 44 mm) at the waist. Polyethylene is the predominant base material. Racing skis come in waxless forms, too, with both patterned and mohair bases.

Choosing Your Skis

If you're looking for equipment, it is best to match your skills and the type of skiing you like to do with the equipment. Beginners and off-track tourers tend toward wider touring skis, intermediates and track skiers lean toward light touring, and so on. The most important factor in ski selection is choosing the right camber for your weight and ability.

To test for camber, place the pair of skis to be tested on a flat, level surface. Place a sheet of paper or an index card under the camber of each ski. Now, stand on the skis with your toes on the balance point. With weight equalized on both skis, you, or a friend, should be able to pull the card or paper out with some resistance. This indicates that the middle part of the ski is flattening out onto the floor and will do so when on the snow. If the paper is easily removed, the camber is too strong and you will not be able to flatten the ski out. If the paper cannot be removed, the camber is too soft; you are depressing the ski too much, meaning you will have great grip but very little glide on the snow.

This technique is true for both touring and mountaineering skis. Light touring skis can be stiffer, as the skier's technique allows the skier to depress the skis fully. If you will be skiing a lot of prepared tracks, a stiffer ski is easier to punch down on a stable platform. Racers go for very stiff skis to produce the most glide on the bare minimum of tip and tail surface after each strong downward kick.

Be sure to measure your skis properly. Raise your hand over your head, place the ski to be measured next to your arm, and see where your wrist falls on the ski. If your wrist is close to the end of the tip, the ski is probably the right size for you. This measurement can be faulty, as those with especially long or short arms should measure differently. The best indicators are these: most men's skis are 205, 210, or 215 cms, while most women's skis are 185, 190, or 195 cms.

POLES

Poles are designed for each classification of skiing. The major differences include: the material the pole is made from, the type of grip and handle, the basket type, and the weight. The most popular materials for touring pole construction are tonkin cane (bamboo) and fiberglass. Touring poles tend to be flexible and heavy, with large circular baskets for support in untracked snow. Most of the touring poles use leather or plastic grips with nylon or leather adjustable straps.

When you select touring poles, be sure to buy the best. Inexpensive tonkin poles are made from poor quality cane, which is susceptible to breakage. Cheap fiberglass poles shatter easily, and the less expensive aluminum and metal alloy poles bend in a strong breeze. It is best to stay with top products.

Handles should be leather if possible, since leather is warmer to the touch in cold weather. Both leather and nylon straps are equally good, but they must be easily adjustable so you're able to adjust them quickly for different gloves. Poles without adjustable straps are worthless. Make sure the straps are wide and comfortable, and come out of the pole handle ¾ inch down from the top. A strap that emanates from the top of the pole will flop out of the hand on each release. But you can tape top-of-the-pole straps ¾ inch down with electrical tape to make them work effectively.

The gap between the handle top and the strap should fit snugly into the crook of your hand between your thumb and forefinger. In this snug position, the skier can release the pole on every poling motion, a factor essential to smooth poling.

Light touring poles are stiffer and lighter, and have more interesting baskets. Such poles are generally made from light aluminum alloys and fiberglass. Stiffness in a light touring pole means the skier can transmit all his energy directly to the track and snow. Lightness is easier on the body in advanced technique, as it requires less muscle work to carry the pole along on the arm swing. Baskets are aerodynamically designed to create less drag in the air.

Mountaineers generally use touring poles. But adjustable poles are now appearing on the market that have some benefits for the wilderness skier. An adjustable pole can be raised to touring height for skiing on the flats and rolling terrain, and then shortened for Alpine-style downhill runs. Most mountaineers like very large baskets on their poles for deep, untracked powder.

Racing poles are the lightest and strongest. These two requirements are best met in modern *carbonfiber*, a material that is super-light and strong. An added advantage of carbonfiber poles is that they are very rigid for transmitting all the racer's power down the shaft. Baskets are very exotic, from the hoof-shaped types to those conical in shape.

When buying poles, again analyze your needs, and buy the pole best suited to the type of skiing you intend to do most often. Don't buy too exotic a pole and plan to go touring with it. Stay within your skiing ability; poles are specifically designed for particular kinds of skiing.

Sizing poles is not too difficult. Put a pole under your arm, the arm raised perpendicular to your side; then drop the arm over the pole. If the pole is snug in your armpit, then it is the right size. If you are between sizes, take the longer of the two poles. It is better to have a slightly longer pole than one that is too short. Most poles may be shortened if necessary.

WAXING

Equipment in hand, it's time to learn about waxing. Waxing, if you bought a waxable pair of skis, is as simple as you make it. First you must learn about the types of wax and how they work. Then, by trial and error, you will understand how to apply them.

There are two types of waxes: *hard waxes* and *klisters.* Hard waxes come in small cans, color-coded for various snow types and temperatures. For instance, blue wax is used in new snow at cold temperatures. As the colors get warmer on the color spectrum (purple, red), the waxes get softer for snow that is changing from new, cold snow to wetter, older snow. (See the waxing charts in the Appendix.)

Klisters come in toothpaste-type tubes, and are used for snow that is older, snow that has frozen and thawed several times, or extremely wet and mushy snow. Klisters, which are sticky, are used for ice, mush, and newly fallen wet snow. Klister colors correspond closely to hard wax colors.

The theory behind waxing is as follows. Snow crystals have long projectiles when they are new. These projectiles reach up and grip the wax on the ski. So, a harder wax is required for cold, new snow, which has long crystals. As the snow gets old the crystals lose their crystalline formation and become rounded. No longer are there long fingers to grab the wax. So a sticky wax is required for the older crystals to adhere to. Klister does the job. Glide occurs when the ski is pushed forward and a microscopic film of water forms between the ski base and the snow, causing the ski to slide freely.

To gauge the day's wax, first check the type of snow. Is it dry and fluffy, is it transitional (can be easily made into snowballs), or is it wet mush or ice? Having determined the snow type, try to get a reading of the air temperature. After putting together these two facts, look at the manufacturers' advice on the side of the wax can or tube. If the snow is cold and fluffy, we already know that a hard wax is called for. After a temperature check, we can zero in on the color.

Apply hard waxes by crayoning them on the area from just in front of the heel-piece on your ski to a point 30 inches forward (the kicker zone). Don't put too much on, just a light coat. After the wax is on the kicker zone, smooth it out with a cork, as smooth wax works best.

Klisters should be applied in thin lines on either side of the base. Smooth it out with the heel of the hand or with the plastic spatula included in every klister box. Generally, klister can be applied in a short kicker, as it grips much better in the appropriate snow conditions.

A softer wax can always be applied over a harder wax, but the reverse is nearly impossible. If you need to put on a harder wax later, you will first have to scrape off the soft wax.

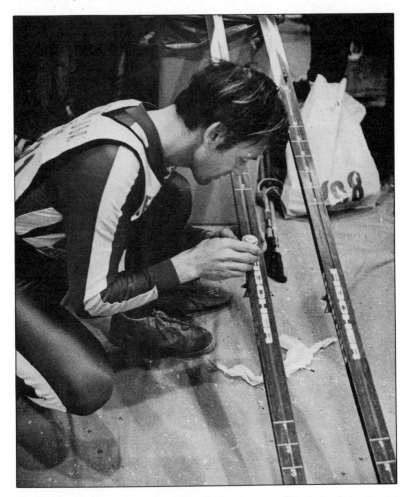

A citizen racer applying a hard wax before a race. (Photo by Peter Davis)

Two other types of waxing are required for modern fiberglass cross-country skis: base waxing and waxing for glide. Don't be alarmed, as both are easy and very necessary for getting the most out of your skiing.

Every poly-based cross-country ski requires a base preparation with a specialized base or glider wax. This base waxing impregnates the base to make it more durable, as well as to set it up for the subsequent application of other waxes. The amount of base wax required varies according to the type of ski. Most touring skis, being nonporous, take a little bit, while more porous racing ski bases require more. Don't forget to prepare the tip and tail sections of your waxless ski as well.

To apply base wax, use a household iron at a low temperature setting, and melt the wax in a thin line along both sides of the ski base. Iron the wax in and let it sit. After a few hours, repeat the ironing. Let the wax cool and scrape the residue off the base with a metal scraper. Draw the scraper toward you, making several passes on the base. Use a plastic scraper or a klister spatula to get the groove and sidewalls clear of spillover wax. If, during the season, the base feels dry or looks discolored, rewax. The life of the base depends on its care and base waxing.

Beginning skiers need not be concerned with glide waxing. But as you increase your skiing skill, it becomes very important. This second type of nongrip waxing is restricted to tip and tail areas of the ski. It can be as difficult or simple as you make it. For simplicity's sake, buy a universal glider wax that accommodates all snow conditions, and apply it to tip and tail sections before each ski outing. The application is done just like base waxing, with the ironing and subsequent scraping. This will enhance your glide, as well as protecting the skis.

If you get more interested in improving glide, there are numerous glider and Alpine ski waxes made just for that purpose. They have colors like cross-country grip waxes. The proper wax for each day's snow has to be determined to get the maximum glide. These are applied like base wax and universal wax and are designed to be almost friction-free at low speeds. This gives the advanced skier the most glide for his effort.

Many companies now market two-wax systems to simplify

waxing. The idea is that most touring needs can be satisfied by one broad-ranged wax for new, cold snow conditions and one for older, wetter snow. Easily applied, these "plus and minus" or "wet and dry" waxes may be layered thicker if a thin coat does not give the desired grip. (See chart in the Appendix.)

Some of the simplified systems have a companion all-purpose glider. Others add a klister from the range of klister waxes for mush and wet snow, conditions not covered well by most simplified systems. Such simplified systems offer a good introduction to waxing. Start with a simplified system, adding hard waxes and klisters as you go, getting a feeling for their properties and how they supplement your simplified system.

CLOTHING

Dressing for the sport is the next task at hand. Cotton jeans are not good for ski touring, because they become wet in snow and feel cold on the legs and lower body. If you want to use something from your regular wardrobe, try a pair of 100 percent wool pants, or a pair with a blend of cotton and nylon if they're available.

The most important part of dressing for cross-country is layering your clothing. Start with thermal underwear, add a turtleneck, and then a sweater, a wool shirt, or a nylon Windbreaker. On the bottom, put on long underwear if you live in a cold climate, and then your pants or knickers.

Suits designed for cross-country are not only fashionable, but functional. They are designed to flex with the skier's motions, to be moisture repellant, and to be wind resistant. Most suits are designed to breathe, so that excess perspiration is expelled. Going light in a suit made for cross-country skiing is far better than donning your Mt. Everest ensemble. About five yards down the track the bulky down jacket comes off, followed by the heavy sweaters, and all the other mountaineering paraphernalia. When touring, you really burn up the calories, and too much clothing can be dangerous. If you want to take a down jacket or vest along, put it in the pack to wear when you stop for lunch.

There are three types of cross-country suits: two-piece, two-piece with bib, and one-piece. The two-piece knicker with top is the traditional cross-country suit. The best material for its construction is 100 percent stretch nylon. Nylon has all the qualities we want in a cross-country suit—stretch, wind-resistance, and water repellancy. Two-piece suits also come in poplin (cotton/nylon), which is windproof but does not flex as well as 100 percent nylon, and is not as breathable for moisture to pass through. If you wear this kind of suit, you can take the jacket off and tie it around your waist if you get too hot. Put the jacket back on if you get cold again, and ventilate with the front zipper. Most traditional suits have convenient pockets in the jacket and pants for storage.

Bill Koch using his equipment to advantage in the North America championships in 1974. (Photo by J. Omholt-Jensen)

An adaptation of the two-piece suit is the bib overall suit and jacket. The bib concept gives vital protection around the kidney area and keeps snow out of your pants when you fall.

One-piece suits are for racing and light touring. They come in two styles: to the knee and to the boot top. Both styles are good for the skiers who want lots of freedom and do not wear a great deal of clothing under their suits. These suits retain heat buildup, and flex well with every move.

Scout out the latest in mountaineering gear if you are a serious backcountry traveller. When you are moving slowly with a full pack, warm expedition gear is required.

Probably the single most important piece of cross-country clothing is the hat. As much as 60 percent of one's body heat can escape through the top of the head. A good wool cap will keep you warm, even if it gets wet from snow or excess perspiration. Take your hat off and on to ventilate.

For gloves and mitts, try mitts first for warmth. Use an over-mitt of poplin to protect the mitt from the wet and wind. As with other clothing, the layer principle works well on the hands. Hands are the last thing to get warm and the first to get cold. After your technique improves and your exercise tempo is increased, switch to finger gloves for better pole control.

Down at the ankle, a gaiter can keep the snow out, especially low mountaineering gaiters or the small Scandinavian ones made for cross-country skiing. The higher gaiters can be a nuisance and serve no real purpose in touring. However, they can be great for kids, since the high gaiter covers a small child's leg completely. This added layer means a lot to a little person.

The key to clothing is to dress in layers: take the layers off if you get hot and put them on again as you get cold. Be sure you don't overdress.

Good touring.

Part II

SKI TECHNIQUE

3

Basic Nordic Technique

by John Dostal

This article on technique is designed to get the beginner skiing quickly and efficiently. For the skier who's been at it for a while, it will help polish the style and maybe suggest a few new tricks. It is developed out of winters at the Trapp Family Lodge, where we developed ways of teaching with skiers and fellow instructors. It's a "how to" article that attempts to anticipate the skier's experiences and questions as he takes technique off the page and onto the snow.

DIAGONAL STRIDE

The kick and scissoring glide of a skier striding down the track are what most of us recognize as cross-country skiing, and it's the way you'll get around most of the time. The sequence of alternating opposite arm and leg forward (a configuration suggesting the *diagonal stride*) is commonly compared to walking. It's thought to be so familiar you don't have to think about it on or off skis. But this exhausts the comparison. It is better to think of skiing as closer to jogging—with a little glide.

Begin your skiing with that notion, and ski in tracks—preferably machine-set—to make your skis run straighter. Shuffle along, getting used to the feeling of gliding with each step. Now start to jog, leaning forward as you take short steps. Reach forward with the opposite hand and push back and through with the pole. Notice how much more glide you seem to get as you lean forward. You aren't being pushed along by a kind of scootering with your rear ski. Instead, you're setting up on it for an instant, using it as a kind of platform from which you can spring out, over, and onto the ski you're sliding forward. Feel your weight through the ball of your foot, pressing the ski onto the snow. Consider the differences in feeling between

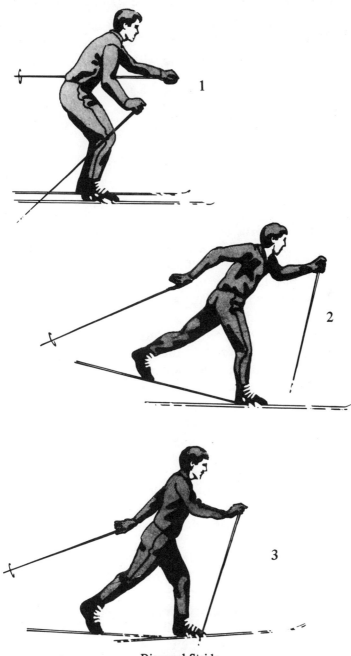

Diagonal Stride
(Illustrations in the technique section are by Bill Yenne)

stepping out to cross the street (a foot advances but there's not a lot of weight over it) and springing across a stream. The latter is more like skiing on the flat on cross-country skis.

A beginner may respond that this dramatic talk of launching onto a ski is an invitation to a nosedive: it feels a little tippy balancing on one ski. But your forward ski will catch you. And if you start off modestly, trying to develop a jogging rhythm, getting completely off of one ski onto the other, your stride will lengthen and balance will improve.

Many beginning skiers observe that they sometimes lose the rhythm of skiing. This is a common and not an irretrievable loss. When it happens, try to be conscious of where your weight is. More likely it will be behind the lead ski, with your hips behind rather than over your foot. A sure sign of this weight difficulty, especially among intermediate skiers, is a kind of slapping sound as the ski slides forward. The skier, unsteady on one ski, will start too early to put weight onto the ski that is coming through, getting support at the expense of glide. Take this problem to the hills, skiing on a gradual uphill, where decreased speed will allow you to bounce more forcefully onto the forward ski. Try to reproduce this feeling back on the flat.

Now it is time to pay a little more attention to the arms and poles. It's not only the thrust down and back that drives you down the track. The forward swing of the recovering arm, pulling your body out over your ski, also aids the stride. Prove this to yourself by skiing without poles. Notice the immediate increase in speed and glide as you swing your arms more vigorously, letting your body follow. It's as if your arms are pulling you down the track. It works best if hands are kept fairly low in front. If you can see them up in front of your face, they're too high, and will push you back off your ski rather than lead you onto it.

Now get some push from your poles. Hold each pole so that it's angled backward, so the basket drops into the snow beside your foot when your hand is extended. (If you wonder why you should angle it backward, try dropping both poles vertically in front of you and pushing yourself forward.) Push down and back past your hip, with your elbows in. If pushing the poles past the hips seems awkward, you may be holding them wrong. This could be an equipment problem. A good pole has an adjustable strap attached under a knob at the top of the grip. When the strap is cinched up tightly enough, the knob will ride between thumb and forefinger so that the pole will hang behind your hand when you release it. If your poles lack a knob and have straps attached at the top of the grip, it will be hard to get them adjusted properly no matter how much you tighten the strap. So make a knob by taping the top inch of strap to the handle with several turns of electrician's tape. This simple adjustment has made many folks' poling freer, easier, and more effective.

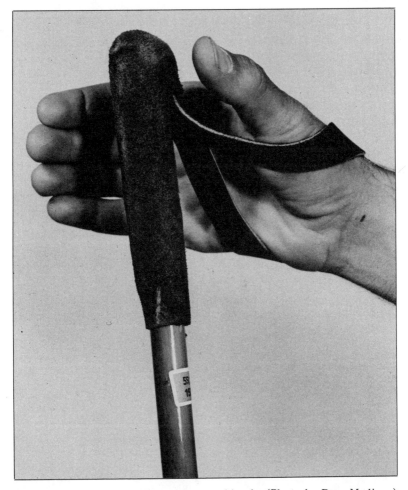

The proper way to grip a cross-country ski pole. (Photo by Dave Madison)

Poles should be used for propulsion, not as canes or outriggers. You may find them an encumbrance and you may seem to ski better without them. To improve your poling, find a section of track with a gradual downhill slope, and push yourself along with one pole at a time. In this exercise, use of the legs is expressly forbidden. If you remember to keep the pole angled backward you won't have to be concerned about getting it clear of the snow. On a bright day, it might help to check your body and pole position by watching your shadow on a snowbank.

UPHILL

There are many ways to ski up a hill. Your diagonal stride, slightly modified, will take you up easy and moderate hills as long as you keep up your momentum. Difficulties with hills are not always due to skis that are too stiff or that are waxed improperly. More often this is a result of using a little less effort than is required. This doesn't mean you have to bound up each hill with gut-straining zeal. Keep up a moderate, shuffling gait. You'll find it necessary to shorten your length of stride and to pole more frequently. Crouch a bit more, as if you're stalking uphill. Some skiers find they can get better grip from their wax if they think about pushing their heels uphill. You'll also find that using the inside edges of your skis will give some extra bite and make a real difference.

For steep hills, the *sidestep* is tedious but secure. With your skis across the fall line (the most direct line down the hill), plant the uphill pole and then bring the uphill ski up to it. Follow with the downhill pole, and then the downhill ski. Roll your ankles, digging the edge of the ski into the snow.

By using the rhythm of the diagonal stride and the edging of the sidestep, you can get up some difficult hills directly using the *herringbone*. Turn the ski tips outward, so the skis make a *V*. Edge to keep them from slipping backward, and chop alternating steps uphill. The wider you spread your skis, the more bite you'll have but the more difficult it will be to move them. Try using as narrow a herringbone as possible.

Success with uphills is ultimately a matter of suiting technique to terrain, getting a feeling for it. A visitor to Vermont, now skiing on the national team, went out for a ski with some

Sidestep

Herringbone

friends on a day when a slick, feathery February snow was filling in the tracks and giving everyone problems going uphill. Since this skier was getting uphill without much straining, he was asked to give some technical advice. "Well," she replied, "I'm just trying to be kind of light on my skis."

DOUBLE-POLING

Double-poling, not surprisingly, involves using both poles at once to push yourself along, thus giving the legs a rest. It's a good way to get some relaxing glide and to keep up speed on a gentle downhill or on a fast or icy stretch of flat track. Try double-poling behind a skier of equal ability who's striding. Note the types of places where double-poling makes more efficient use of the terrain. Double-pole, too, on sections of track where you need a little more stablility on your skis—such as under the trees, where dripping makes the track icy, or where the track is broken and choppy.

While double-poling may look as if it's done with the arms, most of the power is generated by the weight of the skier's body sinking onto the poles. Start double-poling by reaching

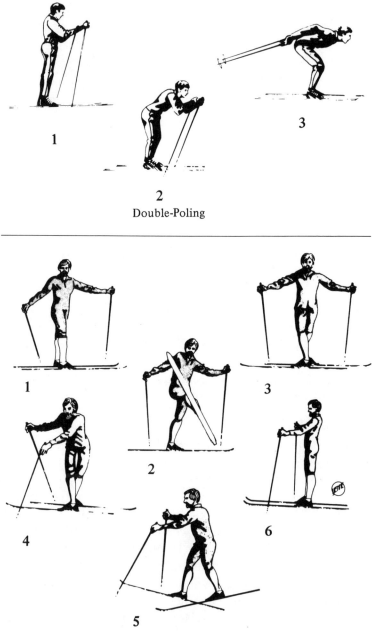

Double-Poling

Kick Turn

forward and planting the poles with a backward angle. Then, hinge at the waist, dropping forward and down onto the poles. Keep your elbows flexed slightly, but at a constant angle. That is, try to push yourself forward without bending your arms any further. Only when you're bent over, with your upper body roughly parallel to the snow, should you straighten your arms with a final push. Then swing the arms forward as you straighten up. Your knees should be relaxed and flexed a bit, but not bent very much. If, instead of hinging forward at the waist, you drop your butt, you'll only absorb the force that would otherwise propel you down the track. Be sure to come back up to your full height, so you can get full benefit from your body weight dropping onto your poles.

TURNING ON THE FLAT

The easiest way to turn skis around is the way most people would instinctively go about it: move one ski at a time, *stepping around*. If you feel there is rather a lot of cumbersome ski to move, concentrate on lifting your toe—and consequently the tip of the ski—and flicking it in the desired direction. Don't worry about what you can't see: the tail of the ski. Use poles to help lead the skis around.

For a quicker change of direction try a *kick turn*—a turn already familiar to most downhill skiers. To turn to the right, plant the left pole by the left ski tip, and the right pole back by the tail of the right ski. This will open up your body for the turn. Pivot the right ski by lifting the knee, cocking the ankle, and flicking the tip up and around. The trick is to get the tip up and then to flip it over; simply turning the ski out makes it more difficult. For those familiar with ballet, you're now in fourth position. Complete the turn by bringing the left ski and pole around, parallel with the right ski. Kick turns are useful for traversing back and forth down a hill.

DOWNHILL

The inquiring downhill skier attempting cross-country for the first time should be aware that: (1) the skis do indeed have "edges" (the bottoms aren't, after all, round); and (2) you do not have to have your heel locked to turn the skis. To the beginner without any Alpine background, the appearance of a downhill stretch need not be cause for immediate alarm. Just work into it, and be glad you don't have to worry that your heel is not locked down.

Before trying to turn or even to check your speed, get a feeling for skiing downhill. Find a gentle slope with a run-out at the bottom to slow you to a stop. If you see only disaster, loss of control, and an inevitable fall at the bottom instead of the flat that is really there, head for a more gentle and inviting incline. After you feel comfortable there, work on a steeper slope.

Keep your skis shoulder-width apart and your poles back, so that they won't catch on brush or on other skiers. Push your knees forward so you can feel the top of your foot press against the tongue of your shoe. This will keep your knees bent and flexible, so you'll be in balance as you ride over bumps and changes in the surface of the snow. Note that bending your knees does not mean bending over at the waist. But you might try bending at the waist, though, and have a friend give you a push on the rump. Then drop your butt straight down, as if balancing a book on your head. Have your friend push you in this position, and compare the stability of each posture. "You can't ski with knees like the goat," is the watchword of one instructor of fifty years skiing experience. Take a few runs, straight down, letting the run-out slow you up. Try lifting one ski, then the other.

Once you have a feel for sliding on your skis, begin to control speed by *snowplowing* or, as the downhill folks call it, *wedging*. Slide the tails of your skis apart into a wedge or *V* by pressing your heels out, and dropping your hands down toward your flexed knees to make it easier. Real braking in the snowplow comes from edging the skis, so that they put up more resistance to the snow. This is accomplished by rolling your ankles inward. Some skiers, eager to check their speed as quickly as possible, edge their skis immediately. As they rocket downhill, knock-kneed on two parallel rails, they wonder why they do not stop. It is better to keep the skis flat on the snow, with the knees pressed forward and shoulder-width apart, as you slide them into a *V*, and then work on some edging. Vary the width of the wedge to modify your speed: the wider it is, the slower you go.

If you're skiing in a track and you want to slow down, try a

1

2

Snowplow

Half-Snowplow

half-snowplow. Lift one ski out of the track and slide it to the side, plowing in the untracked snow with just enough pressure to slow yourself down. It will take some experimenting to determine how much pressure to use. Keep most of your weight on the flexed knee of the ski that is still in the track.

A NOTE ON FALLING

Getting used to all these maneuvers will most likely entail some falls—occasions for high comedy, for learning, but hopefully not for harsh judgment. Rather than gaining experience from the fall or simply enjoying the spectacle, some skiers get down on themselves, equating falls with failure. Since it's pretty hard to get hurt on cross-country skis, it is better to relax and maybe to reconstruct the fall. Hand position has such a great influence on body position that, having dusted yourself off, you might want to recall where your hands were—and be a little more conscious of them next time. If your skis shot from under you, your hands were probably behind you. If you couldn't seem to get enough weight onto the skis to make them carve around, perhaps your hands drifted up by your shoulders.

To get up from a fall, roll onto your side, sling your skis around so they are parallel, and push up onto your knees. If you've fallen in powder, cross your poles and, holding them in the middle, push up using that foundation. If you've taken a headlong pitch, just disentangle your skis by rolling on to your back, and get up using the first method described. If you're on a slope, make sure the poles are below you and pointing across the hill when you get up, so you won't start sliding as soon as you place your weight on them.

TURNING DOWNHILL

You can turn downhill the same way you turned on the flat. Do a *step turn* by picking up the tip of a ski and stepping it in the direction you want it to go. Quickness is vital here; you've got to scamper a bit on your skis. To help get around and to reduce the feeling of being somewhat out of control, use your hands. Lead with your poles, involving your whole body in the turn.

Step Turn

A more flamboyant version of the step turn is the *skate turn*. Skating will be familiar to downhill skiers (and you can skate the same way across windblown flats). But in cross-country skiing, skate turns help you accelerate. Begin by double-poling. While your arms are still back (before you've stood up and re-covered), step one ski in the direction you want to go and aggressively push off the other ski, as if you were skating. If many skiers skate around a particular corner, they will inscribe a deep and obvious rut. To avoid an awkward split in such a rut, anticipate the turn and begin it as your ski slides into the rut.

Along with the step turn, the *snowplow turn* is the mainstay of the cross-country skier. For a right turn, slide your skis into a snowplow (keeping them flat on the snow), and shift your weight onto the left ski—the one that's pointed in the direction

Snowplow Turn

you want to go. The weight change is a shift rather than a lean. Skiers having difficulty with snowplow turns sometimes try to urge their skis around by cocking the head and shoulders to one side, standing straight-legged on their skis. If this is a familiar predicament, try exaggerating it on the flat and then flex your knees more, dropping hips down and over the skis, feeling the increased weight on the skis. It may help to drop a hand down and touch your left knee to weight the left ski for a right turn. To make well-defined, secure snowplow turns, keep up the pressure on the weighted ski throughout the turn. When you're comfortable turning in each direction, try linking turns one after another. Then get a friend and braid some figure eights downhill.

Having learned how to perform a snowplow, a snowplow turn, and a step turn, a skier will still have a few surprises on the trails. The wide snowplow that was such an efficient brake on a packed-out, open slope may not be possible on a narrow trail, where brush or choppy snow catches the tails of the skis. So, try plowing with one ski—remembering how you slowed down in the track—switching skis as the condition of the trail demands. A heavily used trail will have a trough in the middle, and sides humped up with snow from skiers snowplowing down the middle. This is the cross-country version of *moguls,* the bumps in ski runs encountered by downhill skiers. If you can't seem to brake enough in such troughs, try riding the sides, tacking back and forth with snowplow turns, skiing up the bumps, and turning off the tops to check your speed.

The *stem turn* puts a bit more finish on a snowplow turn. It's a quicker turn, one you can use on steeper slopes. Begin by pushing out (*stemming*) the tail of one ski, as if in a snowplow. This weighted ski will come around quickly, and as it does, bring the other unweighted ski alongside for a parallel finish. You may have trouble getting off, say, your right ski and onto the stemmed left ski, so that you end up stamping the right ski into the snow. To avoid this problem, think of the maneuver (for a right turn) as stepping off the right onto a stemming left ski. If it is done sharply, with an emphatic swivel downhill or on the flat, a stem turn can spray a satisfying amount of snow and stop you quickly—like a skater or a hockey player.

Stem Turn

Many skiers use the snowplow on reflex whenever approaching a turn or a bend in the trail. This just isn't necessary. When skiing on trails, take a tip from racers, and *carve* around turns. Keep your skis parallel, drop your hips down into a crouch, and extend your hands in front as if holding a large steering wheel. You will essentially be steering with your hands. If you wish to carve a left turn, reach out and drop your right hand near your right foot, shifting the weight onto your right ski. This way, you will carve around to the left. This is also the position to be in when sweeping around a bend while skiing in tracks.

Skiing down the hills, like skiing up them, takes some work and a willingness to go back over difficult sections and work through them. As you become more adept, the hills will seem slower. Instead of feeling rushed, watching the birch trees click by, you'll look ahead on the trail, anticipating the upcoming squirrelly bumps. Don't hesitate to take your cross-country skis to a downhill area for a workout (check the local regulations), or to step out of the track if the powder looks good down through the trees.

Carving Around a Turn

4

Off-Trail Skiing

by Ned Baldwin

The equipment and technique required for ski touring in untracked snow differ significantly from that used in racing and trail skiing. Skiing off the trail requires sturdier (and consequently, heavier) equipment to cope with the greater turning forces. It also requires more strength and better conditioning if you are to excel. In my judgment, more and more cross-country skiers will be moving off the trail, for it is only there that many of the promises of this sport come true. Only away from trails and other people can one find undisturbed winter wilderness, and test the ability of skis to cope with variations in terrain and snow conditions.

The explosion in numbers that has occurred in cross-country skiing, as in so many other sports, threatens an activity that I always assumed could absorb unlimited numbers. This is largely because recreational skiers have been introduced only to light-weight equipment, suitable for trail skiing. Consequently they have found themselves flocking together on the most accessible trails. In urban areas this leads to insane congestion and some of the worst skiing conditions I have ever seen. As the track becomes worn by hundreds of skiers, the snow gradually turns to dense ice, and becomes rutted and treach-erous. Frankly, I am continually amazed that people go out at all in these conditions. I am certain that many people buy skis, go out once, and then become discouraged and quit.

The other unfortunate result of this emphasis on trail skiing has been the apparent need to develop more trails, form clubs, and exploit the trails commercially. I find the concept of paying simply to use a trail especially abhorrent. The development of additional trails simply reduces the amount of undisturbed wilderness available to explore.

I hope enough skiers will discover the joys of untracked snow in time to reverse these trends. In this article I shall outline what you need to know if you decide to venture off the trail.

EQUIPMENT

Racing and light touring equipment is designed with the assumption that the foot is attached to the ski via a single hinge that opens and closes only in one direction. The shoe sole is therefore very narrow and flexible, like any athletic shoe. When a twisting force is applied to the ski, the sole itself is apt to buckle. This allows the skier's foot to rotate away from the axis of the ski, and the binding itself may become loosened from the ski.

Deep snow skiing increases the likelihood these torsional forces will occur. But good technique should help eliminate it to a large extent. And if you have equipment that can absorb these forces, this places fewer demands on the skier's technique.

In an effort to reduce the weight of cross-country equipment, designers have moved toward progressively narrower skis. Older wooden skis used elaborate shaping techniques, such as side channeling and top rib stiffening, to reduce the amount of wood required to support the desired ski bottom surface. Mass production of cross-country skis has made these hand-crafted features uneconomical. Machine-produced skis have much simpler geometrical properties (such as parallel sides), and to make them lighter, they have inevitably become narrower.

The sacrifices in performance as a result of these changes are quite significant. Side cambering, where the shovel of the ski was dramatically broader than its waist, made it track beautifully and gave it great flotation in deep powder snow. Today it is all but impossible to find skis with these qualities. However, with the developing interest in off-trail skiing, manufacturers are now beginning to introduce features to make the skis more effective in deep powder.

It is important to look for the following features when selecting equipment.

Boots. Look for broad soles that flex easily forward and backward, but are very stiff when twisted. Leather is still the overwhelming favorite for materials. The cut of the uppers should be reasonably high for ankle support. I know some skiers, however, who are happy with low models cut beneath the ankle. But they tend to be expert skiers who seldom stress the sole of the boot, anyway.

Gaiters. These are essential for deep snow skiing, regardless of the height of your boots. Without them your feet will become wet from melting snow.

Skis. Look for breadth above almost all else—70- to 85-mm minimum at the shovel. This width will give you more lateral stability when striding. Unbroken snow is irregular in density, and narrow skis invariably cut in erratically, making control difficult. When downhill running, the greater width will enable you to plane nearer the surface rather than slicing deeply into the mass of the snow, thus increasing your speed.

Obviously the heavier you are the more important these factors become. Length should generally be around 5 centimeters shorter than the length you would select for trail touring or racing. Since arm and leg lengths can vary considerably, the best gauge is to assume the telemark position, and measure from the toe of the trailing foot to the center of the ankle bone of the forward foot. This length will be the distance from the balance point to the tip of the correct length ski.

Poles. Poles up to 5 centimeters shorter than racing poles can be used satisfactorily in deep snow. Baskets should be larger than trail touring baskets to minimize sinking depth in the snow. Tonkin cane is my favorite material, although fiberglass and light alloy poles are almost as good and far more durable. In avalanche country poles with telescoping body probes built within them are a good idea.

TECHNIQUE

Technique for off-trail skiing is essentially the same as that for on the trail, except that there is more variety in movement as a result of continual changes in terrain and conditions.

I have skied hard for 8 hours straight in deep snow, climbing and descending continuously with no ill-effects. But I have suffered leg cramps after 2 hours while running a 50-kilometer race. I often find trail touring monotonous, akin to skiing on a lake for mile after mile.

As a canoeist must read the water ahead of him to choose the deepest and swiftest water, the deep-snow skier must continuously "read" the snow ahead to seek out the easiest and fastest route. Route finding is a great skill, which is only developed by experience. Many neophyte cross-country skiers get into trouble when striking off the trail. They either get lost or find themselves in terrain where their technique is inadequate. It is best, therefore, to plan your route carefully, preferably with someone who has skied that route before you.

Traversing is the key to easy ascents and descents. Many skiers are unable to recognize the fall line, and as a consequence, choose irrational lines. One must develop a good eye for level to understand where the horizontal contour is, and exactly how much snow conditions, your wax, your equipment, and your skiing ability will allow you to depart from it, going either up or down.

Climbing too steeply can lead to exhaustion, excessive perspiration, and chill, resulting in possible exposure to hypothermia. Climb slowly and steadily, attempting to keep your pace uniform. Do not stop and rest, but rather go slow enough that it is unnecessary to stop.

Descending, or downhill running, is for me the raison d'etre of skiing. My objective in any outing is invariably to obtain a fine downhill run toward the end. While descending on a trail is usually a straight run with occasional step turns at the corner, descending in untracked snow offers the opportunity for gracefully steered turns to lengthen the descent, check speed, and avoid obstacles.

The simplest of the steered turns are *edged* (or *parallel*) turns, in which the skier's direction is altered by simple angulation of the ski. By tilting the ski, the tip bites into the snow, causing it to swerve or carve a turn in the direction of the tilt. With this turn, only modest deviations from the fall line are practical.

In deep snow conditions, this is a more practical method for quickly avoiding an obstacle than the step turn, which involves lifting one ski at a time off the snow.

Telemark Turn

The greatest of the steered turns is the *telemark*; for me it is the reason for skiing. No maneuver on skis offers the excitement of a perfectly executed telemark. It is so clean, causing minimal lateral drag on the snow, that it invariably increases one's speed when turning toward the fall line. This feature makes it possible to get a thrilling run on a very modest hill. It offers complete control on the steepest slopes, since the legs are wide apart, giving the skier enormous stability. This stance should always be used when running downhill in unbroken snow, regardless of whether or not you intend to make a turn. Trail skiers are able to ski downhill in the "tuck" position. But one can seldom get away with this in deep snow, where conditions can change rapidly.

The key to learning the telemark is developing lateral balance. Since one's skis adopt a single track there is little, aside from balance, to keep the skier upright. Just as balance comes all of a sudden when learning to ride a bicycle, so it will in learning to do a telemark. On the following pages I have outlined the successive steps in learning the telemark. Do not advance more rapidly than you can master each of these steps. You will suddenly find that you can do it, and that it is not exhausting at all.

Practice the telemark position standing on flat ground without moving, with skis approximately 7 inches apart. Practice moving from a position with the left ski forward to one with the right ski forward. The forward leg should be bent with the knee at a right angle and the shin perpendicular to the ski. The upper body is kept erect, and perpendicular to the ski. The weight is distributed uniformly between the skis, and the arms are kept low and extended outward to provide maximum lateral stability.

Practice switching from one position to the other, smoothly and rhythmically without losing your balance. Do it first with no poles, then with your poles, and finally with no poles and

Telemark Turn

your arms crossed behind your back. The position often seems uncomfortable at first. Only after you have practiced it for some time does it become more comfortable.

Standing on the flat snow in the telemark position feels very awkward. I cannot hold the position for long. But the sense of awkwardness disappears as soon as one is moving downhill rapidly. Then it will seem much more secure than standing erect.

Now move to a gradual hill with 2 to 3 inches of soft powder on a firm base. Practice these same alternating telemark positions, while straight running down the hill. Try to develop the same smoothness that you achieved on the flat. This should seem quite easy, since in the straight running position, the skis can be kept 7 inches apart, making lateral stability less of a problem. After you are entirely confident about assuming the telemark position, you have already progressed a long way in learning how to descend hills. It should be an instinctive reaction to sink into a telemark whenever you are uncertain of the terrain ahead.

The third exercise is to run straight down the same gradual hill assuming a telemark position. On the flat at the base of the hill, make a turn to a stop in the opposite direction from your forward ski. The turn is initiated by tilting or slightly twisting the forward ski in the direction you wish to go. If you wish to turn to the right your left ski should be forward; if you want to turn to the left your right ski should be forward. A small amount of effort will initiate the turn. If the snow conditions are deep powder, it may be necessary to shift some of your weight to the rear ski. This will slightly unweight the forward ski, making the turn easier to initiate.

As the forward ski moves in the desired direction, the trailing ski should slide into the same track, its tip nestling against the forward boot. You should lean slightly into the turn as if riding a bicycle to maintain your balance. This helps offset the centrifugal force that must be resisted to carry your weight around the corner.

If you can manage 6 telemark turns in each direction without falling, you are ready to try them on a hill. Don't attempt them on a hill until you can do them on the flat in the manner described. Don't be afraid to take some speed. Many people try the telemark by assuming the position immediately after they start moving. Some momentum is necessary to accomplish the turn, especially if the snow is at all deep. So make sure you start out aggressively, poling to get started, and have sufficient speed when it comes to making the turn.

Having accomplished the turn, you should now try the same thing on the slope, turning away from the fall line and coming to a stop on the side of the hill. This is basically the same, except that the opportunity for losing one's balance is greater. It is a temptation at first to lean into the hill and fall against it. In trying to overcome this, you may find that you fall down the hill.

It must be practiced coming to a complete stop in both directions. Each time you try, do it in the opposite direction so that you don't develop a propensity for turning in only one direction.

All of these maneuvers should be attempted at first without poles. That way, use of the poles for balance does not become a critical part of your ability to turn. First, simply extend the arms for balance. Then when you feel you have it mastered, try clasping your hands behind your back in each of these maneuvers.

Now you are ready for downhill telemarks, in which you turn from a traverse toward and across the fall line. When you can do this in both directions, actually linking your turns, you can claim to have really mastered the telemark.

When turning toward the fall line your balance must be perfect. The lean to the inside is trickier because you must lean directly down the hill to initiate the turn and maintain your balance as you come around. It is easy to fall either to the inside or to the outside of the turn. Practiced on a gradual hill this really is not difficult. Only when you move to progressively steeper slopes does this balance problem become severe.

Since you are moving from a traversing position toward the fall line, the rate at which you turn can make a great deal of difference in maintaining balance. I like to start beginners initiating the turn only in one direction. Then, they can immediately reverse the position and initiate it on the other side.

Gradually one can deepen the swings as the slope gets steeper.

On very steep slopes I drop my telemark stance much lower, often dragging my trailing knee in the snow. This often results in my rear ski crossing behind the boot of the forward ski, causing a spill. You must develop a sense of exactly how far you can go in dropping your center of gravity close to the snow.

Perhaps the most important thing to remember is to get out over your forward ski if the slope is extremely steep, and actually reach for the fall line. Extend the downhill arm out and twist the upper body in the direction of the turn. The steeper the slope, the easier it is to initiate the turn. The forward ski travels in the direction of the fall line by applying the slightest twist of the forward foot.

Here the whole problem is balance. Once the turn is initiated and you are traveling on the opposite traverse, immediately switch to the opposite telemark position, ready for the next turn. Do not carry across the slope with the downhill ski in the forward position, since it is often hard to prevent the swing from carrying you around to a complete stop.

In very deep snow, or where the slope has a gentle gradient, it is necessary to make your telemarks in complete swings to avoid losing too much speed. The telemark is a steered turn and as such the ski never travels laterally through the snow. Therefore, the skier's speed is diminished only by the fact that he travels a longer route than the fall line, and therefore travels on a less steep gradient. Often, one's speed actually increases in the turn, as you turn toward the fall line and assume a steeper line on the slope.

If you find the telemark difficult, take heart in the fact that very few people today know how to do it all. It actually isn't that difficult if you'll practice each of the steps, progressing through them in a methodical way. When you can accomplish all of them, even without poles and with your hands clasped behind your back, you will have discovered a whole new dimension to skiing.

We have always taken great pleasure in decorating the hills with our telemark tracks. With ingenuity you can completely cover a field with a lacework pattern of intertwining tracks, each one ski width wide.

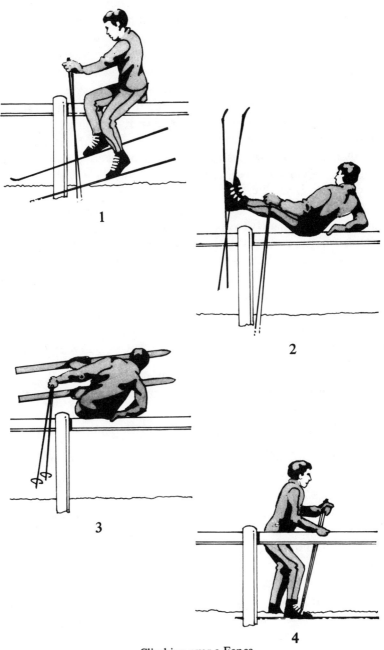

1

2

3

4

Climbing over a Fence

It is not essential to have deep powder snow to do telemarks. Any snow with some loose material on the surface is quite appropriate. Telemarks in corn-snow in the spring are some of the best. Under these conditions one's speed is greater, of course. Then it is sometimes difficult to avoid a slight stemming effect when the turn is initiated sharply to check one's speed.

Telemarks in the woods are a great thrill. One has complete control over direction so long as one is not changing the pattern of telemarks in order to retain balance. If you have mastered the telemark and your balance has become second nature, then you can basically steer in any direction you want with absolute precision.

When skiing in the woods the first thing you will notice is that you are unable to extend your poles and arms out for balance because of obstructions. This makes it extremely important that you are able to telemark with "your hands behind your back." Skiing around trees is always dangerous. One must anticipate the beginning of the turn in sufficient time so that it happens where you want it to, not a critical yard further down the hill.

OBSTACLES

By its nature, off-trail skiing invariably brings the skier into contact with numerous obstacles. The most common of these are trees and bushes. To enjoy skiing, one must learn not to be intimidated by them, especially in eastern Canada and eastern United States.

Usually it is only on the descent that trees and bushes are a problem. It is imperative to wear eye protection. Also, remove pole wrist straps, since a basket hooked on a stump or branch can dislocate a shoulder. One must learn not to shy away from the branches, but only from the trunks of trees. Colliding with an immovable tree trunk, even at a walking pace, can take your breath away. Needless to say, it is one to be avoided. However, skiing through pine branches or brush is not really painful at all, and is almost inevitable at some point if you are to learn downhill running within deep woods. In my part of the country, Ontario, the soft powder remains long after the sun and wind have hardened the open slopes. Thus, we are always in conflict with trees and shrubs. My greatest fear is that I will break my skis by running into a tree trunk or a buried stump. I always wear old clothes that can withstand the beating. It is a regular occurrence for me to return from a tour with burrs stuck all over my clothes.

Crossing fences is also an everyday part of skiing off the trail in the East. One must develop an inherent agility in dealing with these obstacles. Otherwise you will inevitably get soaked, removing skis, sinking into deep snow, and struggling over each obstacle. One must learn to have fun with them instead. I maintain that a good skier should be able to climb a tree with his skis on!

I hope that in these few pages I have managed to convey a bit of the extra scope that off-trail skiing offers to anyone willing to seek out the experience.

5

Parallel Turns on Nordic Skis

by Eric Burr

The first tracks in powder used to indicate christianas, those long graceful turns performed with the legs and skis almost touching. You could hear the skis scraping each other beneath the powder. You were supposed to practice by holding an object like a glove tightly between your knees.

Then along came Jean-Claude Killy with his wide-track parallel that beat the competition and replaced the christiana. Now the first tracks are apt to be made by an expert Nordic skier, quickly climbing high above the lift-accessible slopes to lay down linked telemark turns.

The thing all these turns have in common is that they are all parallel. To ski powder well, especially deep powder, one has to distribute the weight equally on both skis. The tails should go over the same snow that the tips did. Alpine skiers with much heavier equipment can cheat and skid their skis around under light powder. But you can easily spot them by their flaring tracks at the outside of each turn and their advice on how to do it: "Powder is just like regular skiing, only it's more work." Eventually, as the powder gets deeper and heavier, the skidders and heel-pushers are eliminated and only the carvers survive.

Oddly enough, the Nordic carvers do as well as their Alpine counterparts. Skidding one's skis even through light powder is indeed more work; carving, by contrast, is pure, sensuous pleasure. The only time Nordic experts do much skidding is over light spring corn-snow, or when they're side-slipping down a steep, narrow area where there's no room to turn safely. The latter is a survival maneuver, and it's well to practice both forward and backward side-slipping.

66

Nordic skiers have an advantage in powder, in that it's almost impossible for them to skid the skis sideways at any speed. So in parallel skiing, they have to carve right from the start. The only time the carved parallel is not the best turn for heavy snow is when skiing mushy spring corn-snow, when nothing works except a steered telemark or a step turn. This is another advantage of the telemark; it can be both carved and steered, as needed.

COMPONENTS OF PARALLEL TURNS

All parallel turns have two (and, on hard snow, three) separate movements that must be performed harmoniously as the skis pass through the fall line: edge change, lead change, and for hard snow, weight change. The only exceptions are linked telemarks, which do not have the lead change. This is an advanced powder maneuver where only the edges are changed. Failure to change edges usually leads to falls outside the arc of the turn as a result of catching the outside edge. Failure to change lead usually produces crossed tips, as the trailing uphill ski passes over and behind the downhill tip. Egg-beaters are the common result of crossed tips.

Failure to change weight on hard snow usually causes the downhill ski to "wash out." This also tires the legs from having to carry more weight on the inside, uphill leg. The more a leg is bent, the less weight it can comfortably hold. This is why in a traverse the downhill, straighter leg is usually given the most weight to carry.

When turns are linked in tight succession, a good deal of precise coordination must take place, unless your balance is sharp enough to perform the telemark without a lead change—and this maneuver only works when your skis are carving well. Most of us have to break down a parallel turn into its component parts and coordinate each with whatever weighting sequence we're using. Only after each component is mastered are we ready to put the whole thing together through the fall line, complete with rotation, counter-rotation (or split rotation), pole plants, tip pull, and carving or skidding.

The variety of skis, snow, and skiers means that there are a vast number of ways to combine all this. No sequence is sacred, and the following are simply examples of complete parallel turns. You should watch for edge change, lead change, and on hard snow, weight change. Visualize how they mesh with the application of turning forces and the overall weighting and unweighting.

TURNS IN POWDER SNOW

Let's take a wide-track, carved parallel first. This is the classic weighted or compression turn for skiing powder snow on Nordic skis.

Approaching in a traverse, the skier simultaneously sinks down, thereby unweighting the skis slightly. If he thinks a little body English is necessary, he winds up (counter-rotates) just before starting to straighten the legs and driving the bottom camber out of the skis. As the legs push down, the skier simultaneously releases the edges, allowing the skis to drift out of the traverse, and to start seeking the fall line. Meanwhile, the upper body has rotated in the direction of the turn and is beginning to block, transmitting its torsional momentum to the legs.

Parallel Turn

The edges of the skis are now tipped the opposite way, and the tips are pointing into the turn. As the upper body rotation is transmitted to the skis, the skis are equally bowed, reversing normal bottom camber and carving around. By now, the skier is in the fall line and lead must change at this precise instant. The legs are at maximum extension and start to retract in preparation for another turn.

If carving is not enough to bring the skier around as far as desired, he can counter-rotate again with the upper body, causing an equal and opposite reaction to be transmitted to the legs and skis. This rotation/counter-rotation applies maximum torque to the skis, and isn't always necessary. In fact, with so many turning forces going for the skier—tip pull, carving, rotation, and a pole plant—it's very difficult to pinpoint what is causing the rotation. But it becomes easy once you've practiced each of the component parts and gradually put them all together.

The easiest way to break down a turn into its component parts is first to abandon the fall line. That is, practice in the fan or garland pattern to eliminate extreme edge, lead, and weight changes.

In any given snow condition, try an easy uphill turn using each component separately. Perhaps you'll try tip pull first in powder by simply tipping your knees uphill. Next, get some carve into it by pressing on the skis as you point the tips uphill. Then go back, wind up and try rotation alone and pole plant alone. Then start combining them.

Once you have a smooth system going, try steeper and steeper turns, gradually approaching the fall line. Avoid the temptation to go through the fall line; things are complicated enough already. Now try another set of uphill turns in the opposite direction. Then repeat the whole thing on a slightly steeper hill.

Unless you're a super-skier, your body is going to take a while to learn all these moves. Even if your mind can follow it all in theory, it can't possibly keep up as changes in snow condition require technique variations. Your body will feel the snow changing and will react before you have had time to think about it. If you've practiced in many different snow conditions, your body will automatically program in the proper moves. This is the inner skier. Don't fight it; just let it flow. When it all comes together in some silky powder under a sparkling high mountain sky, the experience is orgasmic.

TURNS IN CORN-SNOW

The next best thing to powder is spring corn-snow. Lead and edge changes are the same in spring corn as in powder. But now the surface is firm and weight can be shifted to a new downhill ski every time you cross the fall line. Also, spring corn usually won't hold a carving edge well, so you'll have to change from weighted turns to unweighted. Here you have a choice of up-unweighting or down-unweighting. The latter is faster, but does not give you as much time in the air.

Let's go through a fall-line turn in which you use everything you can throw into it. Approaching the turn, again sink down and wind up counter to the direction you're going to turn. However, this time do not unwind while the legs extend, blocking to transmit the motion to the skis while they carve the snow. This time lift clear of the snow before blocking. The difference is a split-second delay in applying the rotation. This means that tips and tails will rotate at an angle to the direction of travel, and when you come down, they'll be skidding sideways over the snow.

This is how most Alpine skiers turn. We can only accomplish this on Nordic skis when there is a soft surface over a smooth, firm base, such as you find on untracked mountainsides of spring corn after a spell of clear weather. In this situation, there's no carve and no tip pull to help you around. So you'll most likely have to counter-rotate as you sink down. The pole plant is also important, both to swing you around and to help you rise in the air enough for the edges to clear the snow. Starting out, you'll have to eliminate the fall line again. Then, when you go back to skiing the fall line, you'll be leaping about quite a bit until you learn by experience how much lift you need.

To review, during turns, powder snow requires positively weighted carving skis, while corn usually requires unweighted skidding skis. Crossing the fall line in powder necessitates edge change first, then lead change. Corn-snow requires all three: edge, then lead, and finally weight changed together.

LEARNING THE TURNS

A lot of this practice can be accomplished off the snow. In fact, this is a good ankle exercise, too.

Now suppose you can't decide whether that white stuff is powder or corn. There is a vast and only partially charted no-man's-land in between powder and corn called "crud." Those ski crazies who turn in it are called "crud artists." There's really nothing to it except practice—lots of practice!

Try weighted carving turns first. If you don't feel any carve after several tries, then unweight for a couple of turns. Do all this experimenting without crossing the fall line. Maybe only steered telemarks will be successful. Typically, when I cross over a ridge into a new snow condition, I crank out a couple of garlands first until it feels good, and then peel off down the fall line.

Snow is one of the earth's most variable substances, and the ways of skiing it are correspondingly complex. Once you understand the differences between Alpine and Nordic skis, much of the prolific Alpine technique literature may be of interest to you. I want to emphasize, however, that there is no substitute for time on the snow. Practice and approach can be thought out, but split-second body responses on skis are governed by neurological processes separate from conscious thought.

Good ski instruction deals primarily with this inner realm. Nordic instruction is in its infancy regarding downhill technique. In this article, I have tried to introduce Nordic skiing's downhill fundamentals in a way that will give individual skiers some aids to achieving expertise on their own. This approach is necessitated both by the individualistic Nordic temperament and the fact that a cadre of expert downhill Nordic instructors has yet to evolve.

I've tried to take some of the mystery out of off-track downhilling. I hope by now that you're no longer surprised at the sight of skiers with pin bindings coming down the steepest slopes, and that you no longer believe that skiing powder just requires a little extra muscle.

Part III

TRAINING AND CONDITIONING

6

An Approach to Training

by Bob Gray

The last time I sat down to write about skiing and training it was November, and I wrote about the chill winds and the sense of urgency in the air. I was feeling the approach of winter and a natural urge to prepare. Now, at this writing, it is June. The days are warm and easy. Summer seems to stretch out before me, and I don't feel any sense of urgency at all. My training has always been strongly influenced by the seasons and what is going on around me. Consequently, I have leaned toward a natural approach to training. I have always found it difficult to adopt a high-pressure ski training program in summer.

Though it has been four years since I spent a lot of time thinking about training for skiing, you can sometimes see things more clearly from a distance. Still, I haven't found that my ideas have changed much. Some of my ideas have become even stronger.

As you train, I feel it is important that you understand yourself and why you are training. People have many reasons for training, and often you may not realize what they are. You can train to get in shape, or because it simply makes you feel better. You may be training for skiing; or maybe because it is such a good outlet for tensions that build up inside us. Sometimes we train because we don't have anything else to do, and it becomes a form of escape.

Since you need a reason for training, you should spend some time thinking about yourself and your goals. This will help guide you on those days when you wonder where you are and what you are doing there. There are times in your training year when you particularly need a purpose—especially as you progress toward the peak of the season. At that time of year you can't afford to get sidetracked or lose interest. Understanding yourself and your purpose improves your concentration when it is needed most.

In addition, it is essential to have a plan for your training, though not a rigid schedule. You need a year-round plan that fits your own life-style. Don't be too easily influenced by what others are doing. Take some time in laying out your plan, talk with others, and study training programs. But once you decide on a plan, try to stick with it.

Remember, what works for you may not work for others. Enjoy your training, especially in the off-season; it should be the bright spot in your day. If you are a serious cross-country skier, then you are going to be training for a long time. And if you don't enjoy it, you won't last.

In your plan, spring, summer, and early fall are the fun seasons. Almost any type of dry-land training is good, as long as you are basically building skiing strength and endurance. This can include a range of activities: running, bicycling, swimming, backpacking, roller skiing, and so on. As winter approaches, you must settle down to business. By that point, you will be tired of playing around, and ready to settle down to business. You should even be looking forward to it.

By mid-fall (October) you can begin your *progression.* By progression, I refer to the stages of training, as the intensity increases over the course of the ski season. I feel that a progression, both mental and physical, is the most important part of the cross-country ski season, as well as the most difficult to maintain. It offers you a focus during a winter that sometimes becomes scattered with racing, travel, and even sickness. Since progression is difficult to maintain, it is important not to begin it too early in the season. If you are doing X amount of work on November 1, then you should be doing $X+$ so much work on December 1, and so on. You can see that if this continues month after month March could get pretty "heavy." However, there are ways of avoiding this: a progression can be maintained by *intensity* as well by the *amount* of work. If you really think about it, you can work out a solution. But you will have to give it some thought, especially at this most important time of year, with the transition from dry-land training to skiing.

In most cross-country training schedules, November dry-land training is particularly intense. If you shift to snow skiing with rusty skiing technique, this can cause a real setback in

Bob Gray striding out. (Photo by J. Omholt-Jensen)

your progression. A less intense November dry-land schedule might improve this. I have often wondered whether we train too hard in November and not hard enough in January. One possibility is to maintain the same level as the first month of your ski training to help keep your progression going.

Remember that skiing is generally easier than dry-land footwork—especially as your skiing technique and timing improve. It becomes increasingly difficult to get a tough workout on skis as the season advances. Though racing will help keep you progressing, it usually isn't enough. You have to continue training during the racing season as well.

With all the races, sometimes 3 per week, as well as travel, it is hard to get the rest you need so you can train enough to maintain your progression. As a result, your progression may fall apart or you may end up sick. That is why I think you should go easy in the summer and fall. Save all that mental energy for the winter when you really need it. You have to really concentrate those last few months of the season; these are the months that count, the ones you have been training for.

A mental progression, then, is most important of all. It probably should follow a little behind your physical progression. If you can carry a strong physical progression into midwinter, you should be able to complete the season through your psychological resources, even if your training program falls apart through circumstances beyond your control.

Concentration and confidence in your program and your preparation are what you need for strong training. Remember, racing—especially at the end of the season—is what it all boils down to. If you can't finish up the season at your best, your strongest, and your most confident, then your program deserves some reevaluation. More often than not, the problem is one of mental energy and its direction, rather than a physical one. The main thing is to enjoy your training, and to establish a realistic mental and physical progression. It should be such that you can maintain it throughout the season, and conclude at your very best.

7

Physiology, Diet, and Injury Prevention

by Art Dickinson, M.D.

Broadly speaking, the physiological considerations of cross-country skiing are similar to other activities that consist of rhythmic, repetitive, submaximal muscular contractions, such as jogging, cycling, and swimming. There are, however, some important differences. When double-poling, arms contribute directly to forward propulsion, generating 10 percent of the total force on level terrain. Therefore, upper body muscular strength and endurance are more important for skiing than they are to jogging or cycling.

Secondly, a greater variety of physical movements is required than in most other repetitive sports. The long-striding glide traditional to cross-country may alternate with an arm-digging run, a herringbone up a hill, a controlled body tuck on the downhill, or double-poling. It is significant that in skiing the body is not lifted from the ground, as in foot running—a biomechanically connected series of jumps. Therefore the vertical lifting force is less, so the force directing the body forward can be a greater percentage of the total propulsive force. This means that the minimum effort required to get oneself about is much less than in jogging, and comparable to walking or level cycling.

However, because of the arms' contribution to forward propulsion, a maximum effort on level or hill can produce a greater energy expenditure than that generated by running or cycling. Indeed, cross-country ski racers record higher values in physical work (endurance) capacity than any other athletes.

Since skiing offers such a wide range of physical effort, it is ideal for recreational purposes. An elderly couple can hesitatingly shuffle ahead for the first time on skis, using the poles only for balance, while a citizen racer may flash past them, skiing at an intensity requiring a heart rate of almost 200 beats a minute.

THE NEEDS OF THE BODY

Before discussing in detail the physiological requirements and considerations of cross-country skiing, we should briefly review some pertinent facts about the human body. Simply stated, man (or woman) is an oxygen machine; he must breathe in and transport about one quarter of a liter of oxygen each minute to body cells. The cells use oxygen to break down carbohydrates and fats to produce energy for the work of each cell. The energy needed for work and play requires up to several liters of additional oxygen each minute. For muscles to contract, or for the brain, kidney, or digestive system to function a constant supply of energy supply must be available. This energy is formed by the breakdown of nutrients—almost entirely carbohydrates and fats—supplied by food intake. When skiing, the amount and the rate of energy we supply to muscles will determine the extent of work that can be performed. The common unit of measurement for describing human energy gained or used is the kilocalorie (kcal). As an example, a slice of cherry pie supplies 350 kilocalories of energy, while walking the dog requires about 4 kilocalories of energy for each minute of walking.

If a particular task, such as skiing up a long grade, requires 14 kcal of energy per minute, we must supply that amount, or we will fail to complete the task. Approximately 1 liter of oxygen is needed by the body to produce 5 calories of energy. This means that in our example the skier will need to take in, transport to muscle, and utilize 3 liters of oxygen per minute to produce the necessary muscular work. This kind of energy production, where enough oxygen can be supplied to produce the energy needed, is termed *aerobic metabolism.*

Skeletal muscle cells, however, are endowed with a unique capability. When the intensity of effort required to perform a task is greater than the body's ability to supply this energy by aerobic metabolism (as where you have to sprint for the nearest tree when confronted by a bear) additional energy can be supplied by a partial breakdown of carbohydrates without oxygen. This *anaerobic* (nonoxidative) process has decided disadvantages: (1) only carbohydrates can be utilized; (2) it produces lactic acid, which will limit maximum efforts to less than a minute's duration; and (3) it is exceedingly inefficient, producing only 5 percent of the energy that would be released by the normal aerobic process. Conversely, the higher a person's endurance (aerobic capacity), the more effort he can put forth in skiing without having to supplement his aerobic delivery system with anaerobically produced energy. If a person is forced to ski at an energy requirement greater than the aerobic capacity, the higher the person's endurance, the less he will need to supplement it with anaerobically produced energy. He can therefore continue the pace longer before having to slow down, and will recover more quickly on reaching the top of the hill.

Deep body temperature must stay within a range of 8 degrees Fahrenheit or physical and mental work capacity may be impaired. The sea water-like inner atmosphere of the body must be maintained without becoming overly acidic or alkaline. There must be sufficient fluid volume to supply the billions of body cells with the appropriate inner environment, and to transport the solid portions of the blood, oxygen, and carbon dioxide.

The fluid inside of the blood vessels—about 5 liters in total—must constantly recirculate by propulsion of the heart. The blood transports oxygen, glucose from the liver, fatty acids from fat repository areas for the cells' fuel, and transports and buffers the metabolic acids, carbon dioxides, and lactic acid. It is also the chief means of carrying away heat from hardworking areas of the body. By varying the amount of blood flow near the body surface, the person loses or conserves metabolic heat.

THE EFFECTS OF SKIING

There are quite narrow limits within which the body must function. Cross-country skiing can throw off the mechanisms responsible for maintaining this physiological stability. As an example, imagine a skier on an uphill grade that necessitates strong arm movement, with a temperature at 24° F (-4° C) and some breeze for a couple of hours. Additionally, let's place him at a high altitude cross-country resort, such as the one near Winter Park, Colorado, at an altitude of 8,000 feet. In this extreme case, the body muscles will be forced to produce energy greater than their aerobic capacity. This will put an even greater load on the blood to distribute and neutralize the sudden increase in metabolic acid produced to meet the muscular energy needs. The blood will also have to carry away great quantities of heat generated by muscles working at 80 times the resting metabolic rate. This metabolic heat will be welcome to tissues close to the body surface, already supercooled after 2 hours of skiing in a breeze. Hand and forehead skin temperatures are now at 61° F. In fact, for the previous 45 minutes increased body metabolism has been necessary to maintain body temperature against the cooling effect of the breeze, which has depleted more than usual the body's energy supply critically needed to provide forward motion to the end of the track. Finally, larger energy expenditures have been necessary, because at 8,000 feet above sea level the oxygen per cubic foot is about 25 percent less than at sea level.

TABLE 1

Immediate Cardiovascular Adaptations to Exercise

	Rest	Moderate Intensity	Maximum Intensity
Heart Rate (Beats/min.)	45-90	140-150	190-215 *
Cardiac Output (Liters/min.)	4.5-6.0	17-20	25-45 **
Ventilation Volume (Liters/min.)	6-14	30-60	80-170
Oxygen Utilized (Liters/min.)	0.21-0.30	1.8-2.5	2.8-6.2 **
Oxygen Dissociated from Blood to Tissue	5 ml/100	12 ml/100	17 ml/100 **

* Ages 10-25; then heart rate maximum declines with age.
** The maximum varies with genetic capacity and training.

THE BODY'S ABILITY TO ADAPT

The body can make immediate adjustments to exercise such as those shown in table 1. The body can also make a number of beneficial changes over a period of days, weeks, and months, which will result in a stronger, more efficient body, better able to cope with physical or environmental stress. A number of physiological functions contribute to cross-country ski ability, and some can be improved on, with an accompanying improvement in skiing.

TABLE 2
Factors in Ski Performance

Physical Factors	Motor Factors
Endurance (aerobic) capacity	Reaction (response) time
Muscular strength	Muscle speed of movement
Body composition	Balance
(percentage of bone and muscle to fat)	
Flexibility (joint range of motion)	Agility

While motor factors are important to skiing, they are, like red hair or blue eyes, primarily set by genetic makeup, thus not greatly altered through physical activity. This is especially true of muscle speed of movement. Balance, agility, and response time may be improved to a limited degree by practicing motor movements that closely resemble the movement pattern used in skiing. The physical factors, however, can be greatly improved through appropriate physical activity, and I will comment on each of these.

Endurance Capacity

Endurance, or aerobic, capability varies widely for two reasons. First, differences in genetic endowment set our absolute limits. Secondly, there are differences in the type and amount of physical activity a person performs. Striking improvements in endurance capacity can result from sound methods of training. You can improve endurance capacity in several ways.

- Increase the heart's capacity to pump blood to the body, with less energy cost to the heart.
- Increase oxygen transport capacity, with an increase in the

number of red blood cells, as well as an increase in total blood volume. This means that key blood vessels increase in diameter, and metabolic acids are more efficiently neutralized.

- Increase utilization capacity of muscle cells. The most striking changes of all occur here. The capillaries, where oxygen and metabolic acids are exchanged, proliferate. The ability of muscle cells to bind and utilize oxygen increases dramatically. The mitochondria, the energy-producing constituents in the cell, increase in number and capacity, and the enzymes that biochemically break down fats and carbohydrates to usable energy may double in activity.

All-out effort is not needed to produce these beneficial changes. Rather, they seem to occur whenever the intensity of a workout reaches 60 to 70 percent of maximum effort, with the intensity sustained for several minutes. Of course, if the athlete wishes to reach his ultimate capability as quickly as possible, he should work at a higher level than the threshold intensity—about 85 percent of his maximum.

While an extensive conditioning program is not mandatory, many cross-country skiers are active year-round. Research has shown that acceptable aerobic capacity can be maintained by 2 or 3 workouts weekly. If training ceases, aerobic capacity will decline at about the same rate that it improved, although it can be increased more rapidly once training again commences.

Muscular Strength

Muscular strength is second in importance only to endurance capacity for the skier. Muscular force is needed to move the body forward, to produce changes in direction, and to maintain balance. *Strength* is the measure of force produced when thousands of muscle fibers shorten in unison, exerting a pull on a tendon connecting these fibers to a bone. The amount of force produced is regulated by the nervous system, which stimulates the appropriate number of muscle fibers to contract. As we learn a motor skill, such as proper leg drive and glide, many unnecessary muscular contractions are eliminated. Therefore, the movement is performed more efficiently, with a conservation of bodily energy. Over a distance of a few kilometers, the difference is striking!

Body strength is increased by causing muscles to work against a resistance load greater than customary in daily activity. The stress of increased tension, developed by muscle contraction against this resistance, is the stimulus that increases the contractile protein and therefore increases muscular strength. Maximum effort is not needed to produce increases in strength. About two-thirds of maximum effort appears to be the threshold for adaptation.

Muscular strength is not only the ability to lift as much weight as possible in a single maximum effort, but also the ability to contract muscles repeatedly without a significant loss of strength from local fatigue. The type of exercise performed will determine the type of changes that occur within the muscle. Working against heavy resistance will principally increase the ability to generate force, whereas working against a lower resistance that allows more repetitions will increase the endurance, or staying power, of the muscle.

Training programs should duplicate as closely as possible the type of muscular activity required in skiing. For the arms, this means performing 2 or 3 sets of 10 to 20 repetitions each, with an occasional set (once or twice weekly) of 3 to 5 repetitions against nearly maximum resistance.

Good arm and shoulder strength is necessary for the skier, as opposed to the runner, because of the important contribution of the arms to the forward movement of the skier.

Whenever possible, the muscles involved in strength training should be exercised in about the same plane of movement and joint angles as those used in skiing. Research has shown that strength gained in a group of muscles exercised in one plane of motion does not necessarily carry over when the same muscles are exercised in a plane 90 degrees from the first. This is why exercise equipment such as the roller board, Exer-genie, or pushing up with poles from a sitting position are excellent arm and shoulder exercises for cross-country skiers.

Except for the citizen racer, probably no specific resistance exercise needs to be done for leg strengthening. If the skier also jogs, cycles, or swims, then nothing more is needed. If he does not, or if supplemental training is desired, then hiking hills, ski bounding with poles, rope skipping, or stair running are all good leg strengthening exercises.

Strength improvement exercises need not require weight lifting. Using one arm or leg to resist the muscular force of the other through the desired range of motion can be an effective training method. Better yet, two people may pair up for a strength-improvement program, taking turns providing resistance to the other person's movements.

An efficient exercise program produces changes in protein synthesis within 48 hours, shows rapid improvements for 3 weeks, and then plateaus after 6 weeks, progressing slowly after this point. Research has shown that 3 to 4 training sessions weekly produces optimal improvement. Once you have attained adequate strength, it can be maintained by a brief workout once or twice weekly. Even if the program is stopped entirely, our research indicates that the rate of strength never returns to the level measured at the start of the program, but remains 25 to 30 percent greater.

Body Composition

With the exception of Sumo wrestling, above normal percentages of body fat are detrimental to efficient performance in any sport. Fat, other than the 3 or 4 percent essential to protect internal organs and to insulate, serves only as energy storage. Certainly, this is the ideal way to store energy. Fat is essentially free of water, and in such compact form that it produces 9.3 kcal per gram, whereas carbohydrate produces only 4.1 kcal per gram. Yet, fat is dead weight to be moved by the muscular system. The normal ranges of body fat are: 16 to 26 percent for women, and 8 to 16 percent for men. Competitive cross-country skiers average 15 percent fat for women and 7.5 percent for the men, as a few extra pounds carried over distances of 10 to 50 kilometers add significantly to the energy cost of the race.

It has been calculated that cross-country skiing at 5 miles per hour on the level costs between 7 and 14 kcal per minute, depending on skill and body weight. Therefore, cross-country skiing can be valuable as a means of controlling body weight.

A forty-year-old adult with an average life-style loses about ½ to 1 percent of lean body mass per year after the age of twenty-five. If he weighs the same as he did in his early twenties, he can estimate that unless he's led a pretty active life, he's hauling around an additional 17 pounds of fat.

Flexibility

The connective tissue sheaths that surround muscles and joints—not the muscles themselves—set limits on motion. When joints are not moved daily through their full range of motion, some of the connective tissue extensibility is lost. The result is a drop in efficient movement, which means additional energy cost in a distance activity such as cross-country skiing, and a rise in the chance of injury. Indeed, probably one-third of all cross-country injuries would not be significant if there was good flexibility. No area of training is so uniformly neglected, and more easily accomplished. The shoulders, back, hips, thighs, and ankles are the critical areas requiring habitual stretching.

The procedure is simply to use the weight of the limbs or trunk to stretch the connective tissues, one area at a time. For optimal physiological benefit, hold each stretch for 30 to 60 seconds, and then repeat once or twice more. Stretch to the point of feeling tension and mild discomfort, but not pain. Most of the principal stretches are illustrated in chapter 10.

OTHER PHYSIOLOGICAL CONSIDERATIONS

Age

Because of the wide range of effort that can be put forth for enjoyable skiing, the sport is ideal for young and old alike. Some pertinent facts concerning both young and older groups may be of interest.

First, young children have high endurance capacities—not as high as they will have at age fourteen to seventeen, but higher than that of most adults. Because of vulnerable areas at bone growth sites and at tendinous attachments, youngsters are better suited to endurance activities than to activities requiring explosive muscular contractions, such as sprinting, jumping, or shot putting. This country's youngest marathoner was six years old, and no marathon is now run without boys and girls in the ten- to twelve-year-old range. The young do, however, have three functional disadvantages: (1) they are not efficient in oxygen consumption, (2) cardiac outputs are comparatively smaller than for the late adolescent, and (3) their strength levels are still significantly lower than they will be at sixteen.

Most youngsters respond well to weight training routines if the maturational changes accompanying puberty have commenced, assuming they are interested in the program. Prior to the onset of puberty, when significant testosterone levels have not yet appeared, weight training seems to be of little value. A resistance exercise program may help the younger child to experience a strong, all-out muscular effort, which is part of learning.

As we advance into the middle and later years, endurance capacity declines due, in part, to decreases in maximum heart rate and cardiac output. The habitually active person, with an exercise program, can favorably alter the rate of decline of these processes. If skiing, or other aerobic-type activities, are started during the middle or later years, the increases in endurance capacity (about 10 to 20 percent) will not be as striking as those in the thirty and under age-group (30 to 50 percent). A 10 to 20 percent improvement in endurance capacity will result in skiing about twice as far with the same amount of intensity as was initially required.

Muscular strength declines relatively little with advancing age, but flexibility needs constant attention if it is to be maintained at acceptable levels. In both young and old, there is no evidence that vigorous physical activity can harm a healthy skier.

Sex

Differences between the sexes need to be considered, and they all revolve around the hormonal differences. Women, on the average, possess about 70 percent of men's muscular strength; the greatest discrepancy is in arm and shoulder strength. However, women have the ability to improve muscular strength as rapidly and to the same extent as men. Gains in strength will result in greater skill and enjoyment in cross-country skiing.

Men have a 25 to 30 percent average difference in endurance

capacity, due to the female's greater percentage of normal body fat (for the same lean body weight, women carry an additional 10 to 15 pounds), and a smaller muscle structure. But again, men and women have an equal capacity to improve.

Of particular interest to cross-country is the theory, unsupported as yet by research, that because women have a higher percentage of stored fat, they are better suited for endurance work than men. Our recent studies of skiers exposed to the prolonged cold encountered in cross-country skiing indicate that women are better able to maintain body temperatures over long periods of exercise than men. The reason for this is not clear, but it appears to be more than just the higher percentage of fat women possess. Women are certainly more efficient in regulating high temperatures without wasteful sweating than men.

In summary, women are physiologically different from men in their response to exercise, primarily because of hormonal differences. Their metabolic mechanisms are not identical, nor need they be. Practically speaking, unless placed in head to head competition with the male, women are in no way at a disadvantage in skiing, if they possess adequate arm and shoulder strength.

Genetic Endowment and Training

Casual observation of cross-country skiers reveals wide differences in physical work capacity, which are not simply due to differences in skill. One potent reason for these differences is the genetic makeup inherited by each skier. Some people are better suited for endurance activities, while others will have more success as sprinters, jumpers, and throwers. A high-performance heart and circulatory system, with a large percentage of high oxidative capacity red muscle fibers rather than white muscle fibers, are physiological advantages in cross-country skiing. Our national team skiers possess these genetic attributes, but would be at a disadvantage in power sports, such as ski jumping, or hurdling in track. However, in research, it is difficult to separate the relative contribution of genetic capacity from the results of a good training program.

Training involves stressing the various systems of the body

that contribute to performance of that activity. The guiding principles in training are as follows:

1. Overload, but don't overwhelm, the system to produce the desired changes. Improvements in work capacity occur when the sequence involves stress above the usual load, resulting in fatigue, and time for complete recovery. This cycle of stress, fatigue, and recovery will produce the desired changes if the stress is not overwhelming, and if the recovery period is adequate. Careful progression is the rule. The intensity of the training program for the recreational skier need not be the most important consideration. Enjoyment and duration of the activity insure there will be sufficient stress to increase cardiovascular and muscular capabilites. For the citizen racer, however, an accelerated program of graduated intensity is necessary to achieve maximum training efficiency.

2. The stress, or energy, expenditure during skiing or dry-land training depends on four factors: (a) the intensity of exercise, (b) the duration of exercise, (c) environmental factors (altitude, heat, or cold make additional demands on the cardiovascular/muscular system), and (d) relative skill of the person. As we learn to ski efficiently, a good deal of extraneous muscular effort is eliminated, with a decided conservation of effort.

3. Specificity is the key to most efficient training. Exercises that use the same muscle groups, that use the muscles in similar ways, and in about the same planes of movement are the best.

Many physiological changes occur as a result of training. Changes that result from endurance-developing activities include:

- increased stroke volume of heart
- cardiac hypertrophy (increased growth)
- decreased resting heart rate
- increased capacity for oxygen use in both red and white muscle fibers
- increased capillarization in lungs and muscles
- increased fat utilization for energy with reciprocal sparing of carbohydrate

- increased energy stores in muscle
- increased efficiency of oxygen use by heart and skeletal muscle

Submaximal effort produces:
- less lactic acid accumulation
- less heart rate per work load
- less blood flow to the muscles

Maximal effort produces:
- greater aerobic capacity
- ability to tolerate higher lactic acid levels before having to slow or stop exercise
- increased stroke volume and cardiac output

As a result of strength-developing activities there is an:
- increase in tensile strength and density of ligament, tendon, and muscle sheath
- increase in the maximum contractile force of muscle
- increase in nonoxidative energy power of muscle
- increase in cross-sectional area of muscle fibers, predominantly the white muscle fibers

Altitude

At sea level, arterial blood is essentially saturated with oxygen as it leaves the heart. At this altitude, we are also at the bottom of a blanket of air, which exerts a considerable pressure to compact the oxygen molecules more closely together. This concentration of gas molecules decreases as we ascend in altitude to ski. At altitudes over 3,000 feet above sea level, we take in less oxygen molecules with each breath. Starting at an altitude of 5,000 feet there will be a significant decrease in endurance capacity. Three factors contribute to this decrease: (1) lessened lung diffusion capacity (due to a more sparse population of oxygen molecules per cubic inch), (2) a drop in cardiac output (because of a lessened supply of oxygen to the hard-working heart muscle), and (3) an increased energy used in respiration (in an attempt to bring in more oxygen through increased ventilation). This deterioration in aerobic capacity continues at a relatively regular rate until the skier reaches about 9,000 feet, where there is an increasingly steep drop-off in physical work capacity.

The body attempts to make up for this drop in oxygen by increasing the breathing and depth. This increased ventilation releases an increased amount of carbon dioxide, resulting in a shift within the body toward alkalinity. The kidneys can reestablish the acid/alkali balance by adding bicarbonate but this takes time to accomplish. During this period of adjustment, usually a maximum of 72 hours, there continues to be a drop in work capacity. Once this adjustment is made, the acclimatization process improves work capacity toward, but never equaling, the standard at sea level.

There are other, more slowly occurring, changes in the acclimatization process that result from training. Both hemoglobin (the oxygen-carrying part of the red blood cell) and total blood volume are increased. Training increases lung diffusion capacity, probably due to more extensive active capillaries in the lungs. Tissue blood flow capacity increases along with an increase in the oxygen utilization capacity of the muscle cells. The adaptive process is a comparatively long one—7 to 10 days to reach about 90 percent acclimatization at about 5,000 feet altitude.

The higher a person's level of fitness, the less dramatic will be the effect of altitude on his skiing. Symptoms such as headache, minor stomach discomfort, and fitful sleep disappear as soon as the body's acid/base balance is reestablished. None of the high altitude illnesses should be experienced unless the skiing is done at altitudes greater than 9,000 feet elevation.

Cold

One theme that is continuous through the previous pages is the marvelous ability of the human body to adapt and adjust to a myriad of conditions that could otherwise be detrimental to the skier. In fact, the whole basis of training is to trigger these adaptive mechanisms so that an increase in body efficiency results.

In adjusting to exercising in low temperatures, either immediately or over a period of time, the human probably demonstrates his weakest response. A person's experience and savvy in cold weather, his know-how in selecting appropriate clothing, and avoidance of moisture next to the skin are generally more important than the body's adaptive ability in this respect.

Humans have two physiological mechanisms to maintain core body temperature against heat loss: (1) increasing metabolic rate (by shivering, increasing voluntary muscular activity, or adjusting upward the body's thermostat in the hypothalamus); or (2) by shunting amounts of blood flow away from tissues close to the surface of the body, with a consequent reduction of heat loss to the outside environment. For whenever there is more than a 2-degree gradient between the surface temperature of the blood and the skin, body heat will be lost. In temperature regulation, blood is very important for transporting heat away from areas producing high amounts of heat to areas facing critical temperature drops.

When skiing, it would be ideal for sweat to be drawn away from the skin's surface by the underclothing to the outer garments of the body. In this way, it would evaporate without loss of heat to the body, so much of the unwanted heat loss would be avoided. Since water removes heat twenty times faster than air, sweat or moisture collecting from rain and snow can result in serious losses of body heat.

The motion of air across the body, generated by the forward movement, greatly accelerates heat loss in cross-country; so the "wind chill" effect can exist even on a calm day.

In most cases this heat loss results in some discomfort from chilled body parts, or possibly frostbitten extremities as blood flow is shunted away from these surfaces to prevent serious drops in body core temperature. However, if the heat loss cannot be countered by increasing metabolic work, then the potential for clinical hypothermia is present. Below 94 degrees F (34.5 degrees C), temperature regulation becomes difficult for cell metabolism.

The cross-country skier has many defenses against hypothermia. The first is a good level of fitness, for the cross-country ski racer may have to expend energy maintaining body temperature that could otherwise be used in moving him around the race course. Studying this on national team ski racers, both in laboratory cold chambers and under field conditions, we saw an increase in metabolism after about 1 hour of exercise.

The second defense against hypothermia is intelligent selection of clothing. I recommend the type that can provide cooling when needed, yet conserve body heat when necessary. Polypropylene underwear and turtlenecks are superior in "wicking" sweat away from body surfaces through to outside clothing. It would be smart to choose a hat liner of the same material, as well as removable layers of clothing.

NUTRITIONAL CONSIDERATIONS

It is natural for the skier to be concerned about his nutrition, for food intake provides the fuel for muscular activity that propels skiers along the trail.

Food Intake Needs

Protein, of course, is necessary for the amino acids, the building blocks of the body. Beef muscle, milk, rice, and fish are all high in amino acids. After a protein-rich meal, not all the amino acids circulating in the blood are used for new tissue. Some enter the liver, to be converted to glycogen (chains of glucose molecules), so protein can be a secondary source of energy fuel for the body in the form of carbohydrate. However, protein in excess of the immediate needs of the body is excreted—unused and wasted. Only 10 to 20 percent of food intake needs to be protein. Someone on a vegetable, milk, and egg diet has no problem with adequate protein intake. Because protein plays no significant part in skiing such a person should have no difficulty in any type of cross-country activity.

Only about 20 to 30 percent of the food intake needs be fats, one of the two most important sources of energy. In the digestive process fat breaks down to fatty acids and glycerol. If there is adequate oxygen, fats provide large amounts of energy. Because fat is essentially anhydrous (containing no water) much larger quantities of energy can be stored for later use than could be stored as carbohydrate, where each gram must bind with 2.7 grams of water. You can envision what kind of waistlines we would have if we were dependent on carbohydrate storage. Skiers can satisfy from 30 to 70 percent of their energy needs from fat. A small amount is found in droplet form within the muscle cell, but most is delivered by the bloodstream, after being mobilized from the fat repository areas of the body.

Carbohydrate should form the predominant part of the average American's diet whether he skis or not. Much of the carbohydrate enters the bloodstream in the form of glucose, to be used immediately by any body cell for its metabolic needs, or stored for later use in the liver and in muscle cells. An average-sized man may have close to a pound of glucose in his body, about three-fourths of it stored in muscle tissue.

Although inferior to fat in energy per unit of weight, carbohydrate has two significant advantages as fuel for muscular work: (1) it requires less oxygen to produce energy than fat, and is thus 10 percent more efficient in terms of oxygen cost to the body; and (2) energy production from carbohydrate is markedly faster and does not need oxygen to produce a portion of its energy.

The approximate energy stores in the body that are available for skiing at the pace of a 50-kilometer ski racer if used separately are:

Phosphates in muscle	160	yards
Glycogen in muscle (used anaerobically)	1,400	yards
Glycogen in muscle (used aerobically)	10	miles
Fats	630	miles

Therefore, carbohydrate is the limiting fuel of muscular activity; working muscles depend more on carbohydrate stored in the muscles than that circulating in the bloodstream. When the carbohydrate stored in the muscles is depleted it brings physical activity to a halt. To some extent, storage capacity of the muscle can be increased through training. In addition, trained persons utilize a greater percentage of fats in submaximal effort than sedentary folk.

Carbohydrate not immediately used or stored as glycogen will be converted to fat and stored in the body. Unlike protein, none of the excess from immediate needs will be excreted. Carbohydrate should comprise 50 to 75 percent of the total food intake.

The need for water replacement during physical activity occurs before conscious feelings of thirst register in the mind. Skiing at high altitudes requires even greater water replacement than skiing at sea level, so strict attention should be paid to adequate intake.

Minerals are essential elements for bones and for the regulation of many vital physical processes, while vitamins are coenzymes that trigger or regulate various metabolic processes. Skiers need not worry about supplementing either because of vigorous physical activity.

The energy used during a day on skis will have been consumed 1 to 4 days before. The meals on ski day should consist of some protein to dampen feelings of hunger, and moderate amounts of carbohydrate. High carbohydrate intake may elicit an unwanted increase in insulin, with consequent lowering of blood glucose. If a tough workout is expected, allow at least 2 ½ hours for digestion between the meal and skiing.

Snacks and munchies out on the trail, such as "gorp" mixtures, are physiologically sound in principle, and give a perked-up feeling. But these are not nearly as important as fluid replacement.

Carbohydrate Loading

It is possible to increase temporarily the amount of glycogen stored in muscle, beyond the amount that accrues through training. Salton and associates have shown that if an athlete switches to a high-carbohydrate diet the muscle stored carbohydrate will double, from about 1.5 grams to 3 grams per 100 grams of muscle, or more.

Various forms of carbohydrate loading have been done formally or informally for years, and can be valuable whenever ski races last longer than one hour. After the intensive workout that depletes the muscle glycogen, the workouts must be light so that glycogen can again be stored in large amounts. If the athlete follows a high fat and protein diet for two days after the intensive workout before switching to a high carbohydrate diet to gain the maximum supercompensation level, then at least 2 training days will be sacrificed. The athlete will have to resolve whether the carbohydrate loading is more beneficial than the training workouts lost. From my viewpoint, the extra loading during the two-day fat and protein diet is not worth the additional training time sacrificed. A high-carbo-hydrate diet is appropriate for 24 hours following the activity. If you ski several days in a row, you should eat high carbo-hydrate meals. Such a diet will largely replace muscle glycogen within 24 hours.

Costill and associates have shown that the caffeine found in 2 to 3 cups of coffee will stimulate free fatty acid mobilization, and therefore can reduce glycogen use in the early stages of a ski tour or ski race. We used small amounts of caffeine during the in-race feeding of our national team ski racers during the 1976 race season, including the XII Olympic Games. We subjec-tively felt that it lessened fatigue and made the feeding more effective. Subsequent research in our laboratory by Sparks, Haynes, and myself has shown that not only did caffeine dimin-ish perceived exertion stress, but improved the rate of emptying of liquid, dissolved glucose, and electrolytes. In all probability tea could produce the same effect. For the recreational skier who enjoys coffee or tea, these can contribute to the enjoyment of a vigorous ski outing.

INJURIES IN CROSS-COUNTRY SKIING

Cross-country skiing is an activity with a low frequency of injury. Most problems stem from two main causes: (1) overuse or overstress injuries to the connective tissue (muscle sheath, tendon, and ligament); and (2) injury to bones and joints due to inability to maintain control on icy terrain, deep powder, or downgrades. Eriksson and Danielson in Sweden reported 381 injuries among an estimated 3 million skiers during the 1975-76 season. Toney, Baker, and Garrick, surveying American and Canadian skiers, reported injury rates between 1.2 and 1.8 per 1,000 skier days. The Swedish group compared injury inci-dences of downhill to cross-country skiing and found the rates to be 0.6 percent and 0.02 percent, respectively. The U.S. study was completed before fiberglass skis became popular, and prior to the explosion of interest in the sport, so it is highly probable that the injury incidence for cross-country is now somewhat higher. Lyons and Porter have reported that in their locale there has been a substantial increase in severe cross-country ski injuries. Icy or deep powder conditions were contributing factors in most of the cases.

Biomechanically, cross-country is a fine sport for those who have degenerative arthritic changes in the lower extremity or other musculoskeletal problems that are irritated by the jarring of jogging or racquet sports.

In our laboratory, we have used dry-land training devices such as the Nordic Trak, roller skis, or the Norwegian ski simulator as alternative forms of exercise for skiers who develop discomfort from running.

Many overuse and traumatic injuries can be prevented by flexibility and joint structure strengthening exercises. Flexibility exercises help prevent or minimize injuries to: (a) thigh musculature, (b) lower leg musculature, and (c) shoulder joints. These exercises are shown in chapter 10. Strengthening the joint muscles and the ligaments that support the joint are especially important for the shoulder and knee joints.

To minimize injury, it is important to know how to fall and to be able to control the direction of a fall. On downgrades there is a tendency to fall forward, rather than to sit backward, which is safer. In a forward fall, a knee or ski tip digging into the snow can produce considerable force on the knee joint if the upper body continues in motion.

Terrain is important, too. Fallen tree trunks or branches, or a sturdy bush lying close to the trail can be as dangerous to the skier as the grade of a hill.

The Ankle Joint

Ankle joint injury is closely associated with almost all sports. Fortunately, this joint can take a good deal of punishment and come out of it essentially intact. When they occur, fractures are almost always above the ankle joint, at the lower end of the two lower leg bones. Infrequently the ankle will receive an eversion sprain, in which the deltoid ligament pulls off a small chip of bone from the tip of the tibia. Should the ankle become injured, wrap it securely with adhesive tape, as shown in the figure.

A frequent cross-country injury is a sore base of the large toe

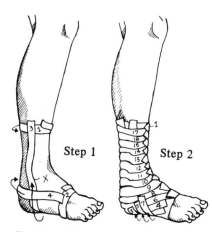

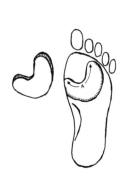

Step 1   Step 2

Taping a Sprained Ankle. Use 1½"
wide adhesive. (X indicates site of
injury.)

Felt Foot Pad. Round off all edges
except the one that borders the big
toe (A).

as a result of a "drive stress" injury, caused by the push-off
motion of foot to ski. Though it cannot be easily prevented,
it can often be relieved by using a felt pad made by placing
two layers of moleskin together to form a ¼-inch pad, shaped
as illustrated in the figure.

The Knee Joint

An injury to the knee joint should never be taken lightly.
There is no room for an error of judgment in evaluation or
treatment of a knee injury. While the ankle joint is forgiving of
errors and will usually heal functionally well, the knee joint can
never be considered in the same way. The most frequent injuries
to the knee joint will be to the connective tissue surrounding
the joint on the front side of the knee. While the amount of
swelling in an ankle injury is a good indication of the severity
of the injury, this is not a reliable sign in knee joint injuries. The
author has seen complete tears of the *medial collateral ligament*
of the knee that required surgery, but essentially had no swelling.
The knee gains stability from the ligaments that cross the
knee, the static stabilizers, and from the dynamic stabilizers, the
large muscles that surround and move the knee. Two groups of
muscles, one on the front and one on the back of the thigh,
supply half the stabilization for the knee joint. The 4 muscles

on the front of the thigh, the *quadriceps*, are joined by a common tendon into which the *patella*, or kneecap, is inserted. These are the principal muscles that extend the leg at the knee joint. As the knee joint bends, the collateral ligaments lose some of their ability to stabilize the knee. So a strong quadriceps musculature can help prevent dangerous lateral or rotary motion.

On the rear of the thigh are the hamstrings, 3 large muscles, grouped together. They cause the knee to bend, and when bent, allow the lower leg to rotate inward or outward. They also prevent dangerous rotation of the lower leg when the lower leg moves forward.

Strengthening of quadriceps and hamstrings will minimize most knee injuries of cross-country skiers. If the muscles and ligaments of the knee are strong, serious problems can result only on downhills or in icy conditions.

The Shoulder

The shoulder area is also vulnerable to injury in cross-country skiing. Actually, two joints are involved in this area: the rigid joint formed by the attachment of the end of the collarbone to the shoulder blade; and the shoulder joint, a mobile ball and socket joint connecting the upper arm and shoulder blade. The former would be injured only by falling on an outstretched arm or elbow, which would damage the two ligaments stabilizing this joint. The shoulder joint is extremely mobile, and can be injured by falling, through overuse, though muscle strains from poling, or by being pulled forcibly when a pole catches on a bush or tree while the body continues forward. The author has even seen an acute shoulder dislocation occur from this type of injury.

Since the shoulder joint has a wide range of movement, this joint cannot be supported snugly by ligaments. Rather it must rely for primary stability on the muscles that move it. Therefore, muscular strength and flexibility are important in minimizing or preventing shoulder injury.

Some good exercises for shoulder strengthening include hanging by the arms and pull-ups with the palms of the hands facing away from the body.

Overstress Injuries

With the increasing popularity of such activities as running, swimming, cycling, and cross-country skiing, overstress injuries have reached almost epidemic proportions. These can occur in muscles, tendons, or tendon sheaths. It involves repetitive stress, and produces inflammation, collection of fluid, and pain. Later, tissue thickening and loss of range of motion may also result. At times, pain starts as a vague discomfort, and only days or weeks later grows into something significant.

The areas most affected by cross-country skiing are muscle attachments on the inner side of the elbow, the large toe flexor, the front and lateral side of the knee joint, and the extensor tendons of the thumb and first finger. Some people seem to inherit a proneness to overuse injuries, but it can affect anyone skiing many kilometers or undertaking a rigorous dryland fitness program. Prevention of overstress injuries involves: (1) stretching exercises both before and after exercise, (2) moderately high repetitions of resistance exercises, and (3) paying attention to good ski technique, especially when fatigued.

Home treatment for overstress injuries involves:

- resting the injured area until painfree passive movement is regained
- heat or cold, whichever feels best, for 10 minutes before activity, followed by 10-15 minutes of cold packs after activity
- cold packs or ice massage twice daily
- stretching to reestablish or increase range of motion
- resistance exercises to strengthen the area

Treatments with Heat, Cold, and Exercise

To minimize the unwanted changes that occur immediately after injury, the skier can do several positive things. As soon as possible, and for the first 24 hours after injury, cold applications are important for reducing pain, and for minimizing the bleeding from damaged capillaries. The less free blood in the area, the faster healing will take place, and the easier it will be to regain painfree movement. If the skin becomes redder than a subtle blush, the application is too cold. Cool applications over a longer period of time are superior to extreme cold for a short period of time. The cold should be applied from 30 minutes to 1 hour.

When cold is applied, you must be able to maintain normal body temperature in the rest of the body. Don't apply cold to an injured ankle or knee that must get you back to the trailhead or home one step at a time; cold at this point may make ambulation more difficult.

The cold can be in the form of cold water, snow, or chipped ice wrapped in a towel. Don't apply ice directly to the skin or wrapped only in a plastic bag, or else frostbite-like damage may result.

During this first 24 hours, take aspirin or similar medication. Wrapping an elastic cloth bandage snugly, but not constrictively, over, above, and below the injury will help minimize unwanted fluid in the damaged area. If the injury is to the lower extremity, elevate the leg when you're not walking, so it's parallel to the ground.

Do not apply any heat for the first 24 to 48 hours after injury. After that period, apply some type of superficial heat to the injury and to the surrounding area. Application of heat increases blood flow, relaxes the muscles, and reduces pain. Start applying heat 24 hours after injury if there is minimal or no swelling, after 48 hours if there is evident swelling in a joint, and after 72 hours on any thigh muscle strain or joint injury with marked swelling.

Heat can be applied with small towels soaked in hot water, and then wrung out. If the injury is to a foot, ankle, elbow, or forearm, soak the limb directly in a sink or bathtub. The handiest way to apply heat is to buy a chemically filled light cloth packet called a Hydrocollator pack. Place it in a pan of hot water for a few minutes, so it soaks up the water. Wrapped in a towel, the pack will provide 20 minutes of effective therapeutic heat. The pack will shape itself to any part of the body.

Keep the heat within tolerable temperatures instead of uncomfortably hot. The skin may remain a mottled red for up to an hour after heating, but no longer. The treatment should be for 20 to 30 minutes, repeated 2 to 3 times daily, if possible.

This is preferable to wrapping an electric heating pad over the area and leaving it on overnight.

If you have access to whirlpool baths, these can be beneficial if swelling is minimal, or after 72 hours if swelling is moderate. Various parts of the body should be immersed as follows: ankle, hand, or elbow for 15 to 20 minutes 108 to 110 degrees F; knee, 15 to 20 minutes at 106 to 108 degrees; thigh, 12 to 15 minutes at 106 degrees; hip, 10 to 12 minutes at 104 degrees.

A nice form of therapy for hand, wrist, elbow, or lower leg injuries involves immersing the area alternately in warm, then cool, water. Start with warm water at a temperature no higher than 104 degrees—soaking for 3 minutes; then shift into cool water—about 55 degrees—for 1 minute. Alternate between warm and cool water 6 or 7 times in each. Always start and finish with warm water. When using either whirlpool or contrast bath, slow, easy movement of the injured area will enhance the effectiveness of the treatments.

Exercise of the injured area is an important part of home treatment. Unless immobilization is required due to the severity of the injury, exercise may be the most valuable form of therapy. Exercise increases blood flow in the area, and it is desirable to work toward motion as quickly as possible. Increased pain or swelling as a result of exercising the injured area is a signal to ease up on the intensity of activity.

A whole series of undesirable physiological changes, grouped under the term *disuse atrophy*, occur when the normal stress of activity on muscle, tendon, and joint is reduced as a result of injury. These begin within 48 hours to 1 week, and can cause a delay in returning to normal activity or a chronic reduction in function. Therefore, it is important to increase use of the injured area as soon as possible.

8

Sports Psychology and Nordic Competition

by Richard M. Suinn, Ph.D.

What can psychology offer a coach and his athlete? Many people feel that psychologists offer only vague abstractions or verbal ambiguities instead of practical help. To alter this picture, I believe it is extremely important to recognize that the high-level competitive athlete is similar to a high-level executive. Both are where they are because of their reliance on their strengths, and both have achieved success through performance. Given this context, psychology must offer the athlete something different from what it offers the average person. For the coach, it must offer something that will enhance the training program and ultimately the performance of the competitors themselves.

A high-performance athlete is a human being who is training himself to be so efficient in his control that he performs to the maximum of his ability. And sometimes he performs beyond his ability. The athlete controls all of those factors that go into performance: use of muscle strength, split-second timing, quick response to visual signals, memory, concentration, and indeed the entire body. In cross-country skiing, the athlete retains control over his body to the extent that mental discipline overrides the pain of effort and fatigue. In ski jumping, the athlete coordinates visual cues with muscular action to culminate in one smooth burst into flight. The athlete controls a wide variety of factors, many of which might be readily labeled as psychological: concentration, discipline, peaking for a performance, overcoming physical stress, and confidence. A finely tuned athlete is able to develop his own ways of accepting and controlling all factors involved in outstanding performances. A successful coach is one who trains his athletes in all factors involved in prompting and insuring outstanding performances.

This article is an outgrowth of my work with Alpine racers, and a recent conference as a member of the Sports Medicine Team with the United States Nordic Ski Team coaching staff. I will focus on a training method, called *visuo-motor behavior rehearsal* (VMBR), which I developed for use with athletes and other persons who have attained a high level of achievement, but who wish to enhance their performance further. The procedure has the advantage of providing training in control of both psychological and physical factors, such as timing.

VMBR is initiated with a relaxation exercise. This exercise teaches the athlete a means of gaining immediate control over muscle tension. As with all other forms of physical training and exercise, the athlete goes through a systematic sequence of muscle movements. Completion of the sequence takes from 30 to 40 minutes, at the end of which the athlete has achieved a condition of muscular relaxation. After the relaxation exercise the athlete is now able to experience visual and motor imagery. Although such imagery is described by the psychological trainer, the athlete is always in complete control of his experience. In this way VMBR is different from hypnosis and is viewed more as an exercise and training procedure.

Learning the relaxation exercise is in itself a proven contributor to performance. Muscle coordination, timing, and endurance are all affected by muscle tension. Although a little tension (muscle tonus) is helpful, too much will interfere with coordinated rhythm, adversely affect timing, and cause more energy to be expended in endurance events. After training with the relaxation exercise, the athlete can develop nearly instant ability to relax muscle groups during performance events.

However, VMBR derives its most beneficial effects through visual and motor imagery. Athletes who have learned the technique have been struck by the vividness and realistic nature of the experience. They have reported that the experiences are so real that they could actually see the course, experience the emotions, and feel the muscular and postural movements. In sum, VMBR is a unique means for providing the athlete with the very foundation of sports training—practice and experience.

The coach hopes to provide his athletes with practice and

experience through both training camps and participation in a series of planned competitions. Improvement in technique and consistency in performance depend on the athlete continually repeating the correct movements. If the athlete can increase the number of such repetitions, he has gained an advantage. VMBR can provide this advantage. Let me briefly show its relevance to a variety of topics.

The athlete must develop proper timing and coordination. In cross-country competition, timing and coordination are responsible for setting the rhythm of the stride. In ski jumping, these are involved in body compression and springing at the crucial moment. Such coordination is best developed through controlled, continuous practice. The athlete practices these movements until it becomes second nature. Yet, the amount of such practice is limited by physical obstacles. For example, the number of jumps possible is a function of the time it takes for the jumper to return from the bottom to the top of the hill. Though a cross-country skier has more opportunity, the terrain or snow conditions may change from moment to moment, so that the track ahead is dissimilar to the one just skied over. Through the use of VMBR, the athlete can actually repeat the same jump in the same way several times through the imagery, while experiencing the same physical sensations and motor activity as if he were actually making the jump. Within a few minutes, the jumper can increase his training experiences tenfold, increasing his muscle memory such that the coordination becomes second nature.

The athlete must develop and retain a confident attitude. Though performance is affected by attitude, little is known about how to manage attitudes. Confidence is affected essentially by two factors: the ratio of previous success and failure experiences, and the nature of the most recent competitive experiences. Unless the athlete is unrealistic about himself, he cannot help but be affected by his experiences. A skier who has always beaten his American competitors will have no trouble believing in his own ability. However, if he has had fewer successes against his European counterparts, it will be difficult to retain a confident attitude in international competition.

Coaches of young professional boxers work on development of confidence by carefully monitoring the ratio of successful to unsuccessful bouts.

Recency is also critical. Two competitors, each with the same ratio, may well differ in their readiness to compete successfully in an upcoming meet. Competitors A and B may have placed well in 7 of 10 contests; however, A may have done poorly in the last two while B may have done well in the last two. Athlete B is likely to feel that he is reaching his peak and will be more ready than A, who is distracted by the nagging problem of recent poor showings.

The outstanding athlete, of course, tries to avoid being affected by previous results and tries each contest at a time. VMBR can be a valuable adjunct to accomplishing this objective. Through VMBR, the athlete can mentally repeat the previous contest, correcting the errors, and thereby establishing a higher ratio of recent success to failure. My experience with VMBR is that an athlete not only can rerun the course through imagery, but can also correct an error and rerun the race with a favorable outcome. There are two advantages to this: first, the athlete now has the opportunity to practice the correct moves under race conditions; and secondly, he is now in a better frame of mind for the next race.

The athlete must have the opportunity to analyze his performance and practice the correct moves. When an athlete performs well, his body communicates this to him; he feels good during the performance. The cross-country skier feels that indescribable state of well-being, that everything is functioning well. The ski jumper experiences the ecstacy of the perfectly executed flight. When the athlete is not performing well, this may be apparent to him, but it is difficult to know precisely what is wrong. The problem may be weight placement, shortened stride, alteration of posture, or hand position. It may be too subtle to notice without reviewing videotape or films.

VMBR permits the competitor to reexamine the performance minutely, and in a step-by-step sequence. Skiers who have participated in my program have reexperienced a previous race in two ways: first, rerunning the course as it really was; and the second time, "watching" oneself running the course and analyzing the movements. This is similar to having the competitor watch a videotape replay of the race. The advantage of VMBR is that the racer can actually review all of the factors involved, including the kinesthetic muscle movement cues during the run.

Once the racer has identified the difficulty, VMBR provides him with the opportunity to practice correct timing and movements under identical race conditions. The racer relaxes, develops the imagery of being at the previous race, and actually runs the course again, but this time practicing the correct technique. One skier, for example, practiced a skating technique out of the starting gate to improve his rhythm, thereby saving time on the slalom course. He developed this after observing his slower performance through VMBR. He adopted the skating in a VMBR scene, and then applied it to the next weekend's race in real life.

It must be emphasized that videotape replay and films are of tremendous help to the coach and athlete in analyzing performances. However, once analyzed, the coach can best provide the athlete with a training course to practice the correct movements. But practice courses are not identical with the conditions of a true meet. Without VMBR, the athlete must wait for the next competitive event to see whether his practice will carry over. Of course, if the competitive event is the Olympic Games, then the athlete cannot really afford to wait until then to find out. VMBR has the advantage of enabling the athlete to practice under realistic competitive conditions.

The athlete must develop the ability to concentrate. Concentration is extremely important to a successful athlete. With it he can remain sensitive to those minute cues that constitute proper timing of a jump, can maintain a determined pace in the face of fatigue on an endurance course, and complete an event using a planned strategy even under adverse conditions. Without concentration the athlete is subject to the doubts, distractions, and disturbances that accompany inefficient performance.

Concentration is a psychological activity inasmuch as it relates to the way the brain is used. Athletes rely upon the brain to monitor and control motor actions. Concentration enhances nerve-muscle coordination and facilitates sensory-motor adjustments. At the same time, concentration is like a physical or motor skill in that it must be developed through continuous practice.

VMBR has been used to help competitive skiers strengthen their ability to concentrate. For slalom skiers, this involves practicing increased concentration during course inspection. For downhill racers, it involves concentrating on output of maximum effort throughout the course. For both groups, it involves training to respond only to those cues associated with winning, and ignoring those that could lead to being psyched out by other competitors, posted times, or course conditions.

The athlete must have experience in coping with the unexpected. As much as an athlete practices his sport, he can never be certain that the circumstances of competition will be as he expects. A sudden gust may catch a jumper in flight, the temperature may dip or rise during a cross-country race, the in-run might ice up unexpectedly, or an obstacle may be suddenly uncovered on a downhill run. Many coaches and athletes assume that exposure to a variety of conditions during training will prepare the competitor for such circumstances. But no matter how accurate this may be, the athlete never has direct training in dealing with the unexpected.

VMBR has been used to train athletes systematically in using their reflexes and technique skills to adapt to the unexpected. During the imagery, the competitor is told that something unexpected will occur during the race and he must cope immediately with the situation. VMBR participants have reported such circumstances as sudden appearance of ruts, unexpected terrain, ice, gusty winds, spectators' actions, and situations leading to weight shift. In the VMBR program the athlete is exposed to unpredictable events that enable him to practice adjusting repeatedly until he is confident he can cope in almost reflex fashion.

To conclude, high-level athletes can profit from training that is directed toward maximum performance under conditions of competition. The VMBR approach aids coaches and athletes in: (1) training for psychological factors not usually subject to training, such as concentration and confidence; and (2) increasing the number of training experiences in motor activities, such as the timing of a jump under adverse conditions. Plans are now underway to develop VMBR training packages through cassette audiotapes. Such tapes could well be the answer for individualized programs designed to suit the interests of each coach and competitor.

9

Conditioning: Preseason and on the Snow

by Steve Williams

Training for cross-country skiing is hard to pin down, as it engenders about as many programs as there are readers of this book. Top-level training for the more serious skier goes on almost year-round, and certainly the accumulation of years of training improves an individual's condition. But, we must also consider the recreational cross-country skier, who enjoys a long ski tour in fresh, untracked snow. But like many Americans he, too, may seek an occasional opportunity to push and even test himself against his own limits, and maybe even against others, as a citizen racer. There are others who simply view skiing as a good way to get themselves into shape for about 4 months. This can include both improving cardiovascular, muscular conditioning, as well as exercising off pounds.

The proper program for each person's motivation, interests, needs, and desires is unique. So this article cannot be a detailed guide to be religiously followed for Olympic success. Rather, I intend to outline and describe many aspects of high-level, even international-caliber, training programs. You should read the conditioning article carefully, but train in a way that simply feels good and is applicable to your needs. By implementing a continual, gradual, and progressive program, any person can improve his conditioning for skiing. Since our primary concern is with what we do on skis, the first section will deal with on-snow conditioning.

ON-SNOW TRAINING

Early season, when the elusive white stuff finally does arrive to stay (perhaps after a few initial teases), all skiers will be eagerly getting out on the snow. But regardless of what degree of physical preparation the skier brings to his first ski effort, the sessions should be carefully planned, or at least controlled, to make the pattern of winter training successful. This does not apply only to the skier with a substantial level of preseason preparation, who must work to ensure that the transition to on-snow skiing is smooth and effective, without wasting the good that already has been done. Likewise, if the skier is just commencing a physical program, he should not be excessive in his initial enthusiasm to get on the snow and catch up in both technique and conditioning. (The word *program* is used loosely here to refer to any plan for the season, regardless of how formal or informal.)

The first workouts should focus on technique, since this is the time when a skier forms or, in the case of veterans, brushes the dust off the movements and rhythm that will characterize his skiing for the winter. This is also a good time to phase out bad habits. Do not practice incorrect movements, but concentrate from the beginning on skiing smoothly and efficiently without concern for speed or intensity. These initial workouts will also naturally develop stamina.

Ski as much as possible the first couple of weeks, staying on good, firm tracks in gentle, smooth terrain. After that, start skiing on increasingly difficult natural terrain (bumps and hills, as well as around corners) until a relaxed balance and rhythm reappears. Don't rush this process, as it takes many kilometers to loosen and relax on skis, with efficient use of momentum and balance. Preparation should not be rushed even if the start of the racing season coincides closely with the arrival of snow. There should be no racing until after several sessions (2 weeks at minimum), since racers need the slow process of reacclimatization to skis. Then look upon the first couple of races merely as training races or timed distance workouts.

During this early on-snow period, serious skiers should maintain a skeleton version of dry-land foot-running workouts. This should include up to three short workouts of 20-25 minutes a week (e.g., 3- to 4-minute intervals) at a good brisk pace. By doing these full-effort exertions during the initial weeks, the skier leaves himself free when he is on skis to concentrate totally on technique. He will not feel any need for additional intensity, since he has already satisfied on foot all needs to reach maximum oxygen uptake in any given week.

More serious skiers will continue to run on foot all season. Even though on-snow speed, tempo, and interval sessions provide good cardiovascular training, a cross-country skier cannot attain as good "pure" respiratory cardiovascular condition as he had at the peak of his dry-land training. Skiing is not as fast a movement as running, and much of a skier's effort is expended in the muscular action of skiing. Thus, with less effort spent on high-respiratory exertion, there is a slight slackening of maximum oxygen uptake. Note that a skier does not breathe as hard on skis as when running. This is not to say a skier is not in as good condition in mid-season, but only that this particular aspect of conditioning has dropped off a bit.

Therefore, serious skiers continue to do occasional foot-running workouts all season (up to twice a week). The workouts should be intense and with a high speed of movement by body limbs. The key factor here is not to cover ground quickly, but to move arms and legs past each other as fast as possible.

Pulse Rate Monitoring

Before discussing on-snow workouts, I want to discuss the use of pulse rate reading. This will apply to any cardiovascular workout (on- or off-snow). Pulse rate is frequently referred to because it is a good indicator of the efficiency of the respiratory system (lungs, for oxygen uptake) and the cardiovascular system (heart and circulatory system, for oxygen transport). I will not attempt a detailed scientific description of the physiological effects of conditioning. But it is generally accepted that, due to the body's remarkable adaptability to stress, the best way to improve the body's capacity for any given workload is to increase its present maximum tolerance. In other words, work hard but only increase the workload at a gradual rate ("train, don't strain"). Suffice it to say that the harder the effort, the harder the heart beats, and the faster the pulse.

Since the pulse rate is so simple to determine—and yet such a good indicator of intensity—you should know how to use the pulse rate to monitor, and thereby control, your expenditure of effort during workouts. Since it is impossible to work at a maximum heart rate for too long, most workouts involve some level of submaximal effort. Effective pulse rate monitoring can help optimize the gains of such workouts. An occasional quick stop to check your pulse rate should be adequate to determine if the body is working as hard as intended for the purposes of the workout. More importantly, this will help the person to recognize the feeling of different levels of effort. The athlete will soon develop a good sense for knowing what level of intensity he is at without checking.

The East Germans believe so strongly in this strict scientific monitoring of training effort that they have resorted to basic animal behavioral conditioning to reinforce it. East German athletes train with a small, portable pulse counter attached to them. This buzzes when their pulse varies from the setting, until they learn how to recognize the level of intensity.

Ski Workouts

Designing a good schedule for on-snow training is difficult, due to the variability of snow, daily weather, and individual race schedules. Nonetheless, we will cover here several realistic training possibilities. Given the essential guidelines of the objectives that need to be met each week, a tentative synthesis will be offered.

Distance training conditions the body's aerobic efficiency and endurance through submaximal stress over long periods of time. In a distance workout, the skier skis for an extended period of time (one hour or more) at a constant pace. Theoretically, heart rate and effort remain constant, while speed varies according to the terrain. Thus, hills would be taken easier than normal. Distance training is done at up to medium intense effort (for the more advanced conditioned skier, at 2/3 effort, with a pulse of about 40 beats/minute below maximum, or 140).

However, in actual distance skiing, speed—rather than pulse or effort—is held more constant. This is known as *interval training* over a distance, since intervals are defined as a series of repeated, intense efforts separated by less intense "recovery" periods. As one skis over open terrain, the intensity of the effort will vary due to variations in the terrain. On flat and on gentle, rolling terrain, a comfortable steady state is attained, as in the theoretical distance model above. But to maintain speed on the uphills requires increased effort, while the down-hills provide recovery periods. So, in reality, most cross-country race courses are a series of linked intervals.

This type of effort is a form of natural interval, or *fartlek*. In the formal sense, skiing natural intervals involves varying the effort to a greater extent than in normal distance skiing over terrain. In other words, the skier purposely makes the effort more intense on the uphills and less intense on flatter, gentler terrain. This is certainly the single most popular training activity of all skiers, whether they are of international-caliber or are recreational tourers.

Formal interval training has been more popularly accepted in such sports as swimming and track. In these sports it is advantageous to work at higher levels of effort over a longer accumulated period of time than would be possible in a single, continuous effort. This form of training is more flexible than was initially recognized.

There are four basic features, and hence variables, to any interval workout: length, pace (intensity), recovery time be-tween efforts, and number of repetitions. Any one or all of these factors can be adjusted to tailor this type of training to the needs and capabilities of any individual or group.

In the context of this article, it is impossible to recommend specific workouts. Nor is it wise to have too fixed an expecta-tion before a workout. This is one instance in which pulse rate monitoring is particularly useful. As with distance, a function-ing pulse rate is suggested for each type of interval workout, and a resting pulse rate is used to indicate recovery. If the pulse takes noticeably longer to drop to a level that indicates recov-ery, or does not decrease at all, the workout has ceased to be effective and should be stopped.

Intervals should generally be at least 3 minutes in length and perhaps up to 10 minutes long. The pulse after each effort should be about 10-12 beats/minute below maximum, and should slow to between 115 and 130 beats/minute before the start of the next repetition.

There are two specific variations of the general format of interval training—tempo and speed.

Tempo intervals. These are done over distances shorter than race length at racing speed to accustom the body to such speed. The intervals should be at least 5 minutes long (to insure respiratory and aerobic equilibrium), but for not more than ¼ of race distance. The total distance skied in the workout should not exceed race length. Since the effort is near maximum, the pulse after each effort should be only 5-10 beats/minute below maximum. The recovery pulse should indicate rest, slowing to about 120 beats/minute before the next repetition.

Speed intervals. These are also known as anaerobic or oxygen debt training. They are designed to increase speed and strength, and condition the system to handle the stresses of extraordinarily intense efforts, such as those felt at the beginning of a race and on demanding uphills. An *oxygen debt* is accumulated when oxygen utilization exceeds the immediate level of oxygen supply, disrupting the aerobic equilibrium. Speed training on skis involves all-out sprints at 100 percent effort for 1 to 1.5 minutes. While it is good to maintain some semblance of proper ski technique, the effort should not be restrained any more than necessary to prevent gross thrashing. During this effort the pulse should rise to near maximum. Recovery is complete when the pulse rate drops to about 100 beats/minute.

I will add a word of caution regarding interval training. Recent research indicates an adverse effect on performance from extended anaerobic training due to a large buildup of lactic acid (the waste by-product of inefficient metabolism during anaerobic work). So except for natural intervals, you should limit these workouts to 5 efforts. You should do light, easy skiing between the intense efforts of natural intervals as a warm-down. This gradual idling-down flushes out lactic acid by continuing to stimulate blood circulation. For this same reason, recovery periods between efforts in formal interval work should not be spent standing, but also by doing light, easy skiing.

A Wintertime Program

Even in sophisticated training programs, there are three, but not necessarily more, maximal intensity workouts per week. Beyond that, the program largely involves supplemental submaximal intensity endurance conditioning and technique training.

Distance skiing. Distance or general skiing is the core of any cross-country program. Even for serious skiers trying to meet the weekly obligation of 3 intense efforts, most of the total training time will be spent on distance training. This develops the stamina for extended work, as well as drilling home technique and helping maintain relaxed and smooth skiing form. The distance skied should be at least twice the normal race length, over reasonably challenging terrain (neither too easy nor too hard).

A distance workout is the best time to focus on technique improvements, through the lens of a videotape recorder, if available. The pace should not be so demanding that concentration cannot be applied to efficiency of movement. But pace should be maintained around a general level of 130 to 140 beats/minute. (See natural intervals, above.) It is best to be videotaped when skiing normally, without posing. Ski technique includes anything and everything that gets a skier from start to finish as fast and efficiently as possible. Everything should be scrutinized: not just diagonal technique on the flats, but also downhill tucks, skate or ski-around turns, herringbones, and change-ups over bumps.

The best way to learn any physical skill is by imitation. Whenever possible, try to learn and improve by following, watching, and trying to copy a better skier as he strides, glides, and handles terrain variations. Then immediately attempt to do the same as smoothly. However, this practice should not be overdone, as no two skiers are identical. Each should spend time developing his own style and rhythm.

While distance workouts should generally extend for a specified time or distance, a skier should normally continue only as long as he is skiing with good punch and drive in his stride. When concentration and coordination start to wane, it is time to quit.

The East Germans control or monitor a distance workout by recording the time taken to ski the first steady (post-warm-up) lap, if the skiing is to be done on a repeating loop. Then they stick to that schedule for the number of laps that would make the workout a specific length of time. As with timing intervals, a stopwatch can be used to monitor how well someone is able to continue to function within the objectives of the workout. A drop in the length of time, shown first on a watch, indicates that the workout has ceased to be effective, and thus should be stopped.

Intensity. This section is for those who do wish to meet the weekly quota of 3 high-intensity workouts. Natural intervals are the best. This does not involve distance skiing, as natural intervals call for higher levels of intensity. However, all athletes occasionally rely on formal interval workouts, which offer clearer training objectives. All this speed/tempo or intensity work helps maintain top cardiovascular fitness and speed on skis. What follows is a general outline of one particular pattern for the most serious skiers.

After the first two weeks of transitional training, intensity workouts should start to shift from exclusively foot-running to on-snow training. This includes one tempo workout per week, plus some natural interval work (or regular intervals) twice a week. Foot-running can still be maintained, and will benefit speed of movement, if not intensity.

Once the racing schedule begins, tempo and speed workouts start to take on increasing importance. A race is viewed as a tough tempo-speed day. So in any week with a race, one other such tempo workout is done with one or two natural interval or light interval sessions. If there are more races in the week, this would mean dropping an equal number of intense workouts. This will maintain cardiovascular fitness and speed on skis. However, no matter how full the racing calendar becomes, always do some distance skiing each week to maintain strength and stamina.

As the heart of the racing schedule approaches and the season progresses, careful evaluation could be done to see what is needed to maximize physical potential or overcome specific deficiencies. Intense speed and tempo work every other day can improve stamina. If one already feels in form, it's best to nurture the peak by avoiding excesses in any direction when training.

Rest and diversions. In any article about serious cross-country training, the word *rest* is not as alien as it might at first seem. Though rest is essential for all athletes, the amount depends on the individual. For strong athletes, "active rest" (e.g., a ski tour in or out of tracks, or some easy Alpine skiing) often serves the purpose, both mentally and physically. Conversely, the less well conditioned an athlete is, the more important is rest. But all athletes have days when real and total rest is needed—a time to lie back, thinking about things other than skiing. Other times, rest may be needed just for the mind. If the spark or competitive fire is lacking, reduce the race and training load. It is important to be aware of this need; don't just try to run through it.

I disagree with those who recommend rest the day before a race. If rest is needed, take it two days before. The day before a race, a snappy ski workout is helpful to get the body tuned up for the pace of the following day's race. But avoid undue fatigue.

Alpine skiing was mentioned earlier as a change of pace, offering mental more than physical relaxation. If done with cross-country skis, it can be good fun and training as well. No longer is defensive or survival-style skiing on downhills adequate. A racer has to be comfortable going fast, tucking, skating, and making high-speed parallel turns.

Final thoughts for on-snow training. Warming up is often the most overlooked part of any workout. It is easy to warm up when doing distance skiing: just start out gradually, and as metabolism, and hence internal or core temperature and muscle elasticity increase, the work-load (pace) can be adjusted accordingly. With interval training—and even more so with races—it is important to be warm when the effort begins, so the body can immediately function at its optimal speed. When racing, time is saved if you can go hard from the beginning. A good warm-up is particularly critical when the race course has an uphill early on.

Lastly, be careful about colds. Too often, a skier will waste a whole year's training by catching a cold during the winter. Take care of yourself. Eat right, sleep well, and rest when needed—particularly after workouts and races, when resistance is lowest. Also, take a dry shirt to all workouts and races—and change out of wet, sweaty clothes after exertion to prevent chills. This should be done after workouts during all seasons.

PRESEASON CONDITIONING

This portion of the article is about how to condition best in the off-season when the snow has gone. It is easy to figure out the best preparation in the winter: just ski (as described earlier), and do strength work and running. Other than that, the skier need only monitor how to design and control training efforts on skis to optimize ski performance.

However, while athletes in most other sports can practice their sports almost year-round, there is an off-season for skiers. For best preparation, the skier must do more than just continue to practice his sport. The skier must examine both his sport and the other opportunities available.

As a competitive sport, cross-country skiing places immense demands on the body's strength and endurance by employing almost all the body's muscles in every movement. A good cross-country skier must have strength, endurance, coordination, speed, and flexibility. The more all-around the skier's physical activities are off-season, the better he will be able to meet and overcome the demands of the sport.

However, most sports focus only on certain desired areas, while neglecting others. Some activities emphasize arms, while ignoring the legs; with other activities, the focus is the opposite. Thus, the skier has to develop a blend, using a mixture of various activities adjusted and modified as best fits his specific needs.

However, it is not the intent here to outline a slavish training program for skiers to follow, but only to highlight activities that are natural to a skier and will serve him best in his skiing. Within these activities, many of the methods and techniques of formal off-season ski training will be noted. In addition, the article will discuss modifications of these other activities to increase their effectiveness and applicability. It remains to the the individual to design a balance of all the different proposed activities to blend them into a single optimally productive package.

Running

Running is the best single means to cardiovascular fitness, and probably the most popular and widely accepted method of training for any sport requiring top respiratory functioning. As with ski workouts, all types of running workouts can be practiced—tempo sprints, repeated intervals with intervening rests, natural intervals as dictated by terrain, or endurance over distance.

Cross-country ski racing is increasingly demanding of power, as well as cardiovascular capacity. The successful marathoner with aspirations of cross-country glory greatly needs to modify his program, rather than merely relying on distance running. Good oxygen transport systems are necessary, but that in itself is not sufficient. For instance, the Boston Marathon course has a total vertical climb of only about 500 feet (with the finish 300 vertical feet below the start). But the 50-kilometer course at the 1978 World Ski Championships had a total vertical climb of almost a metric mile (1,500 meters, or about 5,000 feet). This is 10 times the climb of the Boston course. Strength and power are necessary for climbing by any means, but on skis, which have a natural tendency to slide back without extra effort, they are particularly important.

Running around a track or along a typical footpath is productive, but it is not enough alone. Hence, do as much vertical climbing as possible, particularly as fall and winter approach, since it takes much more strength to move the body up, rather than just ahead.

Skiers have designed modifications of natural running, which simulate the basic cross-country skiing movements, and thereby place a greater emphasis on leg strength and power. This is an application of the training principle of *specificity,* the basic guideline needed for any training program to maximize effective and productive use of time and effort expended, without waste. Simply stated, specificity calls for doing related activities that exercise the same muscles used in the subject activity, and with the same movements and ranges of motion. The following ski stride simulation program is an example of such specificity.

Ski Stride Simulation

Ski stride simulation involves related ski movements utilized in both hiking and running, and calls for leg strength and power.

Ski striding (ski-walking) is a brisk stride forward with the hips lowered. The forward moving leg goes by the pushoff leg strongly, and fully extends and stretches out behind. The body is carried in a relaxed, supple position, a bit forward, with the hips (the center of gravity) always above the leading leg. The arms swing naturally. This is particularly effective when you encounter a long medium-gradual hill when hiking.

Ski bounding is similar to ski striding, but is done on a steeper hill, with more vigor and explosion. The hips are kept low, with the center of gravity over the leading leg. The bound or thrust is a springing movement from one leg to the other, landing on a slightly bent front leg, with the trailing leg fully extended to the rear. Arm swing is coordinated with leg action.

Ski bounding with poles.

Ski bounding with poles is the first formal workout that should be added to any preseason conditioning program. This is the same as ski bounding (as described above), except ski poles are used as well. This exercise is particularly effective for developing upper-body strength and skiing coordination. Ski bounding with poles can be done as a workout itself by doing a tempo workout of repeated 35- to 75-second efforts, with full attention to technique. A few shorter (10- to 20-second) sprints can also be done, though in these no regard is given to technique. This can be done by repeated runs up the same slope. Or if a long slope is available, horizontal walks across the slope can be used for recovery before you continue to bound up the slope.

"Hesitation" ski bounding with poles: Each time you land on the ball of the front foot in the ski-bounding motion, hesitate so that the next movement involves a definite and distinct thrust with opposite leg and pole. The hesitation should be long enough to insure that no momentum carries over from the previous step.

Indian dance (skipping): Bound up a hill without poles in a vigorous skipping motion. The hand should move with the opposite leg, both coming up high strongly, rather than ahead.

All of the above workouts can be combined into a single all-inclusive workout. Close attention should be given to technique as well as conditioning benefits, as there is a close correlation between these exercises and actual skiing. For example, you should emphasize an explosive thrust ahead with each kick, complete weight-transfer from one leg to the other, and proper arm extension (reaching ahead, not across). Also, in ski bounding, no hill should be used that will be steeper than any encountered during a cross-country ski race.

Other Sports

Hiking, likewise, is a productive off-season activity. It improves leg and lower-back strength and overall endurance, particularly when ski stride simulation is emphasized on the uphills. Hiking is also a good diversion from the mental strain of competition. It offers one the inspiration of a good view,

Ski Bounding with Poles

seen only after putting in hard effort. When hiking, be careful to avoid knee deterioration from long, extended downhills, as well as simple twists of both knees and ankles.

Biking also has much merit for off-season training. It is excellent for development of the quadriceps, the muscle that is needed for steep uphills and for the thrust or downward kick of the stationary leg each stride on skis. Biking is particularly effective when aggressively done standing up, pushing on the pedals on the uphills. This assures dynamic movement, much like basic cross-country skiing. Bicycle racing was a major off-season diversion of several members of the U.S. Ski Team in the early 1970s.

Swimming is also good for developing arm and leg strength, and heart/lung endurance. Its usefulness is limited as it is made easier by the natural buoyancy of the body in water. Different swimming diversions can be practiced: water games like polo or races, or swimming using only arms or using only legs. Running in the water along a beach is a good combination of two activities noted here. This is particularly good for improving leg strength.

The paddle sports—rowing, kayaking, and canoeing—are exceptionally good for upper-torso development, particularly the latissimus dorsi, the muscle essential to poling on skis. They are also good for heart/lung development and endurance. The merits of rowing are often overlooked, due partially to the inaccessibility of necessary equipment. Unlike its counterparts here, rowing places stress on the whole body, the legs even more than the arms. Pal Tyldum, for instance, the Norwegian 1972 Olympic gold medalist in the 50 kilometers trained with rowing the summer before the Olympics, while recovering from a knee injury.

Strength Training

It has been stressed throughout this article that cross-country skiing requires strength, or more specifically, upper body strength and leg power. However, this is not just regurgitation of an old, tired song. Increased speeds on skis are now possible, due to the straighter, firmer tracks set by mechanized trail-setting equipment, and the use of Alpine "hot" wax on P-tex ski bottoms. There is hence increased reliance on double-poling. Upper body strength is as important as leg power, and is often a critical factor in racers. Leg power can be improved by incorporating a great deal of hill work into running workouts. But upper body strength training is not usually found in everyday living, so it often needs to be a disciplined and formal part of a determined cross-country skier's training.

Strength training takes many forms, including weight training. If you practice formal weight training, it is recommended that you focus on conventional exercises, such as bench press, standing press with bar resting behind the head, both upright and bent-over rowing, curls, pullovers from behind the head on a bench, and one-legged hops with weight on the shoulders. If a Universal gym machine is available, pull-downs (lats-pulls) should also be included.

Although formal weight training is the most common type of strength training, it is not the only means to accomplish this objective. You can do natural strength training, such as pull-ups, dips, and extensive vertical running, all with a weighted pack or sand bag. Armbands, Exer-genie, and wall-pulley weights are all highly useful methods for developing upper body strength through the simulation of the poling action. Armbands can be made out of inner tubes, surgical tubing, shock cords, or springs and attached to any stationary object (tree, pole, or wall) at about eye level. With one end in each hand, pull in an alternating fashion to simulate single-poling, or pull both to simulate the double-poling action. Remember to stay flexed at the knees and hips. The Exer-genie is now the most accepted method for pole simulation and upper body development. It is mobile and can serve as a complete weight program exerciser.

Most physiologists and coaches agree that twice a week is adequate for strength training. But to gain in strength requires three days of effort a week. Regardless of what program is followed or how it is streamlined, the following areas deserve top priority:

1. abdomen and back: do sit-ups and back-raisers
2. shoulders and triceps: do dips, and use Exer-genie or armbands

3. leg strength and speed: do hill runs on foot with or without
ski stride simulation

These exercises should head the list of exercises practiced, even
through the winter.

With any type of strength training, a good warm-up and a
thorough warm-down, including stretching, are essential for
maximum muscular development with adequate flexibility.

Plyometrics is a new term in the cross-country skiing vocabu-
lary that describes a previously unexplored dimension of
strength training. Plyometric exercises focus on the explosive
functioning of muscles—taking pure strength and moving quickly and powerfully with it. The essence of such exercise is to
stretch a muscle before contracting it explosively. Ski bounding
and "hesitation" bounding are two such exercises that have
been long practiced. The compression before a standing vertical
jump and stationary hurdle hops are two applied examples
of compression before explosive extension. The imagination is
the only limit to the possibilities of other specific applications
of this newly articulated concept of cross-country strength
training.

Roller Skis and Roller Boards

Roller skiing, now widespread as a dry-land training technique, is becoming increasingly essential to a total preseason
conditioning program for the serious cross-country skier. International athletes the world over are now spending a large
portion of their off-season training time on roller skis, some
as much as half their total training time.

There is, however, disagreement as to whether to use roller
skis only for double-poling, or for diagonal striding with the
single-poling action, as well. While double-poling does much for
upper-torso development, single-pole action is also essential for
gaining the full benefits of roller skiing. While the Norwegians
and Finns only practice double-poling, most nations, including
the United States, train on roller skis just as they would on
actual skis.

Cross-country skiing is a very difficult sport to train for
because it requires total body conditioning, good pulmonary/
cardiovascular efficiency, endurance, upper-torso strength, and

Roller skiing simulates actual ski technique in the off-season.

explosive power in the legs. With one exception, the various requirements of cross-country can be met by a combination of conventional training activities that focus on one or more individual areas (e.g., running, hill bounding with or without poles, weight training, and even double-poling on roller skis).

However, only diagonal-stride roller skiing allows the skier to work dynamically on the hip flexor, the muscle needed for the "recovery" action of the kick. The powerful swing and forward drive of the "recovery" leg produces a strong forward thrust (if the body stays above the knee), and provides a strong, long glide. This, briefly stated, is the essence of a good diagonal stride: a kick forward, with the hips over the "recovery" leg, while the other leg contracts isometrically as it pushes down (not back) to give the "recovery" leg a good base around which it moves forward.

Roller skiing is done on paved roads, wherever they're to be found and wherever they lead. The terrain encountered dictates the technique used. Incidentally, the roller skier observes the same rules of the road as bikers: going with the traffic on the right side, but as much to the side of the road as possible. Through intelligent route planning, it is easy to find good, seldom-traveled roads.

Long gradual, or even medium-grade, uphills are particularly good for roller skiing. Almost all roller skis are faster, and have more carry than snow skis. The increased gravitational resistance when skiing uphill adds enough resistance to make either diagonal striding or double-poling an overload situation, and particularly good for training.

Long tours of up to 40-50 kilometers are not unheard of, though tours of that length should only be done by the best skiers in top physical condition. The usual tours are in the order of 10-20 kilometers of nonstop, steady-state roller skiing.

Specific intense workouts, such as tempo (race-speed, full recovery) or interval (repeated efforts with moderate recovery, pulse 120), can also be done on roller skis. The same principles apply here as in foot running. The shorter and faster the repeated efforts, the less attention can be paid to technique (and the more likely only double-poling will be used).

One favorite workout is a series of intervals for approximately 300 meters, over a gradually steepening uphill (or whatever distance takes a skier at full speed just over one minute to ski). Hopefully, coasting downhill to the start will allow the pulse rate to drop to 120. Twenty of these intervals makes a very tough 40- to 45-minute workout.

I should add a note of caution regarding roller skiing on downhills. Though experience and confidence will dictate what hills can be skied down, use your good discretion. While long pants and gloves are good protection for low-speed falls (and recommended), they may not be much help in a fall at high speed. The scrape and resulting wound from a bad fall can actually restrict training for a while. A skier should feel free to take off the skis and walk down steeper hills, particularly if there are corners in the road or if there is traffic.

Roller skiing is limited, however, in how much it can do for the beginning skier. While roller skis are tremendous for conditioning and technical modifications, they are not good devices for introducing a beginner to the sport. With the ease of movement on roller skis, it is easy to begin the bad habit of a late kick, and just push back as with a scooter.

Every skier has to make technical adjustments when roller skiing, since the "recovery" roller ski is not directed or guided ahead by a track, as in snow. Also, once the roller ski has its wheels on the ground it cannot be slid laterally to get it under the skier's center of gravity. Thus, the skier has to make a conscious physical adjustment as he recovers his roller ski to ensure that it's headed straight ahead and is under him. For the novice, this results in not extending enough or not fully transferring his weight from one ski to the other. This can be much like the wintertime track skier who pushes instead of driving his skis ahead. This is something to be guarded against by all skiers, from the beginning of the season.

One last training device that merits mention is the roller board. The apparatus is simply an incline plane and mobile sled, on which a skier simulates double-poling by pulling on the "poling" ropes in a full arch from overhead to the rear. As in normal double-poling, the arms are extended, with the hands and forearms going below the level of the board at mid-stroke. The work load is adjustable by varying the angle, and hence the height, of the board or inclined plane.

In combination, a program of systematic on-snow and preseason conditioning will improve a skier at any level. It is essential for you to tailor your workout to your level and to the goals you hope to attain. Remember, the main thing you are trying to achieve is competency in skiing. The preseason workouts are just a means to that end.

10

Stretching Exercises

by Art Dickinson, M.D.

A warm-up should consist of two parts. The first is a muscle and joint readiness routine of stretching (flexibility) exercises. These stretches should include the back, front, and inside of the thigh, as well as the hip, calf, back, and shoulders. I recommend a "static stretch" routine, using the body weight to stretch the muscles and connective tissue, rather than bouncing up and down. Hold a position in which tension, not discomfort, is felt for a 30-second period. Repeat each stretch at least twice.

The second part of the warm-up consists of using the muscles involved in the activity to trigger adjustments in the cardio-vascular system, thus increasing its efficiency. For cross-country skiing, this is usually done by easy skiing of the course or part of it, sometimes accompanied by foot running. The warm-up intensity should build up to about three-fourths of maximum race pace, and then taper off.

The warm-up usually ends when the racer makes any final change in wax, or enters the ski marking area. The last 10 minutes of a warm-up is for "tapering off" intensity, but movement should never stop.

There is no uniform or prescribed warm-up for the U.S. Ski Team. It is left to individual preferences. Team members vary widely in their warm-up requirements. And the prerace warm-up is a period for both a physiological and psychological preparation. Warm-up times average from one-half to one hour.

Some generalizations about warm-up: the better the physical condition, the longer the warm-up; the colder the day, the more intense the warm-up; and warm-ups are more often too short and too sedate rather than too lengthy and too intense.

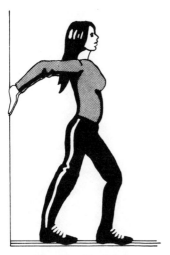

Shoulder Stretch I

Shoulder Stretch II

Shoulder Stretch I. Door jamb may be used to stretch both arms at the same time. Arrows show direction of force in order to apply stretch tension on the shoulder joint.

Shoulder Stretch II. Using a door jamb, stretch each arm and shoulder individually.

Heel Cord Stretch

Lower Leg Stretch

Heel Cord Stretch. Do this stretch, pressing against a wall, with the back leg straight. Keep both feet flat on the floor and alternate legs.

Lower Leg Stretch. This is similar to the heel cord stretch, except both knees are bent.

Posterior Tissue Stretch

Thigh Stretch

Posterior Tissue Stretch. Cross one leg over the other and rest toes of the crossed leg at the outer edge of the other foot. This will put only one leg at a time under tension. Alternate legs.

Thigh Stretch. Back-reclining position to start, with one leg extended. Bent-knee leg has toes extended to rear. Lift hips upward to stretch thigh of bent leg. Alternate legs.

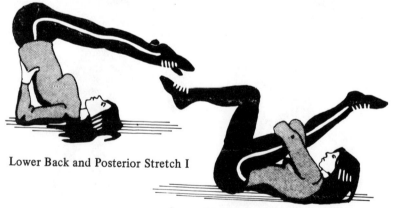

Lower Back and Posterior Stretch I

Lower Back and Posterior Stretch II

Lower Back and Posterior Tissue Stretch I. Support lower back area with both hands.

Lower Back and Posterior Tissue Stretch II. Use both arms to pull straightened leg gently in toward chest. Let opposite leg hang in bent position.

Posterior and Leg Adduction Tissue Stretch

Posterior and Leg Adductor Tissue Stretch. Traditional "hurdle stretch." Forward leg does not have to be fully straightened at knee joint.

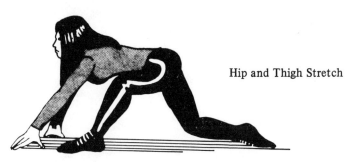

Hip and Thigh Stretch

Hip and Thigh Stretch. Let forward knee rotate outward until stretch is felt on inner side of thigh (adductor muscles).

Back and Shoulder Stretch

Back and Shoulder Stretch. Grasp towel, ski pole, etc., and use alternate arms to exert gentle stretch at several joint angles.

Part IV

SKI TOURING

11

Day Tours and Snow Camping
by David Beck

DAY TOURS

Whether you are starting out on your first ski tour or if you have been ski touring for years, there is always a certain feeling when you put on your skis—the magic moment when you're heading out. We all have a feeling of anticipation when a ski tour begins. The winter environment is unusual and new to most of us. We only see it through windows or have brief tastes of it while walking between buildings. But skiing brings us outside in the winter.

Part of our fascination with winter results because it is the least forgiving of the seasons. Cold, darkness, and deep snows are hazardous to the unprepared.

Whether you're striking out on your own, or if you're skiing on a busy track, ski touring is always refreshing. But as with any sport involving travel, beginners as well as experts need to make careful plans and preparations to ensure a safe and enjoyable tour.

The biggest problem that beginning skiers have is learning how to pace themselves. Skiing is much tougher for the beginner who is always falling, generally tense, using new muscle combinations, and working much harder than it is for the more casual, experienced skier. Deliberately pace yourself on your first few ski tours. Don't try to keep up with a skier who is faster than you are. Never let anyone, including yourself, push you to the point of exhaustion. I always tell beginning skiers to pretend that they are 10 kilometers into a 50-kilometer race; to think of those remaining 40 kilometers. Don't waste energy. You don't have to master the technique of a good racer. But you should be aware that Nordic skiing requires considerable energy, and that you and your party have only so much energy available. We teach beginning skiers the "Sierra shuffle," a simple, short stride in which skis are pushed, not lifted, and hands are kept low with poles behind.

Skiers are always asking me how well they have to ski to go on a trans-Sierra tour. My answer is that they don't have to be expert or even very good intermediate skiers. They do have to be able to ski all day at a reasonable pace without falling too often. Some of the most adventurous skiers have a rather modest ski technique.

Plan your tour so you won't push your energy limits. Remember that, unless you are on a loop tour, you have to return on your original route; so multiply the distance by two. Let the weaker members of your party take turns leading. Many beginning skiers return from their tours late and tired because they ignored their return distance and the time it would require. Pick an easy objective for your tour and stick to it. Beginners should never ski more than 2 or 3 miles at a stretch. The more energetic members of your group can practice their skills on a hillside while the others watch.

Wanderlust often affects some skiers. That's fine, but don't abandon your friends. You don't have to ski tip to tail, but your party should stay intact. Don't let it spread out, especially during storms, darkness, or periods of avalanche hazard. Exploration is certainly one of the most enjoyable aspects of ski touring, but if you are going to explore an area include the exploration as part of your initial objective. Exploring after dark is not fun.

Inform someone about your plans. Always leave word with a responsible person about your tour destination, your route, and the time you expect to return. If you get into trouble on a tour, rescue or assistance will take place much quicker if the rescuers know when and where to look. A tour party has to be self-reliant, since many rescues don't take place until the day after the party gets into trouble. Rescuers do not usually head out until sunrise. The reason for this is that most tour parties aren't due back until dark, and once rescuers are notified it is after dark and too late to head out. So when you go on your tour, you should be prepared to survive the night out if need be. You should carry the necessary items in your day pack even on a warm day. A sweater or parka and a waterproof shell are useful in case of a storm or an emergency bivouac. The gear in the equipment list in the Appendix is essential.

Many day skiers carry a lightweight sleeping pad. Snow, unlike still air, can drain away body heat; the insulating pad conserves warmth. It's also handy for sitting on during noontime picnics. However, don't load yourself down with too much gear. The day-tour equipment listed in the Appendix is fairly complete, but there are a few exceptions. For instance, in a cold climate you need warmer garments, while on a ski center track system with lots of skiers and a Nordic patrol you need little of the equipment listed.

The skis used by snow campers are different than most of the Nordic skis made for track skiing. Since snow campers make their own tracks, they need skis that handle well in variable snow conditions. Skis made for tracks are straight sided; they don't have any side cut. Skis with side cuts are wider at the tip and tail than in the middle, making them much easier to turn—a definite asset. A snow camping ski should also have a flexible tip, since skis with stiff tips won't ride well over the bumps. Metal edges are essential on ice or a hard snow surface. Many snow campers mistakenly buy skis that are longer or more highly cambered than they would regularly use. A longer, over-cambered ski is more difficult to manage. So I recommend using the same length ski for snow camping as for everyday skiing.

If you are going to ski on hills, a stiff-soled boot is essential. Your heel should not be able to slip off your skis. The *loipus device* is handy for downhill skiers. It consists of a plastic spur that fits into a raised plastic slot mounted on the ski. This helps keep the heel planted on the ski for better control. Boots should be sturdy enough to allow you to kick steps up hillsides and to hike on rocky trails. We have found that pin bindings are quite adequate with stiff boots and we use them on trans-Sierra tours.

SNOW CAMPING

Day tours are limited: you can only go so far, and see and do only so much in a day. You have to return to your lodge in the evening. That far ridge that has been beckoning to you is out of reach unless you camp. Nordic skiing frees one; it allows one to wander almost at will. Snow camping enlarges this freedom. The winter camping skier is limited only by his knowledge and ability to carry and use food and gear, as well as those limits imposed by natural elements, such as terrain, deep snows, storms, and avalanches. Most of the really good skiing and scenery in western North America are found either in real wilderness or in legally mandated wilderness areas. There are no lodges and only snow campers visit these areas in winter.

Most people's first snow camping experience is horrible. Miserable discomfort and constant cold keep pulling at the novice snow camper's ears, fingers, and toes. Cold seeps through the bottom of the sleeping bag. Even the novice camper who manages to avoid the cold has a difficult time staying comfortable in the awkward environment of a tent or snow cave. There may be no way of avoiding discomfort the first experience. But don't give up, because a warm and comfortable snow camp is not an impossibility. Experienced snow campers have many little tricks that help them out. They have adequate equipment and they know how to use it. And they have an established routine that helps them live comfortably in the cold.

One of the most important tricks is to wear the correct amount of the appropriate clothing. Wool and synthetic materials keep you warmer than cotton when wet. During a tour, you should expect to get wet or at least damp. Sweat and melting snow and frost are all sources of moisture. Keep your clothes as dry as possible. Don't wear thick layers that cause sweating. Also, don't waste heat; if you begin to feel cold, stop and put on a new layer. When you stop for a rest, automatically put on another shirt or sweater: it's easier to stay warm than to get warm after you are already chilled. Ski touring often involves putting on and taking off a lot of layers. Change clothing at the end of the day when you make camp. One damp layer next to your body will keep you uncomfortable.

I carry a warm Creslan acrylic shirt, which I put on every evening after removing my skiing clothing. (I bought it at Goodwill for $1.50.) I also put on my more expensive Norwegian noitch woolen long johns, which I picked up at a ski shop ten years ago. Clothing is often an exception to the rule that you get what you pay for when you purchase gear.

Down garments and sleeping bags have never been successful on long tours in damp climates. When down becomes wet, it loses its insulating characteristics. The new Polarguard or fiber-fill insulating materials have the advantages of keeping all of their insulating qualities when wet and drying quickly. However, these synthetics are more bulky than down, and pound for pound are not as efficient an insulator as dry down.

A new concept in insulation is called the *double-vapor barrier.* It works for sleeping bags as well as boots. If your ski boots often get wet, causing your feet to become cold, you can make your own insulated, waterproof shoes. On each foot, simply wear a light wool sock, a plastic bag, a heavy sock, another plastic bag, and then your boot. The insulated dry socks will keep your feet warm, regardless of how wet your boots or inner socks become. Mountaineers are using the same double-vapor barrier for camping in cold climates. They keep their down bags dry by using waterproof covers and liners. If the temperature is too high a waterproof bag can cause excessive sweating, but most of the time it is surprisingly comfortable.

Besides moisture, wind can also be a "heat robber." Wind robs warmth from any surface it passes over; the higher the wind the more rapid the heat loss. So it is essential to shelter yourself from it. Most skiers don't understand the importance of protecting their heads and necks from the wind. When you are cold, your body shunts increased amounts of blood (which carries heat) to your vital organs and your brain. The colder your head, the more heat your body will transmit to it, at the expense of your legs and arms. Hence the saying: "To warm your feet, put on your hat." A wool scarf can be invaluable for maintaining body warmth. I always carry mine, even if I'm only going on a day tour.

Packs

Soft packs are much more suited to skiing than frame packs. A well-designed pack must be large enough to hold your gear. The size of the pack will depend on the length of the trips you expect to take. Two- or three-day tours rarely require carrying loads over thirty or forty pounds, while a seven-day tour necessitates a pack that will allow you to carry sixty-five pounds. If you're in doubt, go for the larger pack, but resist the temptation to fill it on shorter trips. A good soft pack, like a good frame pack, must have a comfortable waist belt to allow you to transfer the pack's weight to your hips. A good pack must be waterproof. Packs that wrap around your back are often too warm. I use a well-made narrow pack, with a good belt. There are large side pockets for additional gear for longer trips. Compartmentalized packs are handy, but if you use one be sure that it will still be usable if the zippers fail.

When you shop for your pack, be sure that it fits well. There is no one pack that is perfect for all people, since skiers come in too many different shapes and sizes. Your pack should be comfortable with both small loads of a few pounds and larger loads of thirty to fifty pounds.

When you pack your pack, always place the heavier items close to your back, since the center of gravity should be as close to your body as possible. If you are going to ski on the level or climb, place the heavy items higher in the pack. If you expect to bushwack or ski downhill, pack the heavy items low so the pack won't be off-balance. Always be sure that the drawstrings are tight, the zippers zipped, and outside items tied or strapped securely. At first, don't be too fussy about where to place items. After a few days a natural system will develop, and you will carry your lunch, camera, lotions, and spare clothing in the most convenient locations.

When skiing downhill, place your camera in your pack, rather than around your neck. I made that mistake at the beginning of a thirty-day tour. On the second day I fell on the camera, cracking two ribs. I had to continue the tour very carefully.

Shelter

There are some specific requirements for a good snow campsite. If your campsite has wood and water nearby, you are much better off than if you have to melt all of your water. The tent should be set up on a level site. If you can't find a level

spot, dig a level platform. Bumps or irregularities in the platform will freeze hard under your body and make your night
uncomfortable, so be sure that it is smooth and hard. Always
pack the snow down with your skis. In soft snow you often
have to pack it down first with your skis, then with your boots,
and finally again with your skis.

Timber also provides shelter from wind. But never camp
directly under a tree, which might dump its snow load on your
tent. "Snow bombs" probably destroy more tents than any
other single cause. An ideal campsite would be in a small clear-
ing on a knoll or ridge, near a stream but above cold, frosty
down-channel night winds. Meadows, while pretty during the
day, usually become lakes of cold frost-laden air at night.

For extended stays and during storms, snow caves or igloos
are much more comfortable than tents. But remember, it isn't
always possible to build a snow shelter in shallow, soft, or very
hard snow. The disadvantage of a snow shelter is that building
one is a wet, time-consuming process. The quickest snow shelter
to build is a *T*-shaped trench dug into a hillside. Use skis or
poles to support an overhead tarp, which will hold about a
foot of snow. Make the doorway, or the long end of the *T*,
lower than the sleeping platform, and block the door with
packs. There should be a vent the size of a pole basket in the
top of the shelter. A candle will cheerfully light and warm the
shelter. If you have ever sat out a windy storm in a tent, whose
sides are flapping in the wind or on the verge of collapsing under new snow, you will appreciate a warm, cozy snow cave that
is a good shelter even in the worst of storms.

A good tent for snow has conflicting requirements. It must be
lightweight but roomy. It must be low and flexible enough to
spill the wind, but it must be high, steep-sided, and strongly
guyed to shed snow and stand up under deep, fresh snow. A
good tent is a compromise between all these different requirements. A tent should not have loose side panels or seams that
will flap in the wind.

Be selective in choosing a tent. See if it meets the conflicting requirements. Are there baggy panels or seams? How well is
it stitched? Are the poles strong enough? How long does it take
to pitch the tent? Can you pitch it while wearing mitts?

Skiers setting up camp in Mont Tremblant Provincial Park in Quebec. (Photo courtesy of the Tourist Branch of the government of Quebec)

I use a well-made tent that meets my requirements nicely. I can stand up in it. It can sleep four, yet it weighs only seven pounds when I use my adjustable avalanche-probe ski poles for the center pole. Unless you know that it absolutely never rains in your touring area, always carry a rainfly for the tent. A frost-liner is handy in cold climates, but there is no tent in which some frost doesn't form. It is best to avoid waterproof tents, since they are extremely frosty. They constantly frost up on the inside, regardless of the outside weather.

In a tent or snow cave, chaos is always the order of things. There never seems to be enough room for gear, sleeping room, and space for cramped muscles to stretch and bend. In all this confusion, you will have to be careful about cooking and melting snow for drinking water.

Sleeping Bags

Most campers in dry, colder climates prefer down bags. For long trips or for wetter climates it is impossible to keep your bag dry. You need a synthetic-filled bag, or a down bag with a double-vapor barrier. Baffles are important for ensuring good loft, or thickness. Be sure your bag has a constant loft; in the middle of the night, thin spots are very noticeable. If you stop for lunch and the sun is shining, shake out your bag and other damp garments and dry them out. In cold weather, a roomy mummy bag is recommended. A tight-fitting bag will be cold at the points where knees and shoulders compress it.

Sleeping pads are essential. A half-inch Ensolite pad provides adequate protection from the heat-absorbing snow. Two pads are even warmer. Some good pads are available, made of a layer of high-density foam, with a bottom layer of foam plastic.

When you go to bed at night, take all of your damp clothing inside the bag with you. Damp socks and mitts will be dry in the morning. Take your water bottle inside too. Some dedicated campers even sleep with their boots inside the bag.

Stoves

All camping stoves are cranky—some more than others. You should never quite trust your old and faithful stove; be aware of its quirks and inconsistencies. Light it outside and, whenever possible, use it outdoors. Practice using it in different places and situations. The pumps that can be purchased to replace fuel caps of the Svea, Optimus, and Primus camp stoves increase their performance and reliability. Prime your stove carefully before turning it on, and watch for flare-ups from overpriming.

Remember, gas doesn't freeze; it is the same temperature as the air around it. Skiers have frostbitten their fingers by spilling cold gas over them. When a stove is used in a tent, there should be a minimum of movement. Spills or burning are always a hazard. I remember when I spilled a gallon of scalding water on my down bag. The temperature was below zero that night but I couldn't use the bag.

Always shelter stoves from the wind, but never overinsulate one or use two stoves under one pot. The tanks can overheat and explode.

Food

On long tours or even short ones, discussion topics vary. But one of the main themes is usually food—both its quality and quantity, or the lack of either. On long or strenuous ski tours the best way to calculate food needs is by calories per person per day. The calories a person needs can vary from about 1,500 to almost 4,000 calories a person per day. On trips like a midwinter trans-Sierra tour or a long Alaskan tour, you should plan for at least 3,000 calories per person per day. You can shortchange yourself on food quality or quantity for a few days, but your body will need adequate fuel after you have used your reserves of city fat and are skiing long, hard days.

Winter travelers need fats or oils and protein in their diet. North American Indians and arctic explorers used to live on *pemmican*, a mixture of dried meat and rendered fat. It is a very concentrated and surprisingly nutritious food; the early explorers thrived on it for long periods. But a word of caution: don't change your diet pattern too rapidly. When you go out on a tour, your body and mind will already be worked and challenged more than usual. Don't make your job difficult by trying to live on pemmican. If you need more fat, put an extra dollop of margarine into every meal. For instance, I find that a quarter-teaspoon of margarine will really mellow the taste of a cup of instant coffee.

There are many brands of dried foods on the market. Most of them are adequate, but all of them lack oils and tend to be bland. Since all the prepared foods are expensive, we prefer to make up our own meals.

For breakfast, granola will last you through the morning. Breakfast should be quick. I don't like dirty pots, especially in the morning.

We melt snow and boil water in one pot, and in the evening we cook dinner in another pot. If you are tired and in a hurry, don't waste time on the evening meal. A quick pot of instant mashed potatoes with tuna and gravy is excellent. Another easy dinner is macaroni and cheese.

If you have time for a more relaxed dinner, one of our favorites is curry. The recipe for six is as follows:

1 Box MJB Quick Brown Rice
4 Tbls. chicken stock base
Handful dehydrated onions
Envelope of cream of mushroom soup
Canned or freeze-dried meat for 6
2 Tbls. curry powder
Margarine
Condiments: Raisins, peanuts, banana chips, coconut, bacon bits

Simply bring water to a boil, and add rice, chicken base, and onions. Boil ten minutes, and add margarine, meat, curry, and soup mix. Sometimes we even add an envelope of dehydrated milk when rice is tender to make the mixture more creamy. Fill everyone's bowl and top with the condiments.

If you don't like curry, make a stroganoff. Use noodles rather than rice, substitute beef stock base, and add mushroom soup, dehydrated sour cream, onions, and freeze-dried beef. We buy much of our camp foods in number 10 tins from a bulk food store, which sells dehydrated sour cream, buttermilk, vegetables, fruits, and freeze-dried meat.

A small amount of such condiments as Italian seasoning, chili powder, curry, and beef or chicken stock base can rescue many meals. I have a friend who is addicted to Louisiana hot sauce. She says it always makes bad food good and good food better.

We plan on consuming about half our daily calories at lunch and in trail snacks. Salami is nothing more than an expensive pemmican, with spices and preservatives added. I love cheese, and peanut butter is a sort of vegetarian pemmican. Vary the lunches, and if weight is important eliminate items high in moisture, such as jam and sardines. *Gorp*, a mixture of raisins, nuts, and candy, has been the standby trail snack of wilderness travelers for years.

John Muir was famous for living on biscuits during his early wanderings through the Sierra. Like Muir, after a few days on the trail, most of us crave bread. We carry RyKrisp or hard breads that can take being battered in a pack. We have also carried dried bagels or dried San Francisco sourdough bread.

We also cook bannock, a traditional and filling trail bread. Make a stiff batter from a biscuit or buttermilk mix. For a richer taste, add margarine, sugar, and dry milk. Pat the batter flat and fry it slowly over a low fire. A greased, lightweight Teflon frying pan is useful for this purpose. When the bannock has a thick brown crust on both sides, split it open. While steaming hot, spread it with jam or margarine and devour.

For years Logan bread has been the traditional mountaineering hard ration. It is basically a mixture of whole-wheat flour, rye flour, cornmeal, oatmeal, honey, molasses, dry milk, nuts, raisins, and oil. You mix the concoction together, spread it on a cookie pan, and bake it one hour at 300° F. Leave it in the oven with the door open until it is tooth-breakingly hard. We have a recipe that is both tastier and easier to knaw on than the classic one. We call it Way bread.

Way Bread Recipe

1 cup soy grits
1 cup dry milk
1 cup whole-wheat flour
1 cup blackstrap molasses
¾ cup oil
¾ tsp. soda
1 tsp. salt
1 tsp. nutmeg
1 tsp. vanilla
2 cups oatmeal
2 cups raisins (optional)
1 cup walnuts (optional)

Mix the dry ingredients, except for the oatmeal. Add molasses, oil, and enough milk to make a thick cookie batter. Then fold in the oatmeal. Cook for 20-30 minutes in a 325° oven, and then oven-dry for several hours. The finished Way bread should be firm and should not be crumbly. Add more molasses or honey if you wish to make it harder.

Always carry sufficient emergency high-energy food to see you through any tough periods when you may not be able to cook. There is some sentiment against refined sugars among many skiers. But if you are wet and shivering, there are times when a dextrose tablet or a quick-energy candy bar will give a needed boost.

Air in winter is cold and dry. Dehydration affects many skiers who aren't aware of the low humidity. They don't feel thirsty, and as they become dehydrated they just lose their strength and health. With the exception of late-night drinkers who don't wish to climb out of a warm sleeping bag in the middle of the night, it's impossible to drink too much liquid. Carry a liter water bottle and constantly drink from it. Carry it next to your body and every time you take a drink refill the bottle with snow. When carefully managed, the bottle will always be full.

We recently did a trans-Sierra tour and experienced fatigue going over the passes, falls due to skiing with packs, dinners that weren't perfect, crowded tents, cold feet, and all the other annoyances inherent to winter camping. We also skied some incredible runs, saw the most awesome mountains, and as one of our group put it, "If I was a kid, I'd say, 'It's better than going to the moon.' " In short, there is simply nothing to compare with going to bed in the backcountry in winter, waking up, putting on your skis, and heading for the next pass. If carefully planned with the right equipment, overnight or longer ski tours let you see the backcountry in its most spectacular season.

12

Winter Safety
by Lito Tejada-Flores

Before dealing with the nuts and bolts of winter safety, avalanche awareness, first aid, and so forth, we should take a moment to think about safety itself. What is safety? What can make ski touring safe?

As in most wilderness sports, safety in ski touring does not result from following a fixed set of rules. Rather, safety derives from good judgment.

Now, granted, it takes a fair amount of experience to develop good judgment, but experience alone won't do it. Good judgment is the result of a certain attitude toward the wild or semiwild environment through which the ski tourer moves—a calm, respectful, responsible attitude.

Excitable, nervous people simply aren't safe´ in the backcountry in winter. Their assessments of problem situations tend to be hasty, overdramatic, and often wrong. Their responses are too often exaggerated, too quick, and inappropriate. And it's usually only a matter of degree between overreacting and panicking. I'm not saying that excitable people should never go ski touring. But a calm, steady person must be in a leadership role, responsible for the safety of others in the party.

The next ingredient for safe touring is to take the backcountry seriously, in winter even more than in summer. For the alpinist, if you don't respect the mountains they may kill you. The ski touring environment may seem less fierce than that of mountaineering, yet the two have many similarities. Any landscape in winter—snow-covered and isolated—has its own harsh realities. To ignore these is to be at one's peril. As the terrain steepens from gentle touring country to major mountains, the danger from avalanches, bad weather, and even ski injuries increases. Unless the touring skier respects the potential danger in the environment, safe touring is impossible.

149

Finally we need to maintain a responsible attitude. You must be responsible for preparing for various eventualities, problems, and hazards, as well as for caring for the other members of your touring party. Consider, for example, that very few things really do go wrong on most ski tours. Nine out of ten tours are quite uneventful, except for good skiing and magnificent scenery; the biggest crises may involve "missing" the perfect wax. Being responsible, however, means considering in advance all the things that might go wrong and how you will react, so that if a crisis occurs you're ready for it. It also means being particularly aware of your companions—are they tired? cold? can they make it?—rather than just skiing on, caught up in your own private world. As in any wilderness sport, ski tourers must provide each other's extra margin of safety—each other's backup system. So, ski touring safety is the responsibility of every member of the party, not just the leader.

In the rest of this article we'll be looking at four specific areas related to ski touring hazards and touring safety: orientation or how not to get lost; emergency shelter and warmth; avalanches and snow safety; and touring injuries, first aid, and evacuation. This will be more of an introduction to these subjects than anything else. Whole books have been written on several of them. But hopefully we will have begun the process of looking ahead, of preparing for the worst. This will make it possible to avoid problems, while laying the foundation for safe ski touring.

ORIENTATION

If you know where you've come from, where you are, and where you're going, then you've solved the problem of orientation. Unfortunately, in a snow-covered landscape it's not always that easy. On the other hand, orientation—finding your way without getting lost—is not a big mystery either. You don't have to be an absolute wizard with map and compass to "navigate" your way cross-country. Your topographical map, and to a lesser extent your compass, serve only as reference materials. The basic way a cross-country skier finds his way from here to there is by using landmarks.

Landmarks are conspicuous, identifiable terrain features by which you can judge your position or progress. They range from the overwhelmingly obvious—say, a major peak with a striking rocky buttress—to the rather subtle—a low, rounded ridge, a shallow stream bed, or a fence marking a property line. In a few situations, none of them pleasant, there may be no landmarks at all. Then as we'll see, the compass can play an important role. But generally, the touring skier keeps tabs on his position by simply observing the terrain around him. You should be constantly scanning the terrain for the best slopes to climb or descend, differences in the snow, or the safest route. That way, it's both easy and natural to pick out major landmarks to gauge and guide your progress.

Topographical maps (topo maps) are useful for positive identification of certain far-off landmarks, and in predetermining (even before the tour) which terrain features you will be looking for once on the trail. In order to use your topo map, however, certain things must be known. You must know your own position, both on the ground and on the map. This will allow you to identify other terrain features once the map has been *oriented*, or correctly aligned north-to-south with the aid of a compass. Or else, you must recognize a couple of prominent terrain features, which will permit you to orient the map with respect to them, and thus locate where you are. It's usually necessary to be sure of two points in order to derive precise information from the map.

But topo maps do more than provide information about precise locations. Once you can "read" them, topo maps offer a marvelous general picture of the terrain: its ups and downs, canyons, ridges, and summits—its shape. This is something you can glean from the map before ever starting your tour. The trick is, when looking at contour lines, to be able to visualize them in three dimensions. Locate the high points first, whether mountain summits or merely the tops of rolling hills. These appear on the map as the centers of sets of concentric circles or contour loops. Then, looking for "stacks" of *V*- or *U*-shaped lines, identify the gullies (*V*'s point uphill) or ridges (*V*'s or *U*'s pointing down) leading down and out from these high points. In this way, you can construct a mental relief image of the terrain. In gentler country, rivers and streams can be of greater help than summits in visualizing the terrain. For very flat country, you'll probably learn more from surface features than from contour lines. Here, look for roads, fences, stands of trees, or buildings marked on the map.

If you have a good mental picture of the terrain, with a couple of landmarks to help you orient your map, you may wonder whether you really need a compass at all. On many tours the answer is no. I always carry a map, but seldom a compass. Of course, if you're skiing across an arctic wasteland, devoid of landmarks or contours, you need to follow a compass bearing. But that isn't often the case. In mountains above timberline, low clouds and fog can produce a true *whiteout,* where nothing is visible. Here, too, a compass might be handy, but it's probably better to sit down and wait until the visibility improves somewhat. Finally, in a relatively flat woods, without distinctive topographical features, a compass could be valuable to hold a direction. However, it's not usually much fun skiing in such conditions. Following a compass course, by the way, is not easy. If you want to learn this subtle art, get a book on *orienteering,* an esoteric and challenging sport related to cross-country running.

Yet what do such basic ideas about orientation have to do with winter safety? Clearly, avoiding getting lost is one step toward a safe tour. It is even trickier to keep from getting lost when sudden bad weather alters your visibility. Reaching your destination in time, and being able to retrace your steps if you need to, have important safety implications.

To protect your sense of orientation from the sudden arrival of clouds, storms, and poor visibility, get in the habit of observing small-scale landmarks as well as major ones. Boulders in a streambed or a group of stunted trees may become quite important if clouds later hide the obvious ridgeline you've been following. Likewise, if you periodically take the trouble to look back at your tracks, you'll be in much better shape if you unexpectedly have to retrace your route. In one sense, successful backcountry orientation, on skis or not, boils down to being aware, not just of the landscape you're moving through, but also of your rate of progress.

Even though cross-country touring, unlike racing, is not done against the clock, time can still be a critical factor. Various questions have a direct bearing on reaching your destination safely, or getting there and back. How long is your proposed day tour, or how far to the next good campsite if it's a long trip? How many hours of sunlight are there in January? Did you get an early start or a late one? Is the new snow slowing you down more than you had expected? Particularly if you're day touring with light gear, keeping track of your progress and turning back in time can save you from dealing with the next winter safety problem—an unplanned night out.

EMERGENCY SHELTER AND WARMTH

There are two sides to the problem of winter safety: knowing how to keep dangerous situations from happening, and knowing what to do if one does occur. An unplanned night out is almost always the result of something unanticipated: you lost your way, you took longer than expected, or someone broke a ski and couldn't repair it. And there you are. It's growing dark and you know you can't get back to the car; it's below freezing and all you've got is an extra sweater and a light parka. What now? Such a situation can turn into a tragedy, or merely result in an uncomfortable night and an easy ski out the next morning. The answer to this problem is: dig in!

Even though we tend to think of snow as a cold substance, it offers tremendous insulation. Although snow is frozen water, and hence is always at least 32º F (0º C), such a temperature may seem warm indeed on a cold February night when the air temperature drops to -20º F. And, in fact, as soon as you burrow into the snow pack a couple of feet, the temperature does stay amazingly close to the freezing point. The idea, then, is to create some kind of snow cave or snow hole in which to bivouac if you're caught out unprepared. (Winter camping, a far more organized and pleasant experience is discussed in chapter 11.) Since you didn't plan on staying out all night, you surely won't have a shovel to help you dig your improvised shelter. But in many snow conditions the curved-up tip of a ski works reasonably well, as does a spare ski-repair tip if you have one.

The ideal is to dig a cave, with a small tunnel-like entrance and a rounded-out dome-shaped interior. This is not as hard as it sounds, especially if you have a steep bank or the vertical side of a wind drift to dig into. Since you only have your body heat to warm this cave, don't make it too big. It should be a burrow several feet in diameter, rather than a real "hobbit hole." (As a matter of fact, you probably won't have time or energy to dig a large cave.)

In some situations—with less snow depth, unsuitable terrain, or little time—you won't be able to make a real cave. But you still want to get as deep into the snow as possible. So try to hollow out a small trench, just big enough to sit or lie in. Possibly, you'll be able to cover the top with your skis and poles, and a few broken branches, and then seal it off further with snow packed on top. In any kind of snow shelter, cave, or trench, try to pad and insulate the floor with branches, twigs, greenery, or whatever you can find. Finally, as you're settling in to wait out an unpleasant, but bearable, night (in which you probably won't get much sleep) take your ski boots off and stuff your feet in your rucksack or day pack; they'll stay a lot warmer. Hands and arms can be taken out of sweater and parka sleeves and folded next to your chest for a bit more warmth, as well.

So much for emergency shelter: dig in and you won't freeze. Far less dramatic, but perhaps just as critical for safe touring, is the problem of staying warm on the trail. One of the real pleasures of Nordic cross-country skiing is that your free-and-easy movement keeps you quite warm, even on cold days. Beginners typically overdress, and are always surprised at the light clothes preferred by experienced tourers. So one would hardly imagine that staying warm on the trail can be a problem. It isn't—as long as you're moving. On short tours, or when running for a few hours in a prepared track, warmth is never a problem. But on longer full-day tours, which require definite endurance and a sustained effort for hours, you may start to run out of steam if you get chilled. The key is to bundle up during rest stops, at lunch, and even when you pause to discuss the route.

Here we return to the fundamental idea of responsibility. Once you've skied more than a few hours away from other skiers (and possible help), you simply have to be ready to cope if something unexpected happens. What if a broken ski or a sprained ankle slows you to a snail's pace? Without your normal kick and glide, what's going to keep you warm? Therefore, a 20-kilometer backcountry tour without a pack might be delightful, but it would also be irresponsible. You really need equipment and clothes, just in case. For a full-day tour, you should carry a sweater, down vest, or parka; simple waxing and repair kit; minimum first-aid material; and food and drink. Hungry or thirsty skiers, like cold, chilled skiers, tend to become exhausted. They can become the most likely candidates for on-the-trail accidents of various sorts. Most ski-touring calamities, however, can be avoided with a little common sense (like putting on extra clothes *before,* not after, you get chilled). But avalanches, perhaps the most frightening hazard to the backcountry skier, require some special background to understand and to avoid.

AVALANCHES

Snow slides, even small ones, are potential killers, and the touring skier must channel all efforts toward avoiding being caught in an avalanche. Don't think about how you'll be rescued if you're caught; concentrate on eliminating the possibility of ever getting caught. But before you get into specifics about avalanches and how to avoid them, just how serious a menace are they for the touring skier?

Avalanches are basically a mountain phenomenon. Everything else being equal, the steeper a slope the more likely it is to avalanche. This means that many cross-country skiers don't really have to be concerned with avalanches. For example, most ski touring in the East and in the North Central states takes place on moderately gentle terrain, sometimes rolling and wooded, but generally not mountainous country. Avalanches just aren't a serious factor for skiers in these areas. Heading west across the country, we encounter the Rockies, a giant chain of ranges and sub-ranges, and the coastal ranges of the Far West and Pacific Northwest—and here the picture changes.

Avalanches pose serious dangers in the backcountry, so it is essential to observe snow conditions. This is a peak in the Sierra Nevada range. (Photo by Paul Emerson)

These are steep mountains with lots of snow and high avalanche hazard. But the hazard is not the same for all ski tourers. Most Nordic tourers, on classical skinny skis with three-pin bindings and light boots, tend to shy away from steep slopes. True, in recent years a growing number of skiers have been experimenting with and expanding the possibilities for skiing down steep terrain on cross-country skis (using both telemark and parallel techniques). But Nordic skis are really at their best on moderate, rolling terrain, and that's still where most touring skiers use them. This type of skier, touring mostly below timberline on low-angle terrain, doesn't have to worry much about avalanches either. As ski touring blends into ski mountaineering, however, avalanche danger becomes a real factor to be reckoned with nearly all the time. In truth, adventurous downhill skiers who leave the lift-served, well-patrolled slopes of a commercial ski area in search of steep out-of-bounds powder skiing are in far greater danger from avalanches than most touring skiers.

Nonetheless, if you plan to tour into higher, steeper mountain country, especially above timberline, you should learn as much as you can about avalanches. All we can do in the following pages is to sketch a few of the most salient features of avalanche phenomena, and only touch on the most basic measures for avoiding them. Any more would take a long chapter in itself, and preferably a whole book. Such a book does exist. It's the U.S. Forest Service's *Avalanche Handbook* (Agriculture Department Handbook 489, available from the U.S. Government Printing Office). This book, written in 1976, is very readable, and contains an amazing, practical wealth of avalanche lore. If you're planning a lot of high-country touring, or if you tour on Alpine skis for the express purpose of finding steep, thrilling downhill runs, you owe it to yourself to get this book and read it cover to cover. But in the meantime, consider the following.

As soon as snow has fallen, it begins to change. Different types of change, or *metamorphism,* affect the strength or weakness of the snowpack—the way one layer bonds to another, and even whether and exactly where the snow will later avalanche. Because of the complexities of waxing, Nordic skiers

tend to be more aware of changes in snow than Alpine skiers.
With a little practice Nordic skiers can learn to identify and
understand different types of snow metamorphism.

A thin, early-season snow cover exposed to extremely cold
air temperatures undergoes what is called *temperature gradient
metamorphism*. This results in the formation of an unstable
unconsolidated layer of "sugar snow," or *depth hoar*. Such
layers of depth hoar (common in the Rockies, but less common
farther west) are often responsible for large climax slides after
the snowpack has built up sufficient depth and weight. More
commonly through the winter, *equitemperature metamorphism*
results in consolidation and stabilizing of the snowpack. In
spring, another type of change, *melt-freeze metamorphism,*
acts on the snowpack to produce the beautiful corn-snow,
which is the skier's delight.

But here we're only scratching the surface. The actual mech-
anism of these changes in the snow cover is a fascinating,
complex, and still only partially understood story. The cumu-
lative history of such changes over a whole winter, plus the
shape and nature of the slope itself, determine whether, and
when, a slope will avalanche.

Avalanches, as you might suspect, are classified into various
types; the main division is between *loose-snow* and *slab avalanches*. Loose snow avalanches occur when new snow piles up
so steeply on a slope that it can no longer support itself. At
that point, it begins slipping down—usually from a point and
fanning out—much as the sand on a beach slips away when you
try to build a steep cone with it. While they can be serious
in themselves, loose-snow avalanches are not too important
for most touring skiers, since they tend to occur either during
or immediately after storms. These are not the best times for
touring, unless you're actively seeking deep powder. But slab
avalanches are another story.

A slab avalanche occurs when a large area of snow slides,
altogether, as a single unit. There are different sorts of slabs,
some formed by wind action, and some by snow piling up and
bonding together storm after storm. Avalanches are classified
as hard-slab and soft-slab slides. Before they slide, such slabs of
snow are held in place, or anchored, by various features on the

slope (trees and rock outcrops, for example), as well as by friction with layers of snow beneath, above, and to the sides. Ultimately, the weight of the slab may become too great for its anchors (with one last snowfall), or the anchoring bonds may be undercut or reduced (for example, by a skier traversing the slope), or both, and the slab slides. Slab avalanches, therefore, have a kind of insidious quality: the hazard can build up over a period of time, and then stay poised like a land mine waiting for some new factor to set it off. Fortunately for the touring skier, typical slab locations and likely avalanche paths are fairly easy to spot, and to avoid. So without going any deeper into avalanche theory, let's turn to a set of practical rules of thumb for avoiding avalanche situations.

Since trees provide good anchors for the snowpack, you can assume that wooded slopes are safer than open slopes. But beware of narrow open chutes cutting steeply down through forested slopes. These are more typical in the Rockies than farther west because the timberline is much higher, up to 12,000 feet. Nonetheless, the most serious avalanche hazard occurs above tree line. Here, one would prefer ridges (virtually always safe) to open faces and steep bowls. The center of a wide valley is usually safe, but the bottom of a narrow *U-* or *V*-shaped alpine valley may be continually threatened from the slopes above.

Steepness, of course, is a critical factor. Avalanches can occur on slopes from 15 to 50 degrees, but above 30 degrees they are common, and below that relatively rare. So if you're in search of steep skiing in the backcountry, it's far better to wait until spring conditions have stabilized the snowpack. In winter conditions, especially in the Rockies, avoid slopes steeper than 30 degrees (which for skiing is respectably steep). Another reason to avoid steeper slopes is that most Nordic skiers tend to traverse on the descent rather than ski the fall line, thereby "cutting" the slope and increasing the likelihood of slab failure.

Although ridges offer the safest routes, steep slopes just below ridge crests are the exact opposite. Wind slabs can form on both sides of a ridge, but the major wind deposition area is on the lee side of a ridge (the side where cornices are formed). Wind slabs are hard slabs formed out of wind-transported, wind-packed snow, and offer a disturbing illusion of solidity . . . before they go. Beware of hollow-sounding wind-deposit areas, and treat the lee sides of all ridges with caution. It goes without saying that if the ridge itself is corniced, you must avoid skiing or walking over the overhanging portion. Stay well back from the edge if you can't see how large the cornice actually is.

Finally, sudden changes in temperature can signal increased avalanche hazard. Continued bitter cold will make existing unstable conditions persist even longer. A gradual warming trend, on the other hand, promotes settling and easing of stress in the snowpack, lessening considerably the probability of avalanche. This is why avalanche danger is so much lower in the High Sierra, with its typically warm temperatures, than in the Rockies, where subzero conditions persist for weeks or months at a time.

The essence of avalanche safety, then, is to choose a route that avoids obvious avalanche paths and is not threatened by other avalanche paths from above. The more you can learn about avalanches, the less this will seem like guesswork (though to some degree that element is often present). Even experienced avalanche researchers and control teams sometimes have to trust their hunches about whether a particular slope will slide or not. And you should, too. If a snow slope gives you a creepy feeling, even though you can't explain why, then don't cross it.

But life being what it is, sooner or later you may be in the position of having to cross a potentially dangerous slope, either through impatience or necessity. Do everything in your power to avoid such situations; spending an extra hour or two to traverse around a bad avalanche slope is a small price to pay. But if you are crossing a dangerous slope, make sure only one skier is exposed at a time, with all the others watching so that they can pinpoint his position if he is swept away. Just because the first skier makes it across without triggering an avalanche, don't assume that the slope is safe. Exposing only one person at a time to possible avalanche danger is an all-important rule.

Although I hope you'll never be caught in an avalanche, or be in the position of trying to dig out a companion, the following points could be important. If an avalanche starts above or around you, attempt to ski to the edge. You only

have seconds to move, so think about the possibility before-
hand, if you are in a touchy situation. In any avalanche hazard
area, you should remove the straps of your ski poles from your
wrists, so if you are caught, swept off your feet, and carried
away, at least your arms won't be trapped. Try to stay on the
surface, using a swimming motion with your arms. If you feel
yourself coming to a stop, thrust one arm as high as you can
toward the surface, protecting your face with the other to
create a small breathing space. The buried avalanche victim
usually can't move, since the snow around him, even if it was
powder to start with, sets up hard and fast. Any effective
help must come from his companions.

If your companion is caught and swept away in an avalanche,
it is critical to keep watching his body as long and as far as you
can see it. When he disappears, try to fix on the point he was
last seen. That way, you can mark the point once the slide has
stopped, and conduct your search for the victim downslope
from there. Time is of the essence, so it is rarely worth going
for help. Avalanche victims buried for more than an hour
have a very small chance of being found alive, and the critical
period is actually shorter than that. The first thing to do is to
conduct a hasty search of the area below the last-seen point
for any protruding signs of the skier—equipment, arms, legs.
Then, if that fails, organize the entire skiing party in a line
across the slope below the last seen point and methodically
probe the avalanche debris, descending the slope step by step.
Ski poles with baskets removed make adequate probe poles.

But before going any further, I want to emphasize that
the average touring skier should never find himself in this
situation. The nature of Nordic touring, as opposed to Alpine
touring and ski mountaineering, will fortunately keep most
cross-country skiers out of serious avalanche country. If,
however, you wish to explore peaks and steep slopes, you
simply must take the avalanche problem seriously. In that
case, you ought to be prepared with the following things.

First, learn more about avalanches in general, as the information in this chapter is not sufficient to keep you safe. Obtain
the Forest Service *Avalanche Handbook* and study it. Second,
try to do most of your serious high-mountain touring in spring,

when the snowpack is greatly stabilized, and avalanche danger is limited to predictable wet snowslides in the afternoon. Finally, if you insist on touring in steep, deep powder in mid-winter, carry a full kit of avalanche gear and learn how to use it. This includes an avalanche cord (15 meters of light, red line that the skier can trail behind him, and which, hopefully, will remain visible on the surface if he's buried), and a "beeper" (a small transceiver worn inside your clothes that emits a beeping radio signal, enabling other members of the party to locate a buried skier by switching their beepers to receive). Other useful avalanche paraphernalia include special ski poles that screw together to form long probe poles and lightweight snow shovels for digging out a victim. But even when armed to the teeth with such special gear, you don't have a prayer of survival in serious avalanche conditions unless you develop and use a subtle blend of good judgment and common sense. The best way to deal with potential avalanche situations is to avoid them.

FIRST AID AND EVACUATION

Winter first aid can be an unpleasant subject. If you need to use it, that means you've already made a mistake somewhere. But accidents, like avalanches, do happen; and prudence dictates that we must prepare for them at the same time as we try to avoid them. A general first-aid background is a must for any responsible ski tourer, and the place to start is with the standard Red Cross first-aid textbook and course. If ski touring takes you on longer and longer trips, increasingly farther from civilization and possible help, you will have to expand your first-aid competence to deal with genuine medical emergencies. A good way to do this is to take an emergency medical technician course: a kind of super first-aid course taught by a physician. And if you get serious about emergency medical preparedness, as you should if you take multiday tours, I can recommend one book in particular for reference and study: Wilkerson's *Medicine for Mountaineering,* published by the Seattle Mountaineers. This is a marvelous book, with special insights into the problems of cold, high altitude, and management of trauma when far from the roadhead.

What kind of medical emergencies might you expect to encounter on a ski tour? Downhill skiers typically suffer broken legs and various knee injuries involving torn ligaments and cartilage. Fortunately for Nordic skiers, the free-heel lift and lighter more flexible boots eliminate most of the strain that causes such problems. I sometimes think that you really have to work hard to injure yourself with three-pin bindings. But it can be done, especially with an extra heavy pack, very bad snow conditions (like a breakable crust), and a reckless style of skiing in rough terrain. The knee is still the weakest articulation in the lower body, and when bent 90 degrees or more has very little strength. So with more and more tourers pushing the limits of telemark technique in bad snow, I think it is reasonable to be prepared to treat strained knees. Mild cases can be handled by wrapping with an Ace bandage or taping. But a badly torn knee must be immobilized and the skier evacuated, just as if he had a broken leg (improvised splint and all).

Short of an expeditionary ski-mountaineering situation, most touring skiers don't go high enough or fast enough to run much of a risk of *pulmonary edema,* a severe breathing problem characterized by fluid in the lungs. This can only be dealt with by quickly descending to a lower altitude.

The casual Nordic ski tourer seldom needs to worry about cold, frostbite, and hypothermia. But for the ski mountaineer, climbing a 14,000-foot peak in high winds in January, both frostbite and hypothermia may be of immediate concern. The only thing to do about either of these conditions is to make damn sure you don't get them. Earlier in this article, we talked of the need to carry extra-warm clothes for periods— long or short—when you're not actively skiing. And we discussed how to spend an unplanned night out without getting either frostbite or hypothermia. On the trail, the trick is to avoid getting cold; once you get chilled your body must fight an uphill battle to return to thermal equilibrium. If fingers or toes ever start to go numb, stop right there and take care of it: swing your arms, loosen your boots, change to dry socks, and massage fingers or toes until the feeling returns—but don't wait!

Actually it's the little crises, like a headache with no aspirin, or sunburn, or a broken binding, that are more likely to mess up a ski tour. For this reason, I recommend combining a simple and practical first-aid kit with a sort of mini-repair and emergency kit. This should include wire and pliers to repair a binding, a pack, or a boot; a clamp-on ski repair tip; an extra pair of dark glasses; and a roll of adhesive tape to patch torn ski pants, tape an ankle, dress a wound, or repair a broken ski pole.

If you carry some cord or wire in your emergency kit, you can, if need be, rig up an emergency toboggan out of one or more pairs of skis to haul an injured companion out to civilization. This isn't easy, so if a hurt skier can still function at all, it's probably better to carry his pack and even partially support him as he skis out under his own steam. If you have to improvise a sled, the basic idea is to use two cross pieces (branches, for example): one at the bindings and one at the tips. In order to lash anything across the tapered ski tips and have it stay there, you'll probably have to use a pocket knife and cut notches in the ski tip itself. This is a difficult thing to do to your favorite skis, but in such a situation you won't mind. If someone is hurt very near the road, it would be better to send someone for a toboggan and extra help, rather than improvising a ski sled. Such sleds are neither efficient nor very comfortable for the injured skier, even when liberally padded with branches and packs.

A FINAL WORD

Ski touring, in the last analysis, is a reasonably safe sport, but only, I think, because it tends to attract responsible people. If you begin with the premise that the backcountry in winter is a place to avoid trouble, you'll act accordingly, and safe touring will result. In writing this article on "Winter Safety," I've tried to stress the importance of a responsible attitude over a host of spelled-out safety procedures or "safety gimmicks." I have assumed a great deal of common sense from the beginning. I didn't start with a warning not to ski tour alone, or with the admonition to let somebody always know where you're going and when you expect to return. If such points are not already obvious, then one may not be ready for any sort of backcountry experience, much less ski touring.

So trust your common sense and use it; then you'll be off to a good start no matter what your previous winter experience.

Let me conclude by repeating this one idea: the essence of winter safety lies more in avoiding trouble than in knowing how to deal with it. The problems of safety and self-reliance increase dramatically the further you go off the beaten path. Your response to the winter environment, and your ski technique, should become more thoughtful and more prudent when you're a few days rather than a few hours from the road. As in other wilderness sports, realizing the consequences of a mistake is the best incentive to avoid making one. Besides, a good ski tour is too much fun to chance ruining it. Here's to more touring . . . and safe touring!

13

Skiing and the Winter Wilderness

by David R. Brower

Thirteen years ago a man not quite old enough to vote brought to my house in Berkeley a hand-hewn book, bound in leather, that included color drugstore prints and a text in his own fine calligraphy. Its foreword ended:

Terry and Renny Russell, planet Earth, twentieth century after Christ. We live in a house that God built but that the former tenants remodeled—blew up, it looks like—before we arrived. Poking through the rubble in our odd hours, we've found the corners that were spared and have hidden in them as much as we could. Not to escape from but to escape to: not to forget but to remember. We've been learning to take care of ourselves in places where it really matters. The next step is to take care of the *places* that really matter. Crazy kids on the loose; but on the loose in wilderness. That makes all the difference.

—Terry Russell
Berkeley, February 6, 1965

You may recognize the book, *On the Loose,* published by the Sierra Club the year after Terry was lost when his raft upset in the Green River. His last wilderness experience ended in a double tragedy—his and ours. My family had known him first through wilderness experiences that ended in the high Sierra in summer, in Glen Canyon in spring. So far as I know, he did not ski into the wilderness. He was contemporary with my older sons. How we wish we'd had Terry and Renny along on our memorable experience—being at home on the snow.

The wind had a mean edge on it as it curved across the crest of the Sierra Nevada, and found us two thousand feet above the site of the Donner Party's tragic winter, trying to find out how to camp in deep snow. It was deep snow that trapped the Donner Party members back in 1846. Thirty-six people died, and more would have but for cannibalism. A little more than a century later, deep snow also trapped a train; but all the people aboard the City of San Francisco got out safely. We planned on not getting trapped at all. The ability to contend with winter has progressed steadily since the 1850s. Those were the days when Snowshoe Thompson carried trans-Sierra mail on his 11-foot skis, and his contemporaries set an 85-mile-per-hour record in the earliest American ski races.

The ice-edged wind found us looking at the very peaks upon which the sport of ski mountaineering was adapted to California terrain by the Sierra Club, and then exported to help the armed forces in World War II. I was exported too, and saw how our ski-mountaineering technique and equipment aided the troops, myself included, giving them combat mobility and esprit that should be recorded better than it has been before it is forgotten.

After too long a lapse, I was back in my old Sierra haunts. I brought my sons to this crest, not to expose them to danger, but to show them how to avoid it. I wanted them to feel at home there, far back in the winter wilderness, all around the clock and all around the compass.

Moreover, I also had a suspicion that every generation needs to invent contests that it can be the first to win. This is certainly true of people who look to mountains for their contests. The two generations before mine won most of their contests on the great peaks of the Alps and the major summits of the United States. Those in my generation who could afford such expeditions finished off the Himalayan giants. The less affluent of us settled for little-known peaks or for switching seasons or routes on the well-known summits.

To pioneer, my father had only to find a peak, any peak. In my generation, we could still pioneer merely by finding hard ways up easy peaks—and descending to spend the night in comfort. Today's mountaineers look for the hardest way up the most difficult peaks, and are willing to spend several successive nights trying to sleep partly inside a sack tentatively attached to an entire cliff. The suspense is tremendous! I hope my sons' pioneering will always have more fun in it, no less challenge, and barely enough of the spices of danger. Parents do that.

Not too subtly, on that trip near Donner, I was trying to expose my delegates to the new generation to the good things that could happen if they would turn their skis to the wilderness for a few winter weekends, at least. They would have new frontiers to explore every time there was a new fall of snow. They would find country—especially the western uplands—measured in millions of acres, where skis had never penetrated. They would learn ways of achieving more mobility and safety with less weight. They would also find that in winter one of the finest methods of transportation ever invented is a man's own two feet, lengthened with skis.

They would discover more of what they were already finding out. Ken and Bob liked the look of snow, where the only tracks are those behind them—except for the tracks of wildlife, mysteries to try to fathom. They liked to top a rise and start down into a far valley, knowing that there's no one there, that it is as wild as if creation were yesterday. They weren't antisocial, but they liked changes of scene. They could even endure a series of parental axioms and admonishments, for a while.

So I concentrated on the most important law of winter wilderness—keeping warm. Two light layers of clothing trap more air, I told them, and insulate better than one heavy layer. Look at the stem end of any feather and you'll note that birds have understood this all along.

It is easier to keep warm than to get warm. (Obvious.)

If you don't want a chill, don't work up a sweat. (Almost obvious.)

If your hands or feet get cold, put on an extra sweater.

They looked unbelieving, so I carried on, explaining about the body's thermostats, which will always decrease circulation to the skin and the extremities to conserve heat for the vital organs. I wasn't too talkative, fortunately, because I was reminded of one of the first laws of conservation for older people on the upgrade with a pack—conserve words and wind.

I didn't get garrulous again until we had selected a campsite, leveled a snow platform without breaking any skis, and had pitched and climbed into our new Logan tent. It must have been designed by a recluse who abhorred proximity. You could even stand up in it! They call it a three-man tent, but it could hold our whole family of six and leave room for a friendly guest.

"The perfect tent is yet to be invented," I told Bob, "and a lot of people are going to enjoy trying to invent it." I had amused myself for weeks, long ago, inventing the perfect tent, which I called the "Home-on-the-Snow" model. The U.S. Army stupidly turned it down, so I went into other work. As with tents, so with packs and stoves. There is plenty of room for progress. Whatever the item, the search for lighter, better, and still affordable design can be fun.

I threw the boys this challenge as we lay there luxuriating, and recalled earlier, harder days in the Sierra. "Beat our 21-pound record if you can," I said. "We could take off on a three-day snow-camping trip and spend two nights out with only twenty-one pounds each." That included the food, tents, sleeping bags, stoves, utensils, first aid for us and for our skis, and our extra clothing—for seven of us. But it didn't include what we wore, such as our skis and poles.

A pack as light as that, I could add, doesn't play hob with one's downhill ski technique. More important, it doesn't put too great a strain on the swivel muscles that are the hallmark of the chairborne.

Lightness of pack can also make ski-mountaineering coeducational, as we proved during one Easter week in Little Lakes Valley in the high Sierra. Our party of twenty-two, camping out on the snow at ten thousand feet for five nights, was reasonably mixed. Among the advantages: the food was edible. Ski-mountaineering menus have long been wide open for pioneering, and whatever I am tempted to say about the blending of foodstuffs that were never intended to be mixed in the light of day, and the resulting gastronomic mayhem, are better not discussed at all. Anyhow, things taste better if you work hard enough, and ski mountaineers do. I remembered one thing that never tasted better, and never will: kerosene. We continually struggled, in my early days of skiing, to keep the kerosene out of such food as we had—a struggle that was very much worth the effort—and were never quite successful. The aftertaste is unforgettable; almost immortal.

Having rambled on for quite some time, I thought it about time to become taciturn and try a silent soliloquy. I knew without question that none of my family liked my puns, to my great regret, and I could only admire them for it. I also remembered in time that the less a father tells his own sons the more they are likely to remember. Advice comes best from those who cannot command.

But let me tell you a few of the things I should like to have told them. First, I would have cautioned them: if you ever decide to take up ski mountaineering on your own—and please do—don't go alone, with a weak party, underequipped, or anywhere beyond reasonable expectation of safe retreat. Secretly not wanting them to dash too far ahead of me, I would have warned them that if they were overburdened with energy, they should save it, keeping the party strong in case someone else's underburden should show up (like mine).

Sounding even more fatherlike, I'd have warned them in large boldface italic capitals about avalanche hazard and would have illustrated the warning with a hairy story about how four friends of mine would now be dead, their death brought about by a very simple-minded avalanche, if a fifth friend had not had a cold that day. And there, remembering the attention-getting device of "the Lady or the Tiger," I would have ended the story abruptly.

For a while I would have talked about the first aid—and the second aid—it would be good to know about. They might be amused as I had been about how fast medical certitudes of one year are superseded by medical certitudes of the next, with never an apology for having shown no doubt whatever at the time.

Finally, I would have tried to explain to them what ski mountaineering had meant to my life: about the peaks on which I had made first ascents, for the most part on skis; of the high snow camps I had known and what it was like to be up on top in early winter morning and evening, when the world is painted with a special light; of the kind of competence and maybe even braveness one picks up from good friends and challenging peaks,

Ski tourers cross a lake in the High Sierra. (Photo by Dan Johnston)

up there where the storms hit and the snow pelts the fabric all through the night; of the kind of exhilaration we felt when, after two struggles, the third put us on top of a 14,000-footer and we were first to be there to see how magnificently winter treats a high land we already knew well in summer, but in a lesser beauty; of the long vibrant moments back on our skis, skimming down the uncrevassed glacier on just the right depth of new powder, letting our skis go, finding that every turn worked, hearing the vigorous flapping of our ski pants even though the wind was singing in our ears and stinging our faces, sensing how rapidly the peaks climbed above us, those peaks that we had ascended in the slow day's climb; of the care we had to take after night found us out and we sideslipped and sidestepped down into turtuous little basins and then into the hummocky forest floor that lay in darkness between us and camp. I would have described that hot cup of soup I cuddled

in my hand in exhaustion, sipping slowly to absorb its warmth
and energy at a retainable rate. And I would speak of the morning after: its glow as I looked back to the rocky palisade above
the glacier and was pleased as hell to have been there at last—
pleased with the weather, the companions, and the luck—and
also forgivably a little pleased that I could do it.

But I didn't tell them all that. This is the sort of thing you
find out for yourself, that comes when you escape into the
reality of the wilderness and discover how amazingly well man
has been designed to cope with just such reality. This is the sort
of thing I would want them to find out for themselves. Maybe
then, after that, we could compare notes. That would be the
best reward of all!

When was all the foregoing said and not said? April, I think
it was. But eighteen Aprils ago, before my ski equipment, my
ski technique, and my skiing body had become obsolete. I had
not intended to give up skiing, but I would wake up after some
damned wilderness-saving struggle or other and find the snow
gone. Besides, people began to laugh at my scarred skis—made
of wood, I think it was—and the beartrap bindings. Who ever
heard of a Bildstein heelspring? Don't talk about the boots;
their soles bent.

I did ski fairly well, but fell a lot. The National Ski Association gave me a First Class Skier award in 1942, but that was
for ski mountaineering. I was never a racer, though I knew a
good many. I managed to break seven skis without ever breaking a bone. Having seen Hannes Schroll link christie royals with
the greatest of ease, I tried to do the same for the next twenty-
five years. No way. I was cut out for the winter wilderness, but
it cut out on me, through no fault of its own.

Perhaps going back could be like riding a bicycle; you never
forget how. I can imagine myself on a reasonably steep slope
covered with unreasonably good snow, never falling, needing to
link turns, and when I do my muscles remember how to respond
and I hear the wind in my ears the way I used to. But don't
watch; let me practice by myself for a while. Since touring is
coming back, an old ski mountaineer would hardly be noticed,
especially one who worked hard getting back into shape. If he

could do it for a trek in Nepal at sixty-four, would sixty-six be too late for a ski trek in the Sierra?

But far more important, would 1978 be too late, or the years that are following closely on its heels? Wilderness is being rationed already in our summers. Will there be enough to go around in the winters to come, so that Ken and Bob and you and I can compare notes about what it was like when the world was white and lonely?

When the *Manual of Ski Mountaineering* was first being put together in 1942, Weldon Heald made a wilderness survey for the office of the Quartermaster General and found that there were then only three places in the "lower forty-eight" where you could get more than 10 miles from a road. Glen Canyon dam eliminated one of them. The Disney proposal for Mineral King would get rid of another. It probably wouldn't be hard for some coal operator to end the third in Montana. We would still have Alaska, of course, but it would not take many divide-and-conquer operations like the trans-Alaska pipeline to draw and quarter our last great wilderness. Halve too often, and have not.

It is so easy to lose something as taken for granted as big wilderness was, and to find ourselves wishing so soon that it could be granted back. It won't be. Wallace Stegner summed it up in reply to the late Senator Arthur Watkins of Utah, who once proposed that there be more wilderness near cities, where people could use it, rather than out in places like Utah, where it got in the way. "It is not given to man to create wilderness," Professor Stegner responded, "but he can make deserts, and has."

People have also demonstrated that they can organize and keep wilderness, simply by committing themselves to do just that. Summer wilderness was recently vast. In 1934 a friend and I spent a full month in John Muir trail country in the High Sierra *and saw no one else.* Summer wilderness is not that vast anymore in the United States. It has been disappearing at the rate of about a million acres a year from our national forests (faster yet outside them), and the Forest Service seems perfectly willing to let winter wilderness go fast, as well. Witness their support of the effort to establish at Mineral King a Disney Galaxy. (After Disneyland and Disney World, what else?) This would create one more highly developed ski area, with lots of

Ski tourer winds her way through the Desolation Wilderness in California.
(Photo by Dan Johnston)

high-cost goodies that can be found elsewhere. It would eliminate the only primitive threshold to the longest wilderness in
the "lower forty-nine." The primitive development that now
exists at the climax of Mineral King's challenging road (poor

drivers need not apply) is presently returned to wilderness every winter. It is a magnificent place for ski touring and ski mountaineering provided you are good at avoiding avalanches. Getting there is part of the fun. Virtue can come early to some, late to others. Mine was tardy in these matters. I'll not let myself forget that in 1936 I was advocating major surgery for Yosemite wilderness. I wanted the Tioga Road improved and opened in winter; moreover, to hedge against expected closings from winter storms, I advocated an aerial tramway from Mirror Lake to the summit of Mount Hoffmann. I liked skiing that much, and understood too little what wilderness was all about. But then I also live in a redwood house, voted in 1949 for dams in the Grand Canyon, and was a staunch supporter of nuclear power until 1969. But because you're wrong, you don't have to stay wrong, a friend told me. Better late than never.

It's time to close. Last call for wilderness.

Adventure is not in the guidebook
And beauty is not on the map.
Seek and ye shall find.
—Terry Russell

Part V

SKI TOURING THE COUNTRY

14

Sierra Nevada

by David Beck

Mountains and the sun determine ski touring in California. Although California lowlands are too warm to hold snow, the snow falls in the mountains. There is skiable snow in the Salmon and other ranges in the north, as well as in the coastal and southern transverse and basin ranges. At times there is even good skiing in the Panamints in Death Valley National Monument. But the Sierra Nevada is the foremost mountain range in the state. The Sierra is big and unbroken; it is like one mountain three hundred miles long. The skiing on its ridges and valleys is always interesting and challenging. Every winter, November through May, there is usually skiable snow from 6,000 to over 14,000 feet. During a normal winter a ski tourer can expect to encounter almost every kind of snow.

Californians who use waxable skis tend to be innovative. One useful waxing trick is called tractor treads. When the sun shines on cold, new snow, skis always cake up as the wet surface snow is pressed into the cold snow below it. The best way to wax for this awkward snow condition is to cover the base of the skis with paraffin and then to apply narrow bands of climbing wax across the base of the skis.

THE SUN AND SKIING

The sun also dominates California skiing. Cold powder snow doesn't last, except for a brief midwinter period and at the higher elevations. The best cold snow skiing is during storms. Once a normal storm cycle is over, the sun reappears and things warm up. For instance, if you're skiing during February at seven thousand feet on blue wax in the morning, you will probably be using purple or red wax in the afternoon.

However, there are advantages to skiing under the California

178

sun. There is no unrelenting cold, and for the wilderness skier, there is the best corn-snow skiing anywhere. A corn-snow surface is an unbreakable suncrust that results from many warm, sunny days and cold, freezing nights. As a result of the continual freeze-thaw at the surface, the snow grains are constantly coated with meltwater, which is then refrozen. Skiing on old corn-snow during a spring morning is like skiing on very fine china; it tinkles under your skis. In the Sierra corn-snow forms from late February onward. One advantage of corn-snow is that you don't need to break trail. With a little klister on your skis you can ski anywhere.

In the spring, under the bright intense sun, it is almost impossible to tan; you burn to a crisp. You have to dress like an Arab and use lots of good sunscreen. We have found that sunscreens containing Paba (parabenzoic acid) are by far the best. Skiers on spring tours at the higher elevations even burn the inside of their mouths and nostrils.

MOUNT SHASTA

The ski terrain in California varies widely. The storms that bring the first skiing of the season occur in early November in the northern part of the state—in the Salmon Mountains, on Mount Shasta, and in the Lassen area. The rolling hillsides around Mount Shasta provide excellent skiing. Childs Meadow, a long open meadow just to the south of Mount Lassen is also a prime area. There is lodging available in the meadow, as well as in the nearby town of Mineral. The higher elevations of Mount Lassen have the deepest snowfall in the state, and there is often still twenty feet of snow in May. The volcanic mountains—Shasta and Lassen—provide excellent ski mountaineering. Mount Shasta should be respected, since it can have its own weather patterns, and avalanches are common on its slopes.

DONNER SUMMIT

Donner Summit has been popular with skiers for longer than there have been ski resorts. "Norwegian snowshoes," as skis were once called, were used by the railroad men who built the first transcontinental railroad in 1866. The Donner Summit, at 7,000 feet, has a good snowpack. In the Donner Summit area, there are ski touring centers at Soda Springs, Squaw Valley, Tahoe City, Incline Village, and South Lake Tahoe. Many of the centers in the Tahoe area resemble eastern centers. They provide machine-groomed trails, ski equipment rentals, lessons, races, Nordic ski patrols, and they charge a fee.

Skiers who wish to make their own tracks can find many good areas to ski, as well. On Donner Summit, ski to the north of U.S. Route 40 or Interstate 80. The intermediate ski tour from Sugar Bowl to Squaw Valley has been popular for years. This is actually the first portion of what was once called the Sierra Skiway. A marked ski trail with huts a day's journey apart was supposed to extend from Donner Summit to Yosemite National Park. But only a few huts were ever built, and the trail concept was abandoned. Interested skiers should inquire about trails at one of the touring centers or at the Sierra Club's Clair Tappaan Lodge on Donner Summit. The Sierra Club has the largest ski touring club in California and every large city in the state has a ski touring section of the Club.

SNOWSHOE THOMPSON'S ROUTE

Snowshoe Thompson, who carried the mail across the Sierra for the Pony Express, skied the Sierra south of Lake Tahoe. His route took him from snow line on the Carson River up to Luther Pass and Johnston Pass (now called Echo Summit), and down to the snow line above Hangtown (now named Placerville). He skied the route east to west in two days. With modern gear, most of us would have a difficult time matching his time. Today, Snowshoe's terrain is still good skiing.

Desolation Valley, north of Echo Summit, is popular with snow campers. Hope Valley, and nearby Faith and Charity valleys, offer good Nordic skiing. On Carson Pass there is an interesting monument to Snowshoe. The terrain around Kirkwood Meadows, just over Carson Pass, has mile after mile of good skiing. There is also a small ski center at Kirkwood. Lessons and rentals are available in Bear Valley, on California Route 4. Yosemite National Park has the oldest and largest Nordic ski school in California. In the park, there are many different trails starting from Badger Pass. The view of Yosemite Valley from the southern rim is awesome. Huntington Lake, on

A ski tourer at Carson Pass in the Sierra Nevada. (Photo by Dan Johnston)

California Route 168 out of Fresno, has good skiing. Nearby, the Central Valley Ski Club has marked a trail on Tamarack Meadow.

SOUTHERN CALIFORNIA

Nordic skiing is becoming popular in southern California. When the snow is good in the local mountains, southern Californians can ski nearby. Mount Pinos on Interstate 5, between Los Angeles and Bakersfield, is popular when the snow conditions are good. Wrightwood, Big Bear, San Gorginio, and San Jacinto are all popular with local skiers. The most accessible, consistently good skiing in southern California is in Mammoth Lakes and in Sequoia and Kings Canyon National Parks. Twin Lakes, at Mammoth, is one of the best Nordic ski areas in the state. Its 10,000-foot elevation usually assures good snow. Mammoth Mountain, near the lakes, is the largest downhill resort in the state. However, there are many areas to tour in that vicinity where a skier can escape the downhill resort scene.

There are touring centers at Old Mammoth, Twin Lakes, and June Lake, the latter forty minutes north of Mammoth.

Giant Forest in Sequoia National Park offers a variety of ski tours. The trails follow meadows and wind through groves of giant sequoias. Skiing through a long, narrow meadow surrounded by massive two-hundred-foot trees is a unique experience. The Nordic ski center in Giant Forest offers both equipment rentals and lessons. If the snow isn't good in Giant Forest, the skiing thirty miles up the Generals Highway at Big Meadows is often better.

SKI TOURING

There are many places to ski tour in California. All you need is a plowed road into the hills, a place to park, and the skill and curiosity to go skiing. Before you take off, you should have some knowledge of route finding, avalanches, and other subjects of concern to a winter traveler. Clubs and ski centers offer basic courses in these subjects. A basic technique lesson will help beginning skiers. The Far West Ski Association publishes an annual booklet, listing all California Nordic ski centers, shops, clubs, and ski events. Copies are available for a dollar from Far West Ski Association, Suite 1340, 3525 Wilshire Boulevard, Los Angeles, CA 90010.

Skiing at Mammoth or Yosemite, a skier has a view of the distant high country. The high Sierra has some of the best spring corn-snow, and certainly some of the most majestic scenery in the world. The high country is also difficult to reach. One exception is when the Park Service plows the Tioga Pass Road in Yosemite in the spring, and skiing opens up in Tuolumne Meadows. Summer comes late to the high country, and the corn-snow skiing stays good through May.

Spring is the best season for taking one of the many long loop tours and trans-Sierra tours. The southern Sierra in Sequoia National Park has some of the best high-country skiing. We have a favorite tour, about 40 miles long, across the Sierra. Most of it is above timberline at 11,000 to 12,000 feet. The eastern end of the tour is in the desert on the east side of the Sierra, while the western end is in the sequoia groves in Giant Forest. There is a popular trans-Sierra trip from Mammoth to Yosemite

Valley. Places like Siberian Outpost and the Big Horn Plateau, while difficult to reach, offer some of the best skiing in the world in late spring.

California offers different kinds of skiing for everyone. Racers can use the track systems in Mammoth and Tahoe. Families can enjoy skiing the meadows of Yosemite, Sequoia, and Donner Summit. Wilderness skiers have the entire Sierra to explore. California skiing is unique in that one drives through the orange groves and vineyards to the great Central Valley in order to reach the snow country.

15

Pacific Northwest
by Steve Barnett

Winter in the Pacific Northwest is usually a numbing succession of storms blowing in from the Pacific, with snow levels constantly fluctuating from near sea level to above timberline. The ski tourer is saved from spending day after day in abominable snow conditions by the tremendous variety of terrain and microclimates that allow the imaginative skier to have an excellent ski trip on almost any day of the year.

Furthermore, winter is not the only season for skiing in the Northwest. The best skiing is in spring and summer—using the long-lasting base resulting from the constant winter precipitation. Late-season, trips that would not be possible anywhere else in the U.S. become easy—traveling on huge glacier systems in the most spectacular Alpine surroundings, aided by long, sunny days. By this time, the avalanche danger has mostly receded, and you ski on a pleasant corn-snow surface. Enjoyable ski touring in the Pacific Northwest is then a more complex game than in Colorado, where conditions are almost always excellent and your main problem is to avoid getting caught in an avalanche.

THE WEATHER

The first factor to consider is the weather. A normal winter starts around the end of October. A seemingly endless series of storms blows in from the Pacific, and heads eastward over the Cascades. The prevailing wind is westerly, shifting to southwesterly as the storms hit. Because they have just come over the ocean, these storms are both wet and warm. Seattle rarely gets any snow accumulation, and hardly ever has an accumulation that stays for days. Often the rains extend up past timberline. The mixture of heavy snowfall and occasional heavy rain means that backcountry snow conditions are often abysmal by the standards of the Rockies. There is usually lots of snow—more than many other areas in the U.S.—but it can be deep oatmeal, raincrust, windcrust, ice, or, rarely, pleasant powder.

As you travel east across the Cascades the weather improves. The snowfall comes more in squalls than solid sheets, the snow is often drier, and the sun peeks out occasionally. Also, the snow level drops, so that the valleys and deserts of eastern Washington and Oregon are often white.

The western slope of the Cascades never gets very cold, since the ocean is just too close. For this reason, avalanches are rarely a problem for ski tourers. The temperature is warm enough that new snow usually stabilizes rapidly. Deep, long-lasting instabilities, such as those common in the Rockies, are uncommon. While there are plenty of avalanches, they are fairly predictable.

East of the Cascade crest, temperatures are occasionally low (the record is -50° F in the Methow Valley), but these are never sustained. Cold weather is always clear weather in the Northwest.

After March the heavy rains fade away, but the weather can still be quite stormy till June. Some years, there's sunshine and corn-snow in the spring. But other years there are only two seasons—winter and summer—following each other with a magically sudden transition. Northwest summers, while not as reliable as those in California, still have long periods of clear weather. The ocean is again a stabilizing element: temperatures rarely get to the hot level on the west side of the Cascades, while the east side is often scorching. For this reason, and because the snowpack is thinner to begin with, east-side areas melt much earlier than those in the west. The western extreme, the Olympic Mountains, have the heaviest snowfall and lowest permanent snowline of any range in the United States.

WAXING

Northwest snow frequently falls very wet and at just about 32° F, especially at those areas most favored by tourers, the low passes through the mountains. Since these snow conditions are the hardest to wax for, it's no surprise that 75 percent of the cross-country skis sold in the Northwest are waxless. However, I still use waxed skis because I like their performance, their versatility, and I haven't yet found the kind of waxless skis I want to use.

When I first moved to the area I had many waxing disasters. But in the past several years my touring friends and I have not had much difficulty. It's not that the snow has improved. But we have started using a wide range of wet snow waxes, such as Swix Gray and Jack Rabbit, and have developed enough technique to make them work even when they're far from perfect. These waxes, usually marketed in "starter" kits, seem perfectly suited to Northwest conditions, where the snow is wet and changes considerably in very small intervals of time or distance. They are easily adjusted by either scraping them down or adding layers, depending on the problem. Both of these are much easier than changing waxes.

Waxing and wax corrections can both be done very quickly. When using these waxes over a wide range of conditions, you must learn techniques for both slippery wax and sticky wax. Using a slippery wax requires developing a fine sense of how strong a kick to use, learning to skate efficiently, frequently using a climbing sidestep, setting the wax with a bounce at the beginning of each stride, and kicking with a stronger downward force. When using a sticky wax, you need to maintain a continuous rhythm and use plenty of forward drive to clear the weighted gliding ski. It usually helps to ski in a track. Sometimes, when you're climbing a long ways, you may want to let your skis freeze up, kick them clean at the top of the slope, and then ski down. The beauty of these waxes is that they rarely freeze up so hard you can't kick them clean and then keep them clean while skiing downhill.

If you are climbing through a variety of snow conditions, you may encounter conditions for which it's impossible to wax. For example, it wouldn't be unusual to start out in slush and end up in powder 4,000 feet higher. The klister we'd use in the slush wouldn't work at all in the powder. Thus, for long climbs we usually use "skinny" skins—adhesive-backed mohair strips around 30 mm wide. These have no straps to interfere with edging, can be applied and taken off in seconds, and can be carried in a pocket. They can be bought commercially, or made by cutting Alpine touring Coll-tex skin in half lengthwise and sewing nylon loops on the ends. With the skins, you can climb steep slopes, without undue concern for technique, and glide through short downhill stretches.

The consistent wetness of Cascade snows makes waxless skis easily justifiable. The trick is to get a good quality ski along with your base. Since many manufacturers are really selling a base rather than a ski, there's strong economic pressure to supply a pretty cheap ski. The fishscale base works well in slush and corn-snow. But it isn't so effective in more powdery conditions—and can't be waxed either. The new mica bases, which are found on some excellent skis, appear to work well in wet snow, and, in particular, eliminate the need for klister. They have the advantage of being waxable for colder and drier conditions.

DOWNHILL TECHNIQUE FOR CASCADE SNOWS

Driven by necessity, many Cascade skiers have developed powerful methods for skiing "crud" in all its glorious variety. The Northwest is unlike Colorado, where skiers can say "I'll wait till there's powder" and usually not have to wait long. Cascade skiers must have the attitude that no matter what the snow is like they can have fun skiing it. If they are too selective, they can't expect to go skiing much.

The heart of most Nordic down-hilling is the telemark turn. This turn and its variants can be used in all conditions and on very steep slopes. One will often augment it with steps and strides. The telemark turn is effective for two main reasons.

● Nordic gear is specialized for striding. Telemark skiing is like striding down the fall line; it uses the equipment to best advantage.

● Nordic gear, unlike Alpine equipment, is not specialized for turning. But by using two skis to simulate the action of one, you can attain nearly the same turning efficiency as with Alpine equipment.

To use the telemark in difficult snow and terrain, you should remember that the two skis in a telemark act like a single Alpine ski. Thus, you must edge the rear ski and drive it with your rear knee as you turn. If your knee is allowed to drift too far back,

Skier telemarking down a mountain in the northern Selkirk Mountains in British Columbia. (Photo by Bill Nicolai)

you will lose control of it. The thigh of the rear leg should be vertical and should move forward as you turn. A skier will often step into the turn with his uphill ski (the forward ski of the coming turn), and then step the rear ski into a tight telemark position. This is a very powerful technique, since it gives you an optimal telemark for carving through difficult snow.

In difficult terrain it is crucial to keep your upper body facing down the hill. Then you are always balanced to turn again if your present turn starts going awry. Constant rhythm is a vital part of cross-country stability on downhills. It is possible for each turn in a series to be awkward and unpredictable, even though the whole series is quite stable. The steady body is most easily maintained if you keep the diagonal arm-leg motion of the stride. If the left leg is forward so is the right arm. The left arm is kept back, held down the fall line. This also helps to equalize the weight on the skis. End each turn definitely by striding out with the rear (inside) ski. You can stride into a wide-track parallel if you're not turning again immediately or you can step your ski out into a wide forward stem preparatory to the next turn. A double-pole plant as the turn ends will sometimes help stabilize the transition and help you stride forcefully into the next turn.

Nothing but lots of time on snow will give you the ability to ski the difficult conditions found in the Cascades. But have faith. Even the worst conditions can be skied with the telemark in linked turns down the fall line. Very lovely rhythmic skiing is possible in many snow conditions. It's exciting, extremely enjoyable, and well worth the time it will take to learn. Once you can ski in poor conditions, vast areas open to touring that otherwise would not be possible.

WASHINGTON SKI TOURING AREAS

There is tremendous variety in the Washington Cascades, both north to south and east to west. I'll briefly discuss each area.

North Cascades: West Side

This area is unique in the United States in its heavy glaciation, extreme ruggedness, and wilderness character. Large sections are in either North Cascades National Park or in the Glacier Peak Wilderness Area. In winter, the North Cascades is a forbidding range. Snowfall is extremely heavy and avalanche danger is frequently severe. Visibility is correspondingly often nonexistent above timberline. Skiing the valley floors may be below the snow line and can thus involve unpleasant, wet bushwhacks through areas with many downed logs. For these reasons, long trips, such as those common in the Sierra or the Rockies, are almost unknown in the Northwest.

The principal high access that is kept open in winter is the road to the Mount Baker ski area. When visibility is good, this ski area is one of the most beautiful in the U.S., since it is situated between two majestic mountains—Mount Baker and Mount Shuksan—and is within view of most of the North Cascades. There is some good day touring around the area.

The best seasons for the North Cascades are fall, spring, and summer. October snowfalls can turn high meadows into perfect ski runs while access roads are still usable. In spring and summer you take advantage of the snows that result from all that terrible winter weather. The tremendous snowpack never melts completely; hence the heavy glaciation. The snow stabilizes and develops a corn-snow surface. In many years, one can still ski in various places throughout June. To ski in August, you must look for the most accessible glaciers.

There are many possibilities in spring, but I'll mention only the most obvious: Coleman Pinnacle and Lake Ann near the Baker ski area; Mount Baker via Coleman or Easton glaciers; Mount Shuksan via Sulfide glacier; the Cascade Pass area; tours off the Mountain Loop Highway such as Green Mountain, Meadow Mountain, or Glacier Peak. The last area offers better summer skiing than that found anywhere else in the U.S.

Though it is not often done today, summer wilderness trips involving hiking with skis and then skiing the glaciers can be very enjoyable. This kind of trip makes good use of the light weight of the skis (light touring skis of 3½ to 4 lbs. are adequate), as well as the good hiking qualities of some cross-country boots. Such trips include: hiking over Hannegan Pass to Mount Challenger; hiking into the Chilliwack Range; or hiking into the glaciated area south of Glacier Peak.

North Cascades: East Side

As you travel east in the North Cascades, the altitudes of the peaks stay about the same, but the changes in elevation lessen until you reach the eastern section around Horseshoe Basin, where the climate gets drier and the timberline higher. The eastern side of the North Cascades is the best place in Washington to do long midwinter trips, since you can stay high enough to keep out of the rain zone. The mountains on the east side are rarely socked in as badly as those in the west. Even in storms you can travel in the high forests, which often have beautiful larch and tamarack trees. Long-distance trips on lightweight skis, as well as trips stressing ski mountaineering, are possible.

Even in the lower reaches of the eastern Northern Cascades, around the Entiat, Chelan, Twisp, and Methow valleys, the snow conditions are superior to those on the west side. These areas offer excellent rolling, open terrain for day touring. Many Nordic touring centers are opening in these scenic areas.

Tours Closer to Seattle

The most popular areas for tourers from Seattle and Tacoma are Snoqualmie Pass and Paradise at Mount Rainier. Although Snoqualmie Pass is only 3,000 feet high and is often swept by torrential rains, it nonetheless accumulates a large snowpack. The forest there contains big trees, and is easily traveled by mountain-oriented ski tourers. Since there is much steep terrain in this area, you must keep avalanche danger in mind in many places. East of Snoqualmie Pass, the terrain becomes more gentle, and offers good touring for those not interested in serious downhilling. There is a touring center with maintained trails at Hyak, the most easterly of the Pass ski areas.

Mount Rainier offers all types of terrain, and at Paradise is high enough (5,400 feet) to escape much of the winter rain. It also receives the heaviest snowfall of any measuring station in the U.S., and frequently is either completely socked in or swept by strong winds. There is little forest above Paradise and below it the possibilities are limited. As with the North Cascades (and the other large volcanic mountains), Mt. Rainier is an outstanding ski area in the fall, spring, and summer. The most popular and most accessible high-altitude area is the Muir Snowfield, which offers at least 2,700 vertical feet of skiing at all times of year. Its base is only a two-hour hike from the parking lot. In September or October, tourers can start the next season on new snow and enjoy the fall ambience of blustery days, snow squalls, and occasional sunshine. Only a little snowfall is needed to cover the "sun cups" on the surface of the old snow.

Other Washington Ski Touring

There are many other snow-covered areas in Washington in the winter besides the areas already discussed. There are the Kettle River Range and the Selkirks in the northeast. The Cascades south of Mount Rainier contain good places to ski, including such Alpine areas as the Goat Rocks, Mount St. Helens, and Mount Adams. The Olympic Mountains are unique in the U.S. for their rain forests, their tremendous precipitation and consequent glaciation, and the extent of the roadless areas there. These factors contribute to keeping most people away in the winter.

Rather than providing a detailed list of tours, I wish to stress that the tourer should be imaginative in planning his ski trips. The choice should depend on the weather and the snow conditions. While touring areas at Mount Rainier, Snoqualmie Pass, and the Mount Baker ski area are usually overcrowded in winter (even when conditions are poor), we almost never see anyone at the other areas. Touring skis are wonderful tools for exploring the snow-covered wilderness. You should not be timid about exploring the possibilities open to you.

OREGON

Mount Hood is to Portland residents what Snoqualmie Pass is to those living in Seattle. Mount Hood is only 50 miles from Portland, and shares the same wet snow, rain, and fog as Snoqualmie Pass. But it is a big mountain, and has plenty of good touring on all types of terrain. There are good opportunities for overnight trips on its north side. Summer skiing is excellent and easily accessible.

The Oregon Cascades don't have the kind of spectacular scenery that one finds in the North Cascades. But they do have large areas of excellent touring terrain, and occasional stretches of Alpine terrain, in the form of the volcanoes that extend from one end of the state to the other. Excellent wilderness trips of several days duration are possible in the Mount Jefferson area, in the Three Sisters Wilderness, and around Diamond Peak. All have late-season snow cover.

Eugene residents can find good day touring in the Santiam Pass area; around Big Lake; and around Odell Lake, east of Willamette Pass.

These areas all suffer from the typical western Cascade problems of rain and fog. As one goes east conditions become better. In the Bend area, several touring centers have opened that offer excellent trail skiing, with better snow and weather than that found on the western side of the Cascades.

The best possibilities for long winter trips lie in the ranges east of the Cascades—the Wallowas, the Blue Mountains, the Ochocos, the Strawberry Mountains, Steens Mountain, and the Warners. None is as large as the Pasayten Wilderness Area in Washington, but they offer the same mixture of better weather, higher timberline, open forests, extensive high altitude terrain, and wilderness character. I'd infuriate friends by being specific, so I'll just say that each range has different charms. The Wallowas are the most Alpine, and the Steens are the most remote of these ranges.

BRITISH COLUMBIA

Like the Cascades, which seem to blossom as you approach the Canadian border, so do all the other ranges—the Coast Range, the Selkirks, the Purcells, and the Rockies. British Columbia has everything when it comes to mountains. Huge areas that would be premier national parks in the U.S. are totally unprotected, unheralded, and often lack even hiking trails. In summer, one can ski for days in the grandest surroundings possible without covering the same trail twice. It would be impossible to single out the best places in British Columbia to ski in winter. So it is best just to mention a few, and then to discuss summer skiing, the most unique aspect of skiing in British Columbia.

Vancouver has ski touring areas just outside the city limits at Cypress Park and at Mount Seymour. Forty miles north, along the road to Squamish is Garibaldi Provincial Park, which provides a wide variety of ski touring, both in forest and above timberline. Slightly north of that is the Whistler ski area, which is also surrounded by excellent touring terrain. The accent here is Alpine: the snowfall is heavy, visibility is often poor, and rain is frequent. Manning Park, east of Vancouver, has good touring terrain at a reasonably high altitude. There are lots of rolling meadows, large bowls, and open forest. Trails connect with the Pasayten Wilderness in the U.S. North of Whistler, or east of Manning Park, the weather becomes drier. In the interior, temperatures rapidly drop as you head north, and good skiing can be enjoyed nearly everywhere. The climate of the interior ranges, especially the Rockies, is such that they often have depth hoar underlying the snowpack, and consequently have severe avalanche hazards.

In summer the situation is often the reverse, and the weather gets worse as you go east. Though the weather can be terrible, even in July, you are just as likely to have long periods of settled weather. Since it is possible to ski when the weather is far from balmy, a trip need not be ruined by constant storminess.

The easiest access to glacier skiing in southern British Columbia is found at Garibaldi Park, Rogers Pass on the Trans-Canada Highway, Bugaboo Provincial Park, and Kokanee Glacier Park.

The high areas of the British Columbia ranges are spectacular and have fantastic ski terrain. When combined with the summer charms of corn-snow, long days, and warmth, this area in many ways offers the ultimate ski experience.

16

Rockies

by Rob Schultheis

On the afternoon of November 15, 1806, the explorer Zebulon Pike was crossing the seemingly endless Great Plains of the Arkansas River country. Looking west across mile after mile of rolling grassland, he saw what he described as "a small blue cloud" on the horizon. By evening, as the Pike party rode further west, the "blue cloud" had grown into a great, snowy jumble of mountains stretching north and south as far as the eye could see. Pike had discovered the Colorado Rockies, the heart of that mighty cordillera that forms the spine and ribs of an entire continent, from Canada to Mexico.

By the time Pike made his discovery, other whites had already explored other parts of the Rockies. Lewis and Clark had crossed the northern Rockies two years before in present-day Idaho on their way to the Pacific. To the south, the Spanish had settled in the Sangre de Cristo Range in what is now New Mexico. But the Pike party included the first non-Indians to enter the high, wild heartland of the Rockies, the ranges of Colorado.

The Rockies are much more than a mountain range. They are a sprawling massif, with countless subranges and clusters of peaks. There are places with old, magical names like Wind River, Bitterroot, Medicine Bone, Elk, Rainy, and Snowy; San Juan, Uncompahgre, Saguache, Wasatch, Sangre de Cristo; Eaglebone, Teton, Red, Blue, Mesquite, Cannibal. . . . "There are rivers and mountains without end," as the Chinese Zen poem has it.

The Colorado Rockies are quintessential mountains: landscapes of steep, naked stone; with more than fifty peaks above 14,000-feet high; trackless valleys; wide, forested mesas; snow on the ground a good 7 months of the year. Most flatlanders

A ski party in Rocky Mountain National Park, heading toward Notchtop Mountain. (Photo by Mrs. David Robertson)

find the land desolate, severe, and a bit intimidating: good country for goats, perhaps, or eagles, but not for people. Except for mining, some logging, and a bit of marginal ranching, there isn't much one can do with this steep wilderness. Living in a mountain town like Leadville, Salida, or Telluride has been compared to living in a lunar colony or on a space station.

Almost everything necessary to human existence must be brought in from the world below. The Colorado Rockies are a desolate no-man's land, except . . . to ski. The mountains of Colorado provide probably the biggest, best piece of ski country in the world. The snow, the terrain, the lack of crowds make skiing there perfect, that's all.

HOW IT BEGAN

The first skiers in Colorado were the miners of the late-nineteenth century, who schussed on long, crude skis from the mines into town after work. The Ute Indians and the trappers were already using snowshoes to hunt, to trek from place to place, and to check on their trap lines. Winter backcountry nomadism was a matter of survival, not sport, in those early days. Skis or snowshoes were the only way to travel, when the snow lay ten or twenty feet on the ground and there was work to be done. But there was little joy to it. Occasionally the miners held drunken downhill races on their twelve-foot-long boards, but that was all. It was all work and no play.

It wasn't until the 1950s, when Alpine skiing caught on as a sport, that things began to change. And not until the 1960s did ski-touring—roaming the backcountry on skinny skis—really catch on. It began with a few transplanted Scandinavians and New Englanders like Sven Wiik and Ross and Mike Chivers, and then spread rapidly among the mountaineers, climbers, hikers, and downhill skiers tired of long lift lines, crowded trails, and mountains groomed until they looked like Alpine Disneylands.

In Boulder, for instance, when I first began touring in 1965, there were only a few dozen of us *langlaufers* in town, and we were looked on as something a bit odd, daft, like butterfly collectors or unicyclists. The cross-country craze was in full swing three years later and the woods around Boulder were full of us. Popular touring areas like Fourth of July Valley and Rocky Mountain National Park were actually crowded on weekends. Already, the Nordic "old-timers" were talking about the "good old days," when there was hardly anyone on the trail. Luckily, there was still plenty of skiable wilderness to go around.

THE MOUNTAINS AND THE SNOW

First of all, Colorado is practically empty compared to other touring hot spots like California and New England. Consider the figures: there are only about three million Coloradoans, spread over a 200,000 square-mile state that is half eminently skiable high country. Even Mount Elbert, at 14,431 feet, second only to Mount Whitney in altitude in the continental U.S., can be climbed in winter on the flimsiest touring equipment. Nordic terrain is everywhere, from the Front Range west to Utah: from the open bowls of Mount Audubon near Boulder, for instance, to the vast mesas in the southwest corner of the state. Plenty of country *tierra incognita* everywhere. There are still plenty of places where you can ski a day, a week, or maybe ten days without running into another soul. Just look at San Miguel, Montrose, or Jackson Counties on the map; or Dolores County along Disappointment Creek; or in the deep mountain maze of the Needles Range. There is enough wilderness in which to get lost to your heart's content.

The snow is another thing: Colorado snow is delicate, delicious stuff. It is so light and dry you can take a handful of fresh powder, hold it to your lips, and blow it away like a puff-ball—well, almost. It's like a dream—to Californians used to slogging through waterlogged Sierra plaster, or New Englanders who have been scrabbling and clattering down boilerplate hills for years. This may sound chauvinistic (and perhaps it is), but for Alpine or Nordic skiing there is nothing like Colorado snow. And most years there is lots of it. In fact, the world's record twenty-four-hour snowfall was at Silver Lake, Colorado, where a whopping 76 inches fell on April 14-15, 1921. The old timers mutter darkly of drought, and the old days when it really snowed, but Colorado winters still seem to go on forever. There is an old Colorado Western Slope joke that goes, "I missed summer this year. I was down in Denver that weekend."

Of course, Rocky Mountain weather can be a bit temperamental. Storms hit fast and fierce, and there is treacherous unpredictability to them. The weather can be lukewarm and hazy in one valley, and howling a blizzard the next ridge over. George Frederick Ruxton, the mountain-man-author who traveled the Rockies in the 1830s, described a sudden spring blizzard that nailed him in South Park on the headwaters of the Platte, west of present-day Denver:

> The tempest broke upon us with a deafening roar. The clouds opened, and drove right in our faces a storm of freezing sleet which froze upon us as it fell. The first squall of wind carried away my cap, and the enormous hailstones beating on my unprotected head and face almost stunned me. In an instant my hunting shirt was soaked, and as instantly frozen hard; my horse was a mass of icicles.

These mountain men were known to be liars of prodigious proportion; they multiplied everything by five, then squared it for good measure. If a trout was big, it was so big you had to bait your anchor with a rattlesnake instead of a worm to catch it. If the air was cold, it was so cold the mercury went down out of the bottom of the thermometer and into the ground. But Ruxton's spring storm sounds all too real, too familiar, to one who has skied the Colorado Rockies for twelve years.

A DAY IN THE SAN JUANS

I remember one day in the late spring, in the San Juan Mountains. I decided to ski from Telluride, up across the ski area and the forests of Turkey Creek mesa to the ghost town of Alta Lakes, and back down to the highway by Ophir—an easy, two-hour tour of about ten miles. It was a crisp, sunny morning. The nearest clouds were somewhere far off to the west over Utah. I rubbed some blue wax on my battered Bonnas, stuck an orange, a candybar, and an extra sweater in my day pack, and took off.

By noon, an hour out, cloud shadows were forming on the peaks like dark bruises. Across the valley, above Sunshine Mesa, Wilson Peak was vanishing in a boiling mass of clouds. The treetops were beginning to sway in the wind; a change in the weather was coming. I rewaxed with more blue, where the ice had worn it away, and kept going.

By the time I got up to Alta Lakes, just below timberline, the whole Wilson Range had gone under an end-of-the-world darkness, and the wind was stinging my face with snow crystals as hard and sharp as cinders. The temperature had dropped drastically. My hands, without gloves, stung in the cold, then began to go numb.

I took shelter out of the wind in one of the abandoned mine buildings at Alta, and ate my orange and chocolate. The sugar made me feel stronger, better. I rubbed some feeling back into my hands, and pulled on my extra sweater. Outside, the wind shrieked and the hard snow spattered down.

Skiing the last few miles down to the highway was tough—not dangerous—tough. The wind whipped snow in my eyes and it was hard to see. Twice I caught a ski tip on a rock and went tumbling, getting snow-covered in the process. My hat, sweater, and knickers froze crisp as crystal. I suffered a wrenched knee and mild hypothermia. One boot, caked with snow, kept coming out of its binding. I felt the beginnings of hysteria and rage. The wind blasted headlong into me till I felt like I was skiing on a treadmill going nowhere. The mountains had totally vanished; there was nothing but timber, the snowy road, and that damned white stuff swirling down. If the president of Weyerhauser had come by on a snowmobile and offered me a ride, I probably would have accepted.

At last, below, only two more switchbacks down, was the highway. I skied fast, double-poling, sailing down the frozen ruts. I had one last fall: a rock, a caught tip, and a head-over-heels pratfall to some very hard ice. I lay there, upside-down, one ski off and one ski on, my pack wrapped around my neck, and my knickers full of snow. I cursed, long and lovingly, savoring each word; then I began to laugh.

I hitched a ride home with a hard-rock miner from Rice, who asked me what I'd been doing, said I was crazy when I told him, and then laughed to show he didn't mean it. There was a bottle of whiskey on the floor of the pickup truck. He offered me a snort, "to get the blood circulating." I didn't mind if I did.

To the west, the storm was already breaking. Rags and tatters of clouds were tearing on the peaks and falling away. There was fresh snow up on the crags and on the highest timber. Rain fell on the highway as we drove back down into town. Though I was chilled to the bone, exhausted, and my left knee ached, I was as happy as it is possible to be.

TYPES OF SKI TERRAIN

It would be pretentious, if not impossible, to write a real guidebook to skiing in the Rockies. The Colorado Rockies alone would require a volume the size of the *Oxford English Dictionary*, and would only tell people what they already know—the popular, easy places—or what they shouldn't know—the special, remote, secret places they should seek out and find for themselves. But there are places to shy away from, of course: the avalanche-prone canyons between Ouray and Silverton, for instance, that seem to crop up in every other horror story in that Forest Service avalanche classic, *The Snowy Torrents*. In the winter of 1978, a snowplow and its driver vanished in a slide on the highway south of Ouray.

Rocky Mountain National Park, with its hordes of Denverites and Boulderites on skis, is another good place to avoid if you are looking for solitude. Any of the big basins, such as South Park, are too barren for good skiing: the wind bowls you over, the snow is blown into rock-hard crust, and the scenery is Siberian.

As I said, a guidebook to skiing the Rockies would be impossible. Still, one could say something about the general kinds of terrain in the Colorado mountains. Around Denver and Boulder are the forested hills and valleys of the Front Range, with skiable snow extending as far down as the 5,000-foot level. In a good year, you can ski the Mesa Trail just outside of Boulder, south to Eldorado Springs. This is a lovely, little trip of about 6 miles, up and down tiny valleys and across miniature mesas, with some of the most famous rock-climbing crags in America looming above: the Flatirons, the Maiden, and the Amphitheater.

For those who favor Alpine country, there is touring in all the major high-altitude ranges in Colorado. Several of the state's 14,000-footers—including Elbert, and Lincoln, Democrat, and Bross near Fairplay—can be scaled on touring skis with pin bindings. One of my favorite easy touring peaks is Mount Audubon, in the Indian Peaks area west of Boulder. It is a gentle 13,000-footer that you can ski up in a couple of hours. It has a terrific, laidback run down open tundra slopes, where you can pratfall to your heart's content without much fear of getting hurt. Other Colorado peaks such as Sneffels, Wilson, and Mount of the Holy Cross can be skied, but only with mountaineering equipment: Alpine-style skis, heavy boots, cable bindings, and the like.

But whether the peak is a fierce snaggletooth like El Diente or a mild hump like Pawnee Peak, the Alpine environment creates a unique excitement. Beyond the last wind-dwarfed trees in the tundra and the snow, you can look down on clouds, ridges, timber, and the high sources of rivers. It is a rarefied, luminous country. Skiing above timberline has a special aesthetic quality that makes its hazards—the potential health problems of hypothermia and altitude sickness, the tricky mountain weather, and the avalanche dangers in the high basins worth daring.

Another kind of terrain in the Colorado Rockies is in the great mesa region of southwestern Colorado. Take Wilson Mesa, for instance, where the 30-kilometer Wilson Mesa Classic Cross-Country Ski Race is held each March. This is rolling ranchland, high aspen groves, and elk meadows, with dizzying views of Wilson Peak's north face to the south. The snow is generally good, though in the spring, wind and sun strip away the snow cover in exposed areas. Mesa skiing is relaxed and easy. You can cruise forever, it seems, on rolling country as obstacle-free as a gold course.

During most of the winter, blue wax will get you through. That dry Colorado powder is a waxer's dream, with blue wax perfect for 90 percent of all but the latest spring tours. But waxing can also be tricky at high altitudes. Wind crust alternating with ice and sugary powder can make a single downhill run a nightmare of sudden starts and stops. Skiing from 9,000 feet to 14,000 feet and back again on a single spring day, one may run through everything in the wax kit, from green hard wax to klister and back again. A scraper is a must.

A few good, specific places? Well, there is fine skiing in the hills near Sheridan, Wyoming, they say. There is supposed to be a hot spring you can ski to in the mountains north of Santa Fe, big enough for a hundred people to bask in. And rumor has it there is a mesa southwest of Montrose so vast and deserted that skiing across it is like crossing the Rockies of 300 years ago. Eagles circle in the sky, you spook big herds of deer and elk, and you can find strangely grooved trees where hibernating black bears have awakened and emerged to sharpen their claws. Bears return to the same tree year after year, like pilgrims to a shrine—why, nobody knows.

The best ski touring I've ever done in the Rockies was one long, hardcore winter I spent in a sheepherder's shack high in the San Juan Mountains, at 9,500 feet, doing nothing. The shack had kerosene lamps, but no running water, and a balky, aspen-eating stove for heat. We had to ski in a quarter-mile around a lake to reach the cabin, and it was a 5-mile ski to town, if the truck didn't start. A friend and I lived on skis that winter—hauling jerricans of water, going visiting, and skiing out into the meadows at midnight to watch the full moon on the peaks. It was natural skiing, as easy as breathing out and breathing in.

Beyond that, I don't know. I am no chart-maker, no surveyor, no geometrician of the countryside; just a calligrapher of landscapes, a storyteller, if you will. The high country, the snow country, is out there, and sometimes it seems to go on forever. It takes a bit of nerve, a touch of the blue-ice dancer to set out into it, but it is out there. That is all you need to know: that, a pair of skis, some wool, some wax. From there you can draw your own, ephemeral maps across the high snow of the Rockies.

17

Midwest

by Kathleen Yoerg

Each section of the country has particular qualities that give ski touring a unique regional flavor. In the Midwest, good cross-country skiing is easily accessible to large numbers of people. It usually can be done on pleasant, rolling terrain, with fairly stable daily temperatures, thus presenting minimal waxing hassles. The temperatures are low only in certain areas, thus keeping special preparation to a minimum. The region offers an interesting variety of ski-touring terrain, in a wide range of snow and weather conditions.

This article examines these qualities as they relate to skiing in Minnesota, Wisconsin, and Michigan. The variety of both topography and climatic conditions come as a surprise to persons unfamilar with the region and, occasionally, to residents as well. Natives make good use of their local skiing resources. One needs no special knowledge to see a heavy snowfall, stop what she is doing, and take advantage of the opportunity for exercise and peaceful exploration of an area. When local conditions are unpropitious, however, it can be a great help to know other places that would be fun to explore, as well as regional weather patterns to suggest which direction to head. I will first offer a brief discussion of the accessibility, gentle terrain, temperature uniformity, and cold of Midwest skiing. Then, a survey of topographic highlights and the range of usual winter weather conditions will be given special attention.

ACCESSIBILITY

One of the great advantages of Midwest skiing is the accessibility of snow and ski trails. Snowfall is highly variable, but winter inevitably brings snow, and in recent years has brought quite a lot of it. With 2-3 inches on the ground, it's possible to put on the skis and take advantage of the white transformation of one's immediate surroundings. All urban areas have parks and boulevards, and most have golf courses. In Detroit, ski lessons, equipment rental, and trails are part of the Metropark system. In Minneapolis/St. Paul, the Hennepin County park reserve district has one of the most extensive and heavily used ski-touring trail systems in the United States. The Milwaukee County park system offers trails and lessons. Most midwestern skiers prefer day trips to winter camping. Venturing even a short distance from home, there are state parks, forests, and game areas with designated quiet areas (no snowmobiles) that offer the exploration of additional, less-civilized territory.

TERRAIN

The land is inviting rather than imposing. The terrain most often used for skiing is gently rolling. It is not difficult to find trails that come close to the Nordic skier's platonic ideal trail: one-third up, one-third down, one-third flat. Unlike the long climb and rapid descent of almost all one-day trips in mountainous areas, trails here offer a delightful kinetic balance of ups and downs, mixed nicely throughout the trip.

TEMPERATURE AND WAXING

In Minnesota, northern Wisconsin, and Michigan's Upper Peninsula, it is not unusual to ski for an entire day without changing waxes. Though it may be tiring to climb the often-steep ridges of the Midwest, the elevation changes are not great enough to cause much difference in snow conditions. Skiers carry two or three waxes, in case the midday sun should warm things up a bit, but the elaborate wax-pack required for mountain conditions is superfluous here. For the most part, this is true in southern parts of the Midwest as well. Tricky waxing occasionally occurs here, as elsewhere, when the temperature hovers near 32 degrees F. If this is the case, it is likely to hover there menacingly through most of the day.

Much midwestern skiing is cold weather skiing. This is especially true in the northern parts of the region. While cold-weather skiing makes waxing easier, there are also less advantageous ramifications of the cold. Care must be taken in selecting

Ski touring through the Wisconsin woods. (Photo courtesy of the state of Wisconsin, Division of Tourism)

additional clothing for rest stops. Even with proper clothing, keeping warm while standing still is difficult on near-zero days. You should bring a roomy pack that can accommodate a down parka or vest and bulky mittens (needed to rewarm fingers after eating or waxing). It is a good idea to carry a scarf or face mask, wind pants, Chapstick, and goggles, all of which offer protection if a nasty wind should arise unexpectedly on one of these cold days. You should follow the usual precautions of carrying extra clothing to keep your middle, head, hands, and feet warm and dry.

For delectable, energy-packed pickups, food should be carefully selected that is impervious both to the cold and to other abuse it will take in the pack. A few trips with frozen, wilted lettuce and the matted bread of ordinary sandwiches usually leads skiers to carry cheese and crackers. Many skiers also carry gorp, a delicious combination of sweet and salty things, such as nuts, raisins, chocolate chips, and seeds. Water is always necessary, and an additional thermos of warm liquid is welcome (though this entails additional weight). For fresh fruit, many select an orange, peeling it at home, if it's a near-zero day, to eliminate the necessity of peeling it in the cold.

GEOLOGICAL HISTORY OF THE MIDWEST

All schoolchildren in Minnesota, Michigan, and Wisconsin study glaciers. As adults, they are at least vaguely aware that the landforms and soils existing today are the result of depositions, scouring, or draining by a series of four ice sheets that covered most of the Midwest in glacial times. The glaciers were responsible for a rich variety of landforms: till plains (good farming), moraines (lovely scenery), lake and swamp belts (now covered by northern forests), extensive glacial lake beds, and river valleys wide enough to hold the rivers that drain the huge lakes. The glaciers are responsible for all of the region's topographic highlights except one—the Driftless Area, whose distinctive character will be discussed later. A brief discussion follows of these topographic highlights, and skiing opportunities they offer.*

---

*For more information on the terrain, trails, and wildlife of the Midwest, especially Wisconsin and Michigan, see Kathleen Yoerg, *The Quiet Adventure Guide: to X-Country Ski Trails* (Matteson, Ill.: Greatlakes Living Press, 1975).

Moraines

There are many places in the Midwest where glacial depositions of boulders, pebbles, sand, and clay accumulated in great
clumps or ridges, known as *moraines*. Here scattered wells,
lilac shrubs, and abandoned foundations are sober reminders of
futile efforts of pioneers to farm this glacial mish-mash. The
interlobal land has scattered deciduous woods of second-
growth elm, maple, oak, and hickory, as well as pine planta-
tions. Its open areas of short grasses and shrubs protect rabbits,
mice, squirrels, coyote, and ruffed grouse.

In southwest Michigan, chains of moraines more or less circle
the swamp-belt south of Lansing, and many favorite ski trails
are found on these moraines: Yankee Springs Recreation Area,
Barry State Game Area, Kensington Metropark, Pinckney and
Highland Recreation Areas. In southeast Wisconsin, the Kettle
Moraine area (Kettle Moraine State Forest, Pike Lake State
Park) is a fine example of the interlobal terrain, and is used
extensively by Milwaukee and Chicago skiers.

The Lake Region

Only a few other areas in the world (southern Finland
and Ontario, Canada) have as many lakes per square mile as the
lake regions of northern Minnesota and northern Wisconsin.
The terrain is rolling, with lakes, streams, and swamps scattered
generously throughout dense hardwood and pine forests. The
land is laced with lazy meandering streams and spotted with
various intermediate combinations of land and water: hummocky cedar swamps, tamarack swamps, open marshes, and
cranberry or blueberry bogs. In Wisconsin and the adjacent
section of the Upper Peninsula of Michigan, the area has literal-
ly thousands of small lakes. Here are the headwaters of the St.
Croix and Chippewa rivers in the northwest and the Wisconsin,
Wolf, and Menominee rivers in the northeast. In Minnesota,
most of the larger lakes (such as Lake of the Woods, Rainy
Lake, Red Lake) are in these northern forests. The sources of
three North American river systems are also found here: the
Mississippi, the Red, and the St. Lawrence.

This is deer, bear, and moose country (the latter in Minnesota only). In the winter, deer tracks are seen on ski trails

almost everywhere. Deer trails can be mistaken for ski trails, making compass-reading a good skill to bring with you into these forests. As the snow gets deep and the winter becomes cold, the deer will "yard up," huddling together in low, sheltered areas of hemlock, cedar, and balsam. There they browse, conserving energy by not moving from the yard until the snow has melted enough to make walking less difficult.

There is no shortage of ski touring terrain here. In Minnesota, skiers use the Boundary Waters Canoe Area, George Washington State Forest (Thistledew Lake area), George Crosby Manitou State Park, the Lutsen Resort, and the Superior National Forest (where the Minnesota Outward Bound School is located). In Wisconsin, Nicolet National Forest has a ski trail at Anvil Lake near Eagle River, which was built in the 1930s by the Civilian Conservation Corps. The Northern Highland-American Legion State Forest has two popular trails (Escanaba Lake and Mc-Naughton Lake). Chequamegon National Forest has cross-country hiking trails, wilderness study areas, and the developed trails of the Telemark Resort. In Michigan, the Sylvania Area of Ottawa National Forest offers nice skiing in a mature forest.

Driftless Area

An interesting contrast to the glaciated areas is the Driftless Area in southwestern Wisconsin, southeastern Minnesota, and northern Iowa. This area has the same grassy-area wildlife inhabitants as the glaciated portions of the southern Midwest: cottontail rabbit, squirrels, pheasants, grouse, and deer. In addition, it has the birds of the Mississippi Flyway, thousands of ducks and geese migrating in late fall and spring, and bald eagles, which occasionally rest for a month or two in winter before continuing south.

The ridge and valley system makes for energetic skiing, with far steeper hills than in most of the moraine or lake country already described. There is good skiing west of Madison, Wisconsin, at Wildcat Mountain State Park, Blackhawk Ridge resort, Governor Dodge State Park, and in the Spring Green area generally. Near La Crosse, skiers use Wisconsin Department of Natural Resources' Coulee Experimental Forest, Black River State Forest, Goose Island Park, and Minnesota's Whitewater State Park and Wildlife Management Area.

Lake Superior Region

In the northern part of the region, glaciers scoured away at the hard rock, cutting basins for rock-rimmed lakes, and channels for hundreds of short, swift streams that flowed from one basin to another. This left isolated towers of granite and hilltops of bare rock, and iron and copper deposits close to the surface. This is mining country: Michigan's Porcupine Mountains; the Keweenaw Peninsula; the Huron Mountains; the Gogebic Range; and Minnesota's Vermilion, Mesabi, and Cuyuna iron ranges.

This is the Midwest's most dramatic ski-touring terrain. Here skiers prepare for wilderness skiing, or follow logging roads and abandoned railroad grades. They are apt to find tracks of deer, moose, and perhaps timber wolves, Canada lynx, marten, fisher, and weasel. The area is heavily forested, primarily with pine, white birch, and aspen. In general, wildlife is not abundant in the winter, due to the severe cold, especially as one goes west from Lake Superior.

There is good skiing in Michigan's Porcupine Mountains Wilderness State Park, Keweenaw Peninsula, Ottawa National Forest, Craig Lake State Park, and Lake Superior State Forest. Minnesota's Arrowhead Region, northeast of Duluth, is also recommended.

CLIMATE AND SNOWFALL

Sometime before Thanksgiving, while looking at bare trees and feeling the nippiness of the wind, midwestern skiers may be struck with the annual urge to prepare for the ski season. Those with wooden skis bring out the pine tar and torch and begin the pine tar ritual, rich in tactile pleasures and good earthy smells. For people with waxless skis, satisfying the urge is often more expensive. Preparation may involve a trip to the sports store to purchase the latest breathable gaiters, Norwegian fisherman's mittens, or this year's Trak ski, all of which are conveniently just a bit better than offered last year. Ski season has arrived spiritually. The deer hunters hit the woods Thanksgiving weekend, and from then on one waits for snow. Snowfall is highly variable from year to year; sometimes you may wait until Christmas, or even longer. It is useful to know where to go to find snow when it doesn't seem to be in any hurry to find you.

The prevailing regional winter winds are northwesterly, on a trajectory across the continent from the Gulf of Alaska, passing over the Great Lakes, and into the St. Lawrence Valley. When these cold winds meet the relatively warm water of the Great Lakes, they pick up moisture. As the clouds pass over cold land adjacent to the water, snow falls in great abundance.

Michigan's Lower Peninsula

Two of the most striking aspects of this weather pattern are the abundance of snow and relatively warm weather in the area of western Michigan adjacent to Lake Michigan. Near Traverse City, Michigan, 25-30 degrees F is the normal, delightful, January skiing temperature. The Traverse City/Boyne Highlands area has a long-established reputation for excellent skiing conditions. Back in the 1920s weekend ski trains headed here from Detroit for ice carnivals and Nordic skiing. The many miles of ski trails at Bear Mountain near Grayling, constructed in the 1930s, are reminders of this history. Unfortunately, the quiet of these trails has frequently been violated by snowmobiles in the 1970s. Boyne Highlands gets a whopping and dependable snowfall of 80-140 inches per year; Traverse City a little less. South and east of this snow center, snow conditions are also fairly reliable, with 60-80 inches per year falling from Michigan's northeast coast on Lake Huron, across the state, and along the Lake Michigan shore to Muskegon. Further south, in Detroit and Lansing, the weather is often too mild; the snow there is best enjoyed immediately after falling, before it melts.

Southern and Middle Wisconsin

Compared to southern Michigan, temperatures in the southern two-thirds of Wisconsin are colder and the snowfall is far less abundant. With an annual average of 40-50 inches of snow, it is best to call ahead before planning trips to explore the interesting glaciated and unglaciated sections of this area. Compared to Minnesota on the other hand, this area's midwinter (January-February) temperatures often seem warm. When this region has plenty of snow, the skiing here is attractive to Twin City residents who enjoy the respite from the cold further north.

The North Woods and Southern Minnesota

Moving north in the region, Michigan's Upper Peninsula, southern Minnesota, the "Arrowhead Region," and northern Wisconsin all have colder winter climates. With the dependable snowcover, these areas are principally responsible for the region's reputation for cold skiing. Green wax is the customary ski covering for waxable skis on January expeditions here. The harder light green wax is a safer choice when arriving at the trailhead at the beginning of a day. It may get up to 20-25 degrees F during a day, but it is also frequently near zero. Snowfall varies widely within the area, and once again the Great Lakes are the determining factor. The remote "Arrowhead Region," northeast of Duluth, gets more snow than anywhere else in Minnesota—60-80 inches per year. The Twin Cities do not get the snow of places nearer the Great Lakes. But because midwinter melts are infrequent, there are long periods of snowcover, in spite of the low annual total of 40-50 inches per year.

Again Michigan is favored by the weather patterns, with its Upper Peninsula getting more snow than anywhere else in the Midwest—250 inches on the Keweenaw Peninsula. Winter on the Keweenaw is a unique experience in isolation. Less-hearty souls abandon this busy summer area, leaving the tough locals to stick it out. There, "plowed" roads still have a solid packed snow base, and driving on them is like going on a carnival ride in a weird white, high open tunnel. The numerous logging roads in this area make excellent exploring, and the lonely residents are eager to advise adventuring skiers. But it is best visited early or late in the season, when the snow is more compacted.

More accessible and manageable areas include the Upper Peninsula's Porcupine Mountains, the Huron Mountains near Munising, the Pictured Rocks National Lakeshore area, and the Sylvania Tract. The Sylvania Tract in Ottawa National Forest is a majestic hemlock, maple, and birch forest. This area, largely undisturbed in the twentieth century, contains a lovely string of undeveloped lakes. These Michigan areas have annual snowfalls similar to the warmer Traverse City area (80-100 inches per year). Skiing is usually dependable from mid-December through March.

Northeast and north-central Wisconsin, Wisconsin's snow country, gets 50-60 inches of snow per year. Though this does not at first glance seem remarkable, because of the cold, there is reliable snow. Telemark Lodge, a winter ski resort here with excellent, groomed Nordic trails, is the site of the annual 35-kilometer American Birkebeiner Race. The Eagle River area, with its dense public forests and numerous lakes, gets more snow (over 80 inches per year) than elsewhere in Wisconsin, with a usual accumulation of 2-3 feet by mid-January.

Northern Minnesota

The coldest part of the Midwest is the northern half of Minnesota. Adjacent to Lake Superior, the cold is less pronounced; but moving inland, it increases as the snow decreases. The strip adjacent to North Dakota has an annual snowfall of only 20-40 inches, with sub-zero days the rule. Western Minnesota has undesirable skiing for all but the strongest local residents.

SUMMARY

In summary, the Midwest offers accessible skiing, with uniform if frequently cold temperatures. There is a tremendous variety of conditions: snowfall from 2 to 250 inches; winter temperatures from -10 degrees F to 35 degrees F; terrain from flat river-bottoms to rolling moraines and granite highlands; vegetation from extensive pine and hardwood forests to rolling meadows; and environments from tame golf courses to U.S. Forest Service wilderness areas.

18

New England
by Sally and Daniel Ford

CLIMATE

New England is a grand place to ski, but you have to make allowances. Begin with the climate. New England is cold, especially in the northern tier of states where most of the skiing is found. The forty-fifth parallel cuts through the middle of Maine, placing the state in the company of such demiarctic regions as Minnesota, North Dakota, and Montana. The air is humid, which intensifies the chill. Westerly winds are saturated with moisture as they pass over the Great Lakes, while from the south and east the air is wetted by the Atlantic Ocean. From these reservoirs come New England's snow, as well as its sleet and rain. Generally speaking, it is cold weather that makes New England skiing possible, rather than high altitudes, as is the case in the Rockies and the Sierra Nevada. The highest point in New England is the summit of Mount Washington, which at 6,288 feet is far below such western ski towns as Aspen. Most downhill skiing in New England takes place below 4,000 feet; most cross-country skiing below 2,000 feet. Hence, brute refrigeration is what keeps the snow on the ground.

The first rule of New England skiing is: dress for cold weather. How cold? Well, a thermometer seems to bring out the fabled Yankee perversity, with neighbor competing against neighbor for the coldest reading in town. We long ago learned to carry a pocket Taylor thermometer on our travels; it generally reads about 10 degrees warmer than the reports we get from the innkeeper or the woman next door. Nevertheless, we have awakened to mornings of -20° F, and we once set out on a ski tour at -15° F. We have picnicked at high noon under a brilliant sun at precisely 0° F. This is very cold weather indeed, especially in a damp climate.

For the active skier on a groomed track, such extremes of cold don't matter much, provided the person takes the usual precautions against frost-nipped lungs. (Breathe—like the local joggers—through a scarf or surgical mask.) But for the recreational skier, or for those who like to tour away from the groomed track, warm clothing is essential. The conventional wisdom that wool is too warm for cross-country skiing does not always apply in New England. Since we do most of our skiing in the backcountry, we favor fishnet underwear, wool shirts and knickers, and ankle-high boots. In addition, we carry the following layers on our backs or in our packs as the situation requires: wool sweater, down vest, shell parka and pants, and gaiters. That may seem like a lot of clothing for a heat-generating activity such as cross-country skiing. But there have been days when we wore it all.

Wet weather is always a possibility. The "January thaw" is a notorious companion to New England skiing, but January probably gets a bad rap in this instance. There have been years when everybody talked wisely about the "February thaw," and other years when we were rained out in December and March with equally devastating results. There were even several seasons in the mid-sixties when a thaw was a monthly occurrence in these parts.

Generally, these thaws are produced by a circumpolar vortex that swings to the south, creating a bulge over the American Midwest. That part of the country is beset with arctic air, while tropical air is drawn far to the north along the Atlantic coast. This warm, moist air rides over the local cold air, dumping its moisture as sleet or rain. First the snow-cover melts and the brooks overflow, followed by freezing weather. This results in a moratorium on cross-country skiing that may last for weeks, except at touring centers with trail-grooming machinery.

Since a thaw can occur at any time, we always include ponchos in our backcountry packs. They also come in handy for windbreaks and groundcloths when it's time for lunch.

WAXING

Frequent wet weather also means that New Englanders make greater use of klister than skiers in many other parts of the country, with the possible exception of the Pacific Northwest. During the colder months, snow is often granular as a result of the thaw-freeze cycle, calling for blue or purple klister. In the spring, even "powder" snow can be so soggy that red klister is necessary. A can of hard green wax, on the other hand, can be regarded as something of a lifetime investment. The frustrations of waxing for New England conditions have driven many of us into the waxless legions—using mohair, fishscale, or whatever.* We commend waxless skis to all but the most serious New England skiers—racers especially, and those who customarily go out for the entire day rather than for an hour or so. Better yet, have two pairs in the garage—skis with normal bases for dry snow and lengthy trips, and waxless skis for those afternoons when you'd like to deal easily with snow of varying conditions.

Is there nothing good to be said about New England snow? Certainly there is. Since the stuff tends to be on the dense side, with the high water content, it's a rare storm that leaves more than six inches of snow behind it. Even a full-blown blizzard is likely to metamorphose in a few days to something quite heavy by western standards. Trail-breaking is therefore not the exhausting work in New England that it can be elsewhere. Indeed, a tour through virgin snow is often no more tiring or time-consuming than skiing on a track. Extra-long or extra-wide skis aren't needed for backcountry touring in this region, and you generally need only normal baskets on your poles.

THE MOUNTAINS

Cross-country skiing is possible through all of New England. Every state but Rhode Island has dozens of commercial touring centers and publicly maintained trails. Realistically, though, you must travel to the mountains to find consistently good conditions. We live in coastal New Hampshire, where winter

---

*We personally favor mohair strips because they don't make such a dreadful racket on granular snow; they just quietly wear down to the canvas. Then you must replace the strips. This is almost as messy as applying klister, but at least you can choose your time for the job.

may last from Thanksgiving to Easter. But we can depend on good skiing only in January and February. Otherwise we're at the mercy of the snow gods. So we go to the mountains when the mood is upon us, just as we do for downhill skiing—often enough they are the same mountains.

The New England highlands are the last stand of the Appalachian mountain chain before it subsides into the plains of Quebec and northern Maine. They bear northeasterly, like the New England coast itself: the Berkshires of western Massachusetts; the Green Mountains of Vermont; the White Mountains of northern New Hampshire and western Maine; to the scattered summits of central Maine dominated by awesome Mount Katahdin. Anywhere in this broad swath of uplands is splendid touring country, whether you prefer groomed trails or unbroken snow.

SKI TOURING AREAS

In the annual *Guide*, published by the Ski Touring Council (West Hill Road, Troy, Vermont 05868), we can pick out 33 likely spots in Massachusetts, 66 in Vermont, 54 in New Hampshire, and 25 in Maine. Most of these areas are organized enough to have a trail map; many are full-scale operations with trail-grooming equipment, sales and rentals, instruction, and ski patrols. Some of the more promising areas are:

● *Northfield, Mass.* On Northfield Mountain, site of an electric plant, a power company has opened 2,000 acres of woodland to ski touring, with 25 miles of groomed trails.

● *Windsor, Mass.* Notchview Reservation has 3,000 acres and 20 miles of trails and unplowed roads. A few miles away in Cummington, the Cummington Farm Touring Center has 25 miles of groomed trails, with heated cabins for overnight stops.

● *Bennington, Vt.* The local Nordic ski patrol has mapped about 100 miles of routes variously suited to skiers, snowshoers, and snowmobilers, and also maintains one trail exclusively for cross-country skiing. Their map is available in bookstores and ski shops.

● *Londonderry, Vt.* The Viking Touring Center has 17 miles of trails. For backcountry skiers, the Peru Outdoor Recreation

Club has cut and mapped about 25 miles of trails in the Green Mountain National Forest nearby. (There are maps at Viking Touring Center and the Landgrove Inn.)

• *Middlebury, Vt.* The college outing club at Middlebury College maintains a touring center on the Breadloaf campus, and there are miles of unplowed roads nearby. From Breadloaf you can ski to the Middlebury College Snow Bowl (a downhill area) and from there to Blueberry Hill Touring Center in Goshen.

• *Stowe, Vt.* The capitol of eastern downhill skiing is also the capitol of cross-country skiing, with full-scale touring centers at the Trapp Family Lodge, Edson Hill Manor, and Topnotch Lodge. Experts can strike out for the Skytop trail to the west, the Madonna Vasa trail over the mountains to the north, and a demanding route to Bolton Valley to the south.

• *Waterville Valley, N.H.* The local touring center has 12 miles of groomed trails, notable for their gorgeous settings and ready access to backcountry routes of the White Mountain National Forest.

• *Bretton Woods, N.H.* The resort hotel near Crawford Notch has about 50 miles of groomed trails ranging from easy bridle paths to ridge-line skiing. (One trail is reached via the chairlift at the ski resort.) There's a cabin for overnight stops along one of the trails.

• *Jackson, N.H.* The Jackson Touring Foundation maintains 75 miles of trails over varied terrain. The longer tours are mostly for intermediate to advanced skiers. In Pinkham Notch, nearby, the Appalachian Mountain Club also has facilities for cross-country skiing.

• *Andover, Maine* The ski routes in this White Mountains town range from groomed trails for beginners to a 25-mile loop to Grafton Notch and back.

• *Kingfield, Maine* The Carrabasset Valley Touring Center near Sugarloaf Mountain is one of the niftiest in the region, complete with passive solar heating. There are 50 miles of trails, including one on an old railroad bed. Not far away, the Deer Farm Touring Center offers another 30 miles of trails.

INDEPENDENT SKI TOURS

The independent tourer will discover thousands of miles of unplowed roads in northern New England. Their exploration requires only a few companions, a compass, and a map. You don't even need to be equipped for wilderness if you stick to places like Acadia National Park, on Maine's Mount Desert Island. There, 40 miles of graded dirt roads lace the eastern part of the island, where skiers can travel for days without retracing their steps. Up in the vastness of Baxter State Park, there are more than 60 miles of unplowed roads. But before setting off for Mount Katahdin in that park you'll have to inform the state park rangers. If even Baxter is too civilized for you, there's an entrepreneur who specializes in flying parties deep into the Maine woods—just as canoe parties are flown in during the summer months—then leading them on week-long expeditions from one hunting camp to the next.

Other New England states, lacking the great expanse of Maine (which contains nearly half the land mass of New England) must be content with shorter tours. One of the best is the Wildcat Valley Run in New Hampshire, one of the finest wilderness trails around, albeit a marked route of the Jackson Touring Foundation. You begin at the summit station of a downhill ski area. The trail—cut exclusively for cross-country skiers—drops about 3,000 feet in the course of 9 or 10 miles.

More strenuous still is a traverse of the Pemigewasset Wilderness, which usually entails an overnight stop at the Appalachian Mountain Club's Zealand Falls hut, 6 miles from the highway. On the following day is a 16-mile trek to the Kancamagus Highway near Lincoln, much of the distance on graded railroad beds. One hardy skier from the Bretton Woods Touring Center recently made this passage in a single day, including another 10 miles by proceeding over Mad River Notch to Waterville Valley. His stunt was intended to dramatize the feasibility of a ski route clear through the White Mountains. But we'd recommend that ordinary mortals tackle this route in stages.

Vermont also has its long-distance tours. The Vermont Ski Marathon, launched in 1978, proceeds 38 miles, from South

A lone skier strides across the Vermont countryside. (Photo by Robert F. George)

Lincoln to Brandon. Its route combines regular touring trails and logging roads packed especially for the race. Snow is shoveled across a few intervening highways as well. The winning time the first year was 3 hours and 48 minutes. But the truly astonishing feature of the marathon was that nearly half the 1,000 starters managed to complete the course in the eight hours they were permitted to be on the trail.

Then there are the untracked (and sometimes unmarked) routes between touring centers around Stowe and in the vicinity of Middlebury Gap. Indeed, with sturdy companions and a van to support the expedition, you could ski nearly the entire length of Vermont from Massachusetts to the Canada line. If that's too strenuous, consider a guided tour from one country inn to another, led by Anne Mausloff of Chester, Vermont. That tour covers 8 or 10 miles a day; and your baggage (except for a day pack) is brought around by car to each night's destination. That's touring in the grand style!

ROUTE FINDING

Backwoods skiing has inherent dangers, even though in most

of New England you can seldom ski more than a day's march from a highway. Northern Maine is the dramatic exception to this. We have already described the need for clothing to cope with extremes of cold. Good maps are another necessity. Parts of Maine and New Hampshire have been intricately mapped by the Appalachian Mountain Club (AMC). These maps often prove as useful to skiers as to the hikers for whom they were intended. They should be used in connection with the appropriate Maine or New Hampshire guidebook. The AMC does not extend into Vermont, and the Green Mountain Club's (GMC) cartography leaves much to be desired. The exception is the Mount Mansfield map, which is a foldout in the GMC *Long Trail Guide*. Touring centers are beginning to publish some rather sophisticated maps. But, except for the map put out by the Jackson Touring Foundation, we have yet to see any that equal AMC standards of cartography. Otherwise, the best ones, like the map/brochure published by the Bennington Nordic Ski Patrol, tend to be adaptations of the U.S. Geological Survey maps.

The U.S. Geological Survey maps, however, present some difficulties. The original surveys were done a generation ago; updating has been done mostly through aerial photography. As a result, the location of footpaths and dirt roads tends to be somewhat arbitrary. It takes a good eye to relate what's on the map to what's on the ground.

Then, too, trails marked for summer hikers often vanish in the winter. Once we skied from Jackson up to the AMC's Carter Notch Hut, approaching it from the seldom-skied back route. We managed fine as long as we were in the hardwood forest, where the route had been well marked with frequent paint blazes on the trees. But the blazes ceased once we left the deciduous zone. A summer hiker would simply have followed the trampled ground, scuffed roots, and other obvious traces of foot traffic, but in the winter these are several feet under snow. Even where a trail is consistently blazed throughout its length—as is the Long trail in Vermont—the blazes are normally placed at eye level, say 4 feet off the ground. This may create problems in winter, when 4 feet of snow in the high country of Vermont is not unusual.

It's often possible to ski for miles through the hardwood forests of northern New England, trail or no trail. But this is almost impossible among the conifers. They grow so thick, especially at higher elevations, that bushwhacking is more often than not out of the question. One of the great frustrations of life is to have a ski tip on each side of a tree, and your heels, as you attempt to back off, buried in the snow. It's best to leave this kind of bushwhacking to the snowshoers.

This makes sense when you consider the tremendous distances you can cover through New England on old logging roads, jeep tracks, and abandoned rights-of-way. For example, in New Hampshire's Pemigewasset Wilderness most of the summer footpaths follow the routes of old logging railroads, the tracks having long since been pulled up and sold for scrap. The railroad beds remain, however, graded with consummate skill so that the Baldwin locomotives could haul out their tremendous burdens of pulpwood. Picking up the Wilderness trail near Lincoln, you can ski 9 miles up the East Branch of the Pemigewasset, gaining a mere 600 feet of altitude. This is hardly enough to notice on the ascent, but enough to make your return to the highway an absolute lark. Indeed, the Wilderness trail has become so popular that (in ironic counterpoint to its name) the U.S. Forest Service has found it necessary to divide the trail down the middle, allocating one side to skiers, the other to snowshoers. Snowmobilers, meanwhile, have their own Wilderness trail on the other side of the East Branch.

SPECIAL EQUIPMENT

Whenever you leave the groomed track, some emergency equipment is mandatory. We carry a fairly elaborate first-aid kit. (The more we learn, the more elaborate it gets, but it still weighs less than a pound.) We also pack along a can of Sterno, jellied alcohol (for rewaxing with klisters and as an emergency fire starter), an aluminized space blanket, a whistle, some health-food bars (chosen because they're so unpalatable that we wouldn't dream of eating them except in a pinch), a flashlight, a spare ski tip and binding bail, a jackknife, matches, and 50 feet of parachute cord. Our extra clothing, from poncho to down vest, is also selected with an eye toward the possibility of a bivouac along the trail.

THE UNIQUENESS OF NEW ENGLAND

We've never gone in for ski camping, although we may someday. Certainly the abundance of open-front shelters in Vermont and New Hampshire—and to a lesser extent in Maine— is a continual temptation.

When we look back on seven years of ski touring in New England, the trips that stand out most vividly are those that took us to heights that offered views of the distant countryside. New England is a closed-in land; you never notice this so forcefully as when you do come upon a vista. The hills are rugged and set close together; highlands and lowlands alike are heavily forested. There is a special joy when you succeed in finding an overlook. It's a visual release akin to the physical release of cross-country skiing, and it seems to bring out the pleasures in higher relief. On New Hampshire's Wildcat Valley Run, for example, you can detour a few hundred feet to Hall's Ledge, overlooking the Mount Washington Valley. The Rocky Branch Ridge spreads its great length to the west, and northward stands the white massif of Mount Washington itself. This is the ultimate picnic spot, unequalled in grandeur between the Rockies and the Alps. Just across the Connecticut River in Vermont, there's a vast outlook from the Skyline trail near Woodstock. And there are several remarkable vistas on an arduous route (followed more by snowmobilers than skiers) near Brookfield, Vermont, where you pass from a region of dairy farms to a sudden outlook upon the main Green Mountain range, then back again to the pastoral countryside where you began. This route is called the Cram Hill Loop, and is described in several cross-country skiing guides, including our own.

These are all redoubtable tours. We have gentler memories too—of picnicking in the sun by backcountry ponds, and of tearing along a groomed track from one lodge to another. In Franconia, New Hampshire, a friend of ours has worked out a route that includes five lodges (and five mugs of mulled wine) in the course of a single day. Like ski camping, that's something we haven't yet tried. But it makes you aware of the infinite variety of New England touring.

19

Alaska

by Wayne Merry

Alaska skiing: what's it like? Endless darkness, biting cold, bottomless snow . . . right? Wrong. Ten months of skiing on nothing softer than green wax . . . right? Wrong, again. Those are stereotypes you keep hearing about the arctic and subarctic, and there are times and places when each of them is true. But it's a big country up there—staggeringly big—and subject to nearly as many extremes as any other ski country. Sure, there are times and places when it is light only a few hours each day, and when cold is so intense you can't get a decent glide going downhill. But in that same area, you might wind up using red klister in December for short spells. Out on the coast, you might find that there isn't much use for your hard green wax, since it's too warm. In lots of places the ski season is even shorter than in the "south 48," since there is too little snow on the ground. Alaska is a big, diverse, fascinating country—one you can't classify and put in a box.

Still, the Alaskan and Canadian arctic and subarctic have certain characteristics that tie them together for the skier. For example, you can generalize about the interior, where most of the ski country lies. You find that conditions are much the same everywhere. There is one great common factor that holds true almost anywhere you go in Alaska, away from the few cities. And that is *wilderness.*

Folks don't go to Alaska for track skiing unless they are competitors. There is a strong interest in racing up there, centered in the larger cities and schools, and some well-maintained trail systems around those towns. Even in the Yukon and Northwest Territories, tiny towns like Old Crow and Inuvik have produced some remarkable racers—many of them local Indians, largely due to the pioneering work of Father Mouchet. If you are a

racer, you already know about that. But you don't generally go
north to ski on tracks. You go north to get out on skis and
mingle with the moose and camp with the caribou—and that's
what Alaska has: wilderness skiing. That's what this chapter
is about.

WHEN TO GO

Winters are notoriously long in the north, but that doesn't
mean that skiing is tops all winter. Most of Alaska has an interior climate, which means that it is pretty dry. Snow cover is
often shallow. During the early part of winter, the snow is often
so thin, light, and cold that it doesn't have any body. You may
well find that your skis cut right through a foot of snow and rip
into the rocks below. Later on, toward spring, the long days of
intense sunlight may change the shallow snow cover so rapidly
that waxing becomes a nightmare. Here's a brief rundown of
the ski season.

October

You really have to hunt to find any worthwhile skiing this
early. Some of the local enthusiasts are busy scraping the snow
together for trail systems, but most folks are just beginning to
think about skiing. In the boonies, snow tends to be light and
thin, except, sometimes, in maritime climates up in the mountains along the coast. Generally, October does not offer much
good wilderness skiing.

November/December/January

Skiing slowly improves through these months, as snow slowly
accumulates and settles. But unfortunately, this is the "dark
time," and very often is the coldest time, too. In the interior
and arctic, the cold may be intense, and the snow light and dry.
Track skiing can be excellent. If you are in the bush, skiing can
be excellent on trails packed by snowmobiles or dog teams. But
if you are breaking your own track, you may well break
through to the ground. Lakes and rivers should be well frozen
by now, and offer fine skiing and good routes across the land.
But check locally on this for specific conditions.

My personal preference is to take only short tours—a few

hours at a time—during these months because of the cold and the dark. In December, dawn comes around 9 a.m. and dark arrives around 3 p.m. in central Alaska. This, combined with temperatures that may be below -40° F, isn't frivolous skiing. You need to go out well laden, prepared for anything. Your nose runs constantly and freezes. Frost feathers grow on your eyelashes and ice cakes your beard. You keep moving to keep your toes warm. When you stop, the big down jacket goes on instantly. Lunch breaks tend to be short—maybe nonexistent— or else long, complete with a rough campsite, warming fire, and a boiling pot of tea.

But there are rewards, too. The day is one continuous sunrise and sunset, with pastels so delicate they are almost impossible to catch on film. The sun provides color highlights above a black-and-white landscape. Sounds are unnaturally clear and sharp in the cold. You'll swear you can hear the whistle of every feather in the beat of a raven's wing. Still, these aren't the months to go adventuring in Alaska's outback, unless you are testing cold-weather gear or simply like to suffer. See what I mean? The winter is half gone, and we've hardly started skiing.

February

As the days stretch out, you again become aware of some trace of warmth in the sun. It isn't much—and it still gets terribly cold—but it is enough that warmer days and cold nights may produce a sun crust on the snow. Unfortunately, the great temperature gradient between the cold air and the much warmer earth in many areas produces a thick deposit of depth hoar—a layer of weak, unconsolidated snow crystals that flows like sugar. But toward the end of February, the days lengthen rapidly. Action is picking up in the bush; it is almost time.

March/April

These are the skiing months, the time to go on a trip. While there may still be spells of severe cold, the days are long and the sun is warm. And in many parts of the interior the weather is quite stable. You should still be prepared for nighttime temperatures that plunge to the minus forties. But the bright sun lifts the spirits after such a night and drives the frost from those frozen socks on the back of your pack. Spring is coming with a rush, and it is a good time to be out. Beware of snowblindness, the ice starting to go on some rivers, and of lying awake wondering when it is going to get dark. You will be going through your softer waxes at a great rate around the end of April, even above the Arctic Circle.

May

All the lowland skiing is pretty well gone by now. There may be good skiing on mountain plateaus and glaciers. The rivers are almost all open, and thawing lakes are dangerous. The sun is up most of the night, and the glare and surface thaw are sometimes so intense that you do better to travel nights and camp days. It is madness to slog through sucking slush, panting and getting the roof of your mouth sunburned, when you could be resting in the shade, waiting for the long shadows that bring frozen snow and relief from the glare. Even after May, you'll still be able to ski on the glaciers.

WHERE TO GO

Almost all of Alaska has superb wilderness areas. The type of skiing you will encounter, though, varies depending on the climate of each area. While it is a pretty general approach, let's look at the basic features of the interior, the coast, and the arctic as they affect skiing.

The Interior

The great bulk of "skiable" Alaska and the Yukon has an interior-type climate. This means that winters tend to be extremely cold and dry, and the snowfall light. Lows of -40° F are not uncommon during the darkest months, and may persist for many days or even weeks. Some areas consistently record lows of around -60° F each winter. However, brief warm spells may jolt the mercury up to 35° F or so from time to time. Fortunately for the outdoorsman, temperatures frequently stay in the -10° to $+10^o$ range, which many northerners feel is an optimum range for active outdoor pursuits—barring wind, of course. Around that range, you can often ski comfortably in a single sweater if head and hands are well protected. Normal cross-country boots are adequate then, if worn with two heavy pairs of socks and an overboot. But sensible skiers carry *mukluks* or other superwarm footgear for stops or camping.* And of course, one must be prepared for anything.

Don't expect much snow in the interior. Most areas have from one to three feet on the ground at any one time. Interior weather is generally more stable than that of coastal areas, winds being the prime climatic hazard.

The Coast

Coastal weather affects all areas touching the Pacific, the Gulf of Alaska, and the Bering Sea, and penetrates inland at times to the great weather barriers of the St. Elias, the Wrangells, and the Boundary and Alaska ranges. Interior areas in the "rain shadow" of these ranges will enjoy good (if cloudy) weather, while the windward sides may undergo heavy precipitation and strong winds.

Snowfall is usually heavy along the coast, especially in the mountains, which in many places rise almost directly from the sea. Nearest the ocean, it may snow and rain intermittently. Snowfall is heaviest in southeastern Alaska and the Gulf of Alaska; it diminishes as one moves north toward the arctic. Sub-zero temperatures are uncommon along the southeastern and Gulf coasts, and Juneau experiences average temperatures below freezing only during January and February. The Bering Sea coast is noted for winter weather of high humidity and extremely high winds.

The Arctic

The important boundary between what we might think of as interior and arctic conditions is the Arctic Divide, from which waters flow either north to the Arctic Ocean or south (eventually) to the Bering Sea. The transition is dramatic. On a ski trip across the Brooks Range, from Bettles to Galbraith Lake we were "woods camping" all the way to the divide. We built big fires to cook and keep off the frost, and camped in thick groves of spruce. This persisted right up to the last climb to the

---

Mukluks are sealskin or reindeer-skin boots worn by the Eskimos.

divide. But there we abandoned the ax and went to alpine-style camping, for beyond that there were no trees except low willow—just miles of unbroken whiteness stretching to the horizon; and wind.

Skiing above the Arctic Circle, but still south of the Arctic Divide, is much like skiing in the rest of the interior. Temperatures may be slightly more severe. But south of the divide conditions are generally similar to the interior, with the same flora, wildlife, and precipitation patterns.

The North Slope fits most preconceptions of the true arctic: flat, bitterly cold most of the winter, and exposed to searing winds from the Arctic Ocean. Snowfall is light, and snow is often drifted or wind-sculptured. The tops of gravelly ridges are often blown bare. As you approach the ocean, you enter the range of the polar bear, a creature of the pack ice.

Thus far, skiing has been rare in Alaska's arctic. A few parties have skied across the Brooks Range since 1972, with at least one of them having severe problems with frostbite. Skiing conditions there may often be better than in the interior, since wind-packed snow is more common. The surfaces of the major rivers are sometimes blown free of snow, affording a bare or nearly bare ice surface. This presents strenuous skiing but it is fast traveling, especially if the wind is with you! You may find sand and gravel on the surface of the river ice, though, blown there from exposed sandbars. In that case, good walking!

Come spring, the snow disappears quickly from the tundra. Some days in early May you may have to go from green wax to klister in a few days, and be carrying your skis and wading through water a couple of days later.

Little information is available about skiing on the pack ice of the Arctic Ocean. Pressure ridges are formidable obstacles that reduce any form of surface transportation to a laborious crawl or even a futile struggle. There has been speculation on the possibility of reaching the North Pole on skis. But the pressure ridges and open leads dictate that skis will cease to provide transportation, and will become part of the load for a good part of the journey. Skis were little used by early explorers in this area, who had a sharp eye for the easiest ways of getting there first.

DEPTH HOAR, THE NORTHERN SKIER'S NIGHTMARE

Alaska has more than its share of depth hoar—the bane of off-track tourers. In regions where there is a great difference between the temperatures of the frigid air and the relatively warmer earth, water vapor tends to leave the warmer snow crystals below and accumulate on cooler ones above. This produces a fragile layer of unconsolidated, rounded crystals, which simply cannot support the skier. Around February, there is often a considerable thickness of depth hoar, as well as a sun crust, in protected areas. The combination of breakable crust over loose, sugary depth hoar is simply a disaster for the over-snow traveler.

When it becomes necessary to make a new track over such snow, each person in a party of skiers usually alternates breaking trail. Each may drop his pack and break a hundred yards or more, and then return to the end of the line to retrieve it. There is no problem catching up; it is slow, brutal work. Other parties—particularly those pulling sleds or *pulks*—have found it better to leave camp set up, while part of the group skis ahead, lightly laden, to pack the next day's train. Both systems have pros and cons, but either way progress is dismayingly slow. Some teams carry a pair of long, narrow snowshoes with a sharp upturn at the tip, used strictly for trail-breaking. These appear to work well at times, but are little better than skis at others.

Beware of the old runner's malady *shin splints*, when there is much trail to be broken in such conditions. This appears to be caused by the effort of kicking or lifting the ski out of the depression and sometimes through the crust from below. Each member should break for only a short period. Today's trail-breaking hero can easily become tomorrow's casualty, which would be a liability to the group for the balance of the trip.

The best way of dealing with depth hoar is, obviously, to avoid it. During February, March, and April, it is best to look for wind-scoured travel routes, where the snow is shallow and well packed. This includes rivers, ridges, lake systems, wind-swept tundra, or glaciers—anything to avoid the depth hoar that lies in wait in protected areas.

SKIING WATERWAYS

Very often, the choicest and most logical Alaskan ski routes across the land lie on frozen lakes or rivers. These offer a reasonable way through brush and thick forest, an aid to navigation, and often—though not always—a firm skiing surface of ice or wind-packed snow.

Skiing up the main branch of the Koyukuk River in Alaska.

Waterways offer certain hazards, too. The thought of skiing over an unknown thickness of ice and depth of water conjures up some frightening scenarios, some of them entirely realistic. But the experience of wallowing through a mile of wind-crusted depth hoar up on the bank will convince anyone that the nervous strain is worth it.

Practically everything in the north that will freeze is well frozen by the good traveling months of February, March, and April. But it still pays to tap into local knowledge about danger spots. By and large, glacial streams rarely present problems, as their sources are reduced to a trickle by the cold. (This, however, may not be true in some coastal areas.) Streams of groundwater origin, though, especially big ones, are less predictable.

Overflow

Overflow is the most common problem. As stream ice thickens downward in very cold weather and starts building upward from the cold rocks on the bottom, the water is compressed into an ever-smaller space. Eventually, it must escape to the surface as overflow. There, it too will soon freeze, unless it has flowed up beneath an insulating layer of snow. If that is the case, it may remain there in liquid form for some time. If you ski into this, you've got problems, not the least of which is scraping the ice off. It is a hideous job, requiring an excellent scraper and a lot of time. Always take a good scraper with you in the north, made of metal, not plastic.

If overflow is deep, it is also possible to get your feet wet, the disaster that befell Jack London's protagonist in "To Build a Fire." Overflow is rarely deep on the surface of a large river, but it may accumulate in deep pools under the snow in a ravine or in the hollow beside a small stream that has "glaciered up" above its banks.

I once ran a big closed-cab snow machine into 18 inches of overflow on the surface of a snow-covered road beside such a "glaciered-up" stream. The temperature was -45° F. I was able to throw off enough water and freezing slush only by gunning it unmercifully to keep the tracks from freezing solid in moments. Even at that, we did a few hours of chipping before the issue was settled. If you go into that much water at that temperature on skis, you will have to move fast to keep all your toes. Fortunately, you usually become aware of overflow before the water is over your boot-tops. And it will ordinarily freeze before it penetrates your boots. High gaiters or overboots are a help, too.

Thin Ice

More dangerous yet is unexpected thin ice. Since it isn't common, that makes it all the more dangerous. Most big lakes have their well-known (to locals) soft spots. There's a point near my home where a moose breaks through and drowns almost every year.

Dangerous spots include narrow channels between two lakes (where a slight current becomes prominent), the mouths of streams flowing into lakes, and—rather unpredictably—above fast spots on an otherwise frozen river. You may also find them in totally unexpected spots on both lakes and rivers—places that you can't imagine being unfrozen.

Once, skiing alone up a small river, I felt the snow settle under me and looked back into a hole of black, still water that had appeared as I skied over it. I couldn't reach the bottom with a six-foot stick. Thirty feet away was a rapids that was safely covered by a foot of hard ice. Why the difference? I don't know for sure the reason for the difference. Maybe it was caused by a warm upwelling from a spring. Such an immersion would be extremely dangerous. A lone skier would be lucky to survive in very cold weather, even if he was able to get out.

In the spring, the snow on the ground is vanishing and only the thickly frozen lakes seem to offer much good skiing surface. There is a great temptation at this time to stretch the season by traveling the lake ice, especially if you cut through and find that there are still two or three feet. But it is a dangerous time. As the weather warms, the ice changes daily from underneath, not from the top where you can see it. Very often, nighttime freezes will put a smooth, glassy frozen surface on the lake, but beneath that there may be *candled ice*—ice that has degenerated into parallel columns with no strength of their own.

Once you break through the surface glaze—and your skis will carry you well out onto it—it is impossible to get back on top again. The ice simply crumbles away at the edge of the hole even if you distribute your weight on your skis. It is a desperate trap.

If you ever do break through into deep water, remove your skis and poles immediately and put them on top of the ice, and take your pack off right away. You won't be able to feel anything with your hands or even control them very well in just a couple of minutes, and it will be too late. You had better have a sharp partner at this point. Make no mistake, getting wet at low temperatures is every bit as serious as Jack London made it out to be!

SKIING TRAP LINES

There aren't many places within a hundred miles or so of a northern settlement where you won't come across trap lines in the winter. These are ordinarily run on snowmobiles every few days, and they may provide excellent skiing. There are a few cautions, though. A trapper's catch for the winter may be a major part of his livelihood. Anything you do to reduce that catch may produce a serious hardship for him and his family, and will understandably make that trapper pretty unhappy with skiers in general and you in particular.

It isn't hard to tell when you are on a trap line. Every once in a while you will come to a place where tracks show that the trapper got off his machine (or dogsled) and strayed a few feet off the trail to set a trap. There will usually be some sort of arrangement of sticks, forming an alcove over the scent or bait above the hidden trap. This may be marked by a tuft of fur or something similar nailed to a tree. Regardless of your personal convictions about leg-hold traps, don't bother these sets. The trapper is pursuing an old and accepted vocation, he's usually within the law, and he has legal trapping rights on that line, for which he may have paid a pretty penny.

But the trapper doesn't ordinarily own the land, so if it is public land you have a perfect right to use the trail. But you are still, in a sense, on his territory. Most trappers are perfectly hospitable, and I've spent some nice nights in the warmth and comfort of trap line cabins. But some are fiercely possessive of their lines and may be hostile. I know of one who has threatened to shoot anyone who molests his sets.

Almost all trap lines have shelter cabins at infrequent intervals. In the tradition of the north, these are left open with a supply of kindling and stovewood ready at hand. Many trappers will not object to your using one for shelter—if you leave it like you found it. You are expected to leave it clean, with fresh wood and kindling to replace any you've used, and with supplies intact. If it is possible, though, check and get permission first.

Above all, don't take dogs on a trap line. Dogs will invariably investigate the fascinating scent of each trap, and either disturb the set or get themselves caught in the traps. If the trap is a wolf or wolverine trap, you may have a helluva time getting him out. And the trapper won't be overjoyed that your dog has lost him a potential $200 skin.

Pet dogs can be a liability in the bush at the best of times. They mangle your return trail, bite porcupines and get stuck full of quills, chase away wildlife, get eaten by wolves, get exhausted wallowing in deep snow, get iceballs caught in their pads, pollute the snow around camp, knock over the stewpot, and I've even seen them break through thin ice and drown. When skiing with a dog in late spring, the dog may range ahead of you and bump into an irritable grizzly—and then run to hide behind his ever-loving master, with the bear in hot pursuit. The best advice is to leave the dog at home, unless he is pulling a dogsled.

SKIING WITH A DOGSLED

A sport that is growing in popularity in the north is dogsledding. After a slump, when snowmobiles took over as the workhorses of the bush, dogsleds are returning with a vengeance. Much of the resurgence is in dogsled racing, but I've been seeing more work teams, as well.

A good working team is a pleasure to watch. Its enthusiasm for pulling is amazing. And if the team is hauling your 60-pound pack, you can forgive dogs any number of minor sins, such as tangling the tug lines, taking an occasional snap at each other, and leaving droppings on your ski trail. If you have a dog team, you need only carry a day pack, you can use lighter skis, and on good snow you can actually use a little kick-and-glide technique instead of shuffling along.

However, in some snow you may find yourself breaking trail for the dogs, especially if a sled is used rather than a toboggan. It may even be necessary to dump much of the load, and pack the trail to camp with skis and a light sled. Then the musher will have to dash back for the load over a frozen trail in the evening.

If you have any influence with the musher, encourage him to attach a couple of light, ski-width skegs to the bottom-rear of his toboggan—just thick enough to make a bit of a ski track for those times when you follow the dogs. Otherwise, you will tend to spend a lot of time steering your skis through the tracks and ruts.

SKIING GLACIERS

The most spectacular part of Alaska's scenery is its mountains, and the avenues to and among such mountains are glaciers. The Alaska, Chugach, Wrangell, St. Elias, and Boundary ranges are blanketed by immense icefields, offering some of the most awesome skiing terrain anywhere. Alaska's lesser ranges are lesser by comparison only; many are girdled by large glaciers. All are serious business, the province of the experienced mountaineer. From the air—especially in winter—they look like great flat or gently contoured ski runs, and sometimes they are. But they are invariably riddled with crevasses, and exposed to ferocious weather and sometimes to great avalanche hazards. Roped skiing is imperative on glaciers, if you want to enjoy the sport into your advanced years.

Long tours of one to several weeks have grown in popularity in recent years, and some of the best are on the great icefields of the major ranges. A variety of routes can be mapped on almost any of the icefields. As there is little road development adjacent to the glaciers, most are best approached by landing well above the terminus in a ski plane or helicopter. Such tours must be treated as full-fledged expeditions. A party is very much on its own, and won't be rescued from a miscalculation up there any more than it would be in the Himalayas. But provided you have the necessary mountaineering knowhow, you won't find a more magnificent place to tour.

The old notion that heavy downhill touring gear is the only proper equipment for glacier skiing is fading fast. Many skiers now use skinny, almost unbreakable skis, fiberglass sledges, and have plenty of savvy.

Most icefield terrain is gentle, except for the occasional icefall, the *terminus* of the glaciers, and the mountain slopes—which the sensible skier will avoid, unless he is a very accomplished ski mountaineer.*

Working within these restraints, though, a skier has all the control he needs by using touring gear with pin bindings. The saving in weight is a joy. It isn't necessary to be a cross-country stylist, so long as the glacier tourer is competent in all the basic cross-country maneuvers. But the glacier skier should be a knowledgeable mountaineer, be able to ski while roped, know what glaciers are all about, know crevasse rescue and cold-weather camping, and have the endurance for occasional exhausting work in poor conditions.

Some of the finest glacier tours are within national parks of the United States and Canada, particularly Mount McKinley National Park in Alaska and Kluane National Park in the Yukon. In both parks, you are requested to register at park headquarters. Kluane, which is particularly demanding, classifies most backcountry trips as expeditions and requires extensive documentation of experience and equipment, as well as medical exam certificates. If you plan trips in these areas, contact the parks well in advance. You can write to:

> The Superintendent
> Mount McKinley National Park
> McKinley Park, Alaska 99755

> The Superintendent
> Kluane National Park
> Haines Junction, Yukon Territory
> Canada

*The *terminus* is the extreme point or tip of a glacier.

SNOWMOBILES: BANE OR BLESSING?

Having migrated north from California, the very word *snow-mobile* was initially enough to strain my emotional composure. In places like Fairbanks (and its academic suburb, College), there have been some fierce disputes triggered by ski-trail destruction by snowmobiles. Actual violence has flared in Juneau, where the amount of skiable and buzzable terrain is limited by ocean and mountains. But in much of the bush, skiers just wouldn't get around much if it were not for snow-mobile tracks.

Don't get me wrong, I hate what snowmobiles have done to northern wildlife, to the wilderness, and to people. If there was a chance of outlawing them entirely, I wouldn't hesitate. But if it comes to the choice of wallowing for two days in depth hoar up to my fanny-pack, or making the same trip in two hours on a snowmobile track, I'm certainly going to ski in the track.

The snowmobile is a tool all over the north. Granted, it is often misused, and there is plenty of moronic recreational use around towns. But in the bush it has largely replaced dogsleds for running trap lines, skidding logs, hauling supplies, and simply getting to civilization once in a while. The trails they leave, old or fresh, are often the only reasonable route for skiing through abominable snow.

WILDLIFE

Perhaps the nicest thing about skiing in Alaska is the feeling you get from the wildlife—when you run across a set of fresh wolf tracks in your trail or find yourself transfixed by the unblinking stare of a lynx. Skiing in the north almost demands that you make a study of tracks, or you will miss many dramatic tales written in the snow. Study the deep tracks of moose and wolf: which way were they running? Notice the feathery prints of ptarmigan feet ending at a tracery of wingtips as he erupted into the air ahead of a stalking fox. There are the diagonal tracks left by a loping wolverine. And there are the tracks of a bear heading your way up the trail: how fresh are they? Is it a black bear or a grizzly? It's nice to know things like that.

Following tracks can also help you physically. I've intention-ally skied over the bumpy, pitted trail of a couple of moose for miles. It was rough going, but their passage had packed the snow just enough to support my skis, and everywhere else was seemingly bottomless depth hoar.

If you are nervous about all this big wildlife running around loose, don't worry about it; just enjoy it. Wolves will not hurt you. There's no documented case in North America of an attack by a healthy, wild wolf. You are superbly lucky if you see one up close. If you hear a wild chorus of deep howls out beyond the darkness at night, just savor the genuine wilderness symphony.

Moose, on the other hand, *can* be dangerous. Most of the time, the huge, strangely beautiful animals will trot off when they hear you coming, leaving only tracks and a pile of steaming pellets. Sometimes they will simply stand quietly and watch you pass. But beware of the cow with a calf. She's unpredict-able, and if you ski between them, or even too near, you may arouse her protective instincts.

If a moose is going to charge, her head will go down, her mane up, her ears back, and sometimes a low growl-like sound will rumble out. At that point, get away as fast as you can, possibly up a tree. Those forelegs flash like pistons, and have killed many a wolf and dog. Fortunately, moose are usually satisfied if you just move away, for if they pursued you they would be difficult to escape.

The wolverine is another much-maligned creature. He is extremely wary of man; if you see one at all you are lucky, indeed. They have been known to raid food caches and cabins; but so will ravens, foxes, early bears, and a host of other small animals.

Once in a great while, you may find a bear track while skiing. We found two different sets of grizzly tracks (one set was over our own of two hours earlier) on the North Fork of the Koyukuk in early April 1972. This caused much consternation, as early grizzlies are even more unpredictable than late risers. But such sleepless bears are uncommon in the Arctic. You should be particularly observant, though, if you are skiing

A ski tourer on the Itkilik River in Alaska.

glaciers. Many grizzlies hibernate in south-facing dirt and gravel slopes near the terminus of glaciers. Around late-April they emerge with their new cubs, born during winter, and wander down toward the lowlands. You don't want to meet any of these unexpectedly.

The dangers from winter wildlife are almost nil, though. The birds and animals there are what make it a wilderness. They make skiing in Alaska something special, an experience that is almost gone from our world.

Part VI

RACING

20

Perspective on Racing

by Bill Koch

It takes years to build the training base required to reach one's potential in racing. This base must be built carefully and systematically. A good training program takes careful thought and planning. Each person should ultimately design an individual program that will put him on the right track toward a successful racing season. I design my yearly program to begin at the end of the previous year's competitive season. The competitive season then follows as the culmination of the year's efforts. The training ideas I present should only serve as an example to take into consideration when planning your own program. They are mainly meant to start you thinking on your own about training.

PLANNING YOUR PROGRAM

It would be helpful to keep a training log. Make it as simple and easy to understand as possible. It should tell you what volume of training has been done for the year. For their accuracy, I prefer hours to kilometers as a volume measure. For example, one hour of cycling would be nearly the same as an hour of running. However, one can cover 30 kilometers in that hour on a cycle and only 10 or 15 kilometers running.

When designing your program, there are many things to take into account:

1. What volume of training will you shoot for? How many hours will you train over the year, and how will you spread them out over the month?
2. How much is going to be distance training, interval training, and strength training?
3. Where are you weak? What areas need the most work?

Bill Koch during on-snow training in the summer at Grand-Targhee in Wyoming.

4. What types of training do you enjoy most and which do you consider most necessary?

OFF-SEASON TRAINING

One of the great things about off-season training is that there is such a wide variety of methods you can use to condition yourself. Some methods that come directly to mind are: roller skiing, hiking, cycling, running, summer skiing, rowing, and swimming. There is also strength training, the backbone of which includes work on the Exer-genie and the rollerboard. The circuit training routine can be rounded out with sit-ups, wall squats, dips, back extensors, and plyometrics. Some skiers also enjoy weight lifting. But be careful not to get too bulky in the wrong places! Some activities you might try for diversity are: canoeing, tennis, soccer, rock climbing and mountaineering, kayaking, farm work, and Alpine skiing. These are good strength builders and will help liven up your training.

There is a saying "the longer, the stronger." So don't forget to stretch those muscles! Ballet or gymnastics will keep you very limber and are great for coordination and strength. Flexibility is an important part of ski training, and is all too often neglected.

The major part of your distance hours are likely to be spent with some of the first eight activities, as they are the best ones for developing cardiovascular endurance. The others are mostly for strength and diversity. Use training methods you enjoy most to log the necessary hours you've decided to spend. Cycling is a good activity for spring through early fall. Summer skiing is fun and should be very low profile. It's a good time to get off the beaten trail and go for some fun touring. Many places where you can summer ski also offer Alpine skiing. If roller skiing isn't already part of your everyday program, it is probably a good idea to do a fair amount in the late-summer and fall. This will help tune up those muscles specific to skiing, and will make the transition from dry-land training to skiing easier when the snow flies.

One way to organize your yearly program is to concentrate on distance and strength training from April to November. This will form your base for winter racing. Then, as it gets closer to the racing season, increase the intensity of your workouts. This will cause training volumes to drop. It's all too easy to train too intensely in the summer and fall. It's better to save it for racing!

Build your training volume from year to year at a reasonable pace. A 12 to 20 percent increase each year is enough in most cases, until you reach the volume that's right for you. If you're just beginning to train, and you don't have a very active background, it's probably a good idea to begin with a low volume of about 20 hours a month, or 200 to 250 hours per year. If you are already very active and consider yourself in pretty good shape, start with more—whatever you can handle comfortably.

As you slowly increase the volume each year, be attentive to your body to insure that it doesn't become overtrained. Some people can handle tremendous volumes of around 1,000 hours a year; others reach their capacity at 400 hours. If you compare your training with others, do it objectively. A program that is successful for someone else may not be for you.

Intensity plays an important role. The higher the intensity, the less volume you can handle. It is particularly important for those who race long distances to concentrate on volume during the off-season, while saving high-intensity training for the racing season. This is not to say that there should be no intensity in the off-season; but you should not do as many all-out intervals. The solution is to vary the pace of your distance training on different days from a very slow pace to faster ones. But, don't go at race pace. You might practice monitoring your pulse rate during workouts to see how it varies with the pace. Generally, when you reach 170 beats per minute, this is beginning to get a bit intense. Take your pulse for 6 seconds and multiply by 10.

Listen to your body. It will probably let you know if there are problems with your training program in one of the following ways:

1. continuously feeling tired and uninspired to train
2. frequent sickness like colds or bronchitis
3. frequent injuries, muscle strains, and pulls
4. loss of weight

If you are having any of these problems, there is a possibility you are overtraining, or are not getting sufficient rest and recovery between workouts. Overtraining can mean you're training either too many hours or too intensely. If these problems arise while you are doing double workouts, single workouts may be more comfortable. A happy, well-trained body feels peppy and eager for workouts.

Because it is a total body sport, cross-country requires one of the highest energy outputs of any sport. Combine this with the long hours needed for increasing your endurance and you have quite a combination. For these reasons, it's crucial that your body recover between workouts, or it will begin to break down. Because recovery time is so important to training for cross-country, be extremely careful about altitude training if you are used to training near sea level. It takes longer to recover from a workout at high altitudes (5,000 feet and up) than it does from the same workout at 1,000 feet. If you don't decrease your volume sufficiently to allow for this, you will run into trouble. This will also mean that you cannot ski as fast or as powerfully as before, which could result in a loss of power. This, however, is not a problem for those who live at higher altitudes. This problem will gradually take care of itself as the athlete becomes acclimated, usually in 3 to 6 weeks. While altitude training is thought to be favorable for long-distance runners, its value is still being studied for long-distance skiing, where power and strength become major factors. Endurance is the only significant factor common to both.

When looking for early snow in November, high altitude areas are the only places with sufficient snow. As long as you are conscious of the problems involved, you can make the most of the situation. When the snow begins falling at lower elevations, you should move down to these areas to get tempo and power back into your skiing. When descending, some people notice that they feel especially strong for 3 to 5 days.

One approach to managing the year's training is to make the spring (April to June) an easy, relaxed season. You may benefit from reducing your hours after the racing season. This is the time to get fully recovered, to take care of any injuries or problems, and to plan for the year ahead and the excitement to come. Summer is the time to get in a lot of long slow distance: intensity is low; fun is the key. Fall is also a time for long slow distance, low intensity workouts. Remember, the most important races aren't until mid-January to March. You can begin to get your skiing legs under you in November or December. Until you can start skiing, roller skiing is a good substitute.

RACING SEASON

In December, you might start slowly increasing your intensity. If you have a good distance base to work from, you can easily build to good racing form in a matter of just 4 to 6 weeks. But don't rush; if you want a nice long peak, you must build it slowly. By the end of January, you should be flying. With some experience, you can learn to hold your peak pretty well through the rest of the racing season.

The racing season is not a time to increase your training volume. This is the time to maximize what you have already built up to this point. To perform well, it is essential to be well rested. During the racing season training hours will drop and your intensity will increase, due largely to racing and shorter workouts. The time between races should be spent doing whatever it takes to recover the quickest, so you will be prepared for the next race.

During the meat of the racing season there is very little long-distance skiing. Most time is spent racing, recovering, resting for a race, traveling between races, and maintenance skiing. A typical maintenance workout between weekend races might involve skiing 10 to 15 kilometers, with a few, quick natural intervals to stay in tune—but nothing too long or tiring.

Competition usually creates a lot of pressure and anxiety. I find that the best way to deal with this is simply to do your best. Rather than thinking about beating your competition and worrying about what they have done to prepare for the race, just think about your own strategy. Prepare yourself for the race the best way you know how and race the best you can. After the race, make a fair evaluation of what happened. If it was good, how can you make it happen again? If it wasn't, what should you do differently next time?

It takes a lot of time, experience, and training to race to one's potential. Getting in shape is really only half the battle; this is merely where racing begins. You need to call on the upper limits of your body and mind. They are usually a lot higher than you think!

A relaxed and collected mind is essential at the start and during a race. Only in this state is the racer free to concentrate on racing with efficiency and to receive vital information about the body. Like the race car driver who must be sensitive to the way his car engine is performing, the skier must learn to read and interpret the messages his body sends him as he races. If he is overly tense or nervous and in a panic, the result might be an inefficient "thrash" technique.

Experience will help you understand the variables involved in waxing your skis properly for a race. The conditions for each race will always be different, and several wax combinations will work on any given day. But there is usually one perfect combination; the trick is finding it. Some of the variables to consider in choosing the right wax are: temperature, humidity, track hardness and general condition, and how these factors are likely to change during the race. You must also take into account how abrasive the snow is, the length of the course, and the terrain you must negotiate. Once you think you've found the right wax, you need to determine how it should be applied for best adhesion, speed, and kick. How long should the kicking wax be and how thick? Where should it be applied, given the placement of the camber pocket, the stiffness, and your personal style of skiing?

JUNIORS

Much of the strength and endurance required for racing comes only with full adult maturity. Be wise in how you build your training base during the teenage years. Avoid hurrying and training too hard too early. You should build your training slowly from year to year—so slowly you can't even notice it. The best thing is to ski as much as possible, so that it becomes second nature. During the teens, plan a fun, low-key training program. By doing this, you will build a good base to work from later. You ought to gear yourself for your best performances sometime after age twenty, perhaps nineteen for some women.

A regimented training program should not even be considered for kids under thirteen. Skiing should be very low-key, and fun. Training and racing at this age are best left to the child's own initiative.

21

Training for Racing
by Trina Hosmer

I am not going to write this article from the point of view of a former member of the U.S. Ski Team. Instead, I would like to write it from the perspective of an athlete who races as a serious hobby, like most of the cross-country ski racers. Training at the level of a member of the U.S. Ski Team is an unrealistic endeavor for the majority of ski racers. While on that team, I had most of the day to train or at least it was the most important thing I had to do each day. Now, as a mother of two, and a wife with a full-time job, my whole approach and attitude toward training have changed. Training must fit a life-style that makes many other demands on my time. The vast majority of today's racers are in this same situation, and I hope they will benefit from this article.

First and foremost, training is not the most important activity of each day. Training should be enjoyable, and possibly used as an outlet for built-up tensions from work, from being a parent, and so on. Given that there is limited time to train, one must be well organized and effective during training sessions. There is not time for a half-hour warm-up and warm-down, an hour to travel someplace just to get in two workouts a day, plus 10 hours of sleep a night. Plan what time you have available each day, and then organize a yearly program so you can bene-fit the most from the time spent. My yearly program takes from 1 to 1½ hours each day. It will certainly never get me to the level of performance of the U.S. Ski Team (although I came close in 1976-77), but it does allow me to compete at a serious level and feel competitive. (I must disregard this past season when I was a little too pregnant to charge the hills.)

When the racing season ends, usually in March for me, spring training starts. The first task involves learning to run effectively again. The old legs, cushioned by the soft snow all winter, take some time to adjust to the shock of daily running. Three to four weeks of easy running, trying to average 6-8 miles daily, usually does the job.

After that month, I am ready to do some effective training. By this time, May has arrived, meaning June track meets are only a month away. I enjoy competing and find these track meets an incentive to keep a good training program. To prepare for them, I do interval training on the track once or twice a week. The interval training is excellent for the cardiovascular system, but does little for strength building. To supplement the strength building, I try to pull the Exer-genie daily, do push-ups, pull-ups, and wood-cutting and hauling on the weekends. Because I am a female, I feel that strength training is a very important part of my program. Somehow, though, the thought of going inside a building at this beautiful time of year to carry out a weight program on the Universal gym machine is appalling. I do not have a roller board, but I feel it is excellent for building body strength. This could be installed outside along with the Exer-genie to permit daily use. Serious weight training begins in the late summer and fall.

After the heat of July and August and the summer track meets are over, I begin my roller skiing and hill training. I try to roller-ski twice a week—usually up pretty good hills, rather than doing long-distance skis. I do not have the time for 2- to 3-hour roller-skis, so I concentrate on shorter, more intense workouts. My hill training in late summer consists of hiking with a child on my back. I cannot think of a better workout. Also, this is something I can do with the whole family, so I can spend a longer time working out.

On the days when I do not roller ski or hike, I run. One running workout I do involves intervals over hilly terrain. I try to pick a loop of about a mile, and repeat this several times with a 5- to 10-minute recovery between each loop. During the recovery period, I do light stretching and flexibility exercises. I conclude every workout with 5 to 10 minutes of stretching, sit-ups, leg lifts, and push-ups. Stretching and flexibility exercises are very important, but are difficult to make yourself do when you are pressed for time. One suggestion is to try doing some of these when you are killing time sitting at a desk, sitting in the car, cooking dinner, and so on. If you think about it, there are lots of little stretching exercises one can sneak in throughout the day.

As fall approaches and the days become cooler, I force myself to go inside the weight room for a 20- to 30-minute weight workout, 2 or 3 times a week, followed by easy running. I concentrate on: bench press, military press, pulling weights in double-pull and diagonal motions, and leg lifts. I do 3 sets of each exercise, 10 repeats for each set. As much as I dislike this kind of training (pushing and straining on a Universal), it seems to be the most effective and quickest way for me to gain added strength.

Since the weather has become cool enough, I begin my intense hill training. I pick a steep hill one-quarter to one-half mile long and run this as hard as I can, then jog back down, and repeat. Because it is so steep, my legs are burning when I reach the top. My lungs also burn from hard breathing. I continue with roller-skiing and the longer intervals on rolling terrain.

I get more excited about my training in the fall because the winter and ski racing are not far away. But since my time is still limited, my workouts just become more intense. On weekends, because the fall colors are so beautiful, I spend more time on long, easy runs for endurance training. This also helps to relax me after intense training during the week.

When snow arrives, the real training begins. I would like to think I could just ski for 2-3 weeks daily and then begin racing. But those days only occurred while I was a member of the U.S. Ski Team. In fact, I must admit that my winter ski-training program frustrates me at times. I would like to be able to ski daily because this is what I love to do. But time just does not permit this luxury. So I end up skiing a couple of times during the week and both days on weekends—which is not enough. On the days I am not skiing, I run, continue to weight train, and do intervals on the steep hills. Since I spend so much more time on days that I ski, these have to be shorter workout days.

If I were able to ski daily, I would vary my routine as I do with running. Some days I would concentrate on interval training, hill training, tempo training, or just long ski days. I race almost every weekend throughout the winter, so I have at least

Trina Hosmer strides out on her skis.

one good speed workout a week. However, during the winter race season I feel I get out of shape, cardiovascularly. I do not do enough hard running, and skiing just does not demand as much from the heart as running. But during the winter one should ski daily, if possible. The need to ski daily becomes evident as the season draws to a close. The females I was beating earlier, who have been skiing daily in their collegiate programs, become closer to me and some even beat me.

Though I love to ski and race, when the racing season is over I am quite happy. I now have another free day on weekends to catch up on house chores, plus it is now time to plan a training program for the next year. First I sit down and evaluate last year's training program. Some of the questions I ask myself are: If I had a good racing season, what new training techniques did I employ to produce this? If I had a poor year, what in my training was lacking? Or was my problem that too much was going on in my life to concentrate on skiing? In addition, I pick up some new training ideas throughout the winter, from talking with other ski racers and reading ski articles. After evaluating the previous year's training program, and prepared with some new ammunition, I am ready to plan the following year's program. I find it very satisfying to plan a year's program and goals, and then to gauge how successful my planning is on a day-to-day basis. This gives me an indication of how well I know myself. One of the greatest benefits of competitive sports is learning about yourself and the conditions under which you perform your best.

22

Citizen Racing

by Peter Davis

The citizen cross-country ski racer is a new breed. Only in the last five years or so have the numbers of races and participants in each of these events grown to become fairly commonplace. This, of course, reflects the tremendous growth of cross-country skiing. This growth is due largely to the increased consciousness about fitness, and to some extent disenchantment on the part of some skiers with the highly commercial aspect of downhill skiing.

In any given citizen race in the winter, skiers line up 200 to 300 strong, poised and ready to dash away at the sound of the gun. Such races may be anywhere from 10 to 70 kilometers. This represents a drastic change from five to ten years ago, when competitors were hard pressed to find a race every weekend. Whatever races could be located included the same few hard-core racers each time out. Now the picture has changed and there are races all over, each with hundreds of competitors.

DEFINING SOME TERMS

But before I go too far, a few terms need to be defined. The term *citizen racer* has come to refer collectively to all non-classified competitors in general—that is, recreational racers. The distances in these races are relatively short—10 to 40 kilometers. *Classified racers* include those who have joined their respective divisions of the United States Ski Association (USSA) and pursue racing somewhat more actively than citizen racers. Of course, one does not preclude the other, and many classified skiers enter recreational races (if they are sanctioned by the USSA). Similarly, many citizen skiers join their divisions of the USSA for various benefits and to support the sport.

One other term that needs clarification here is *ski mara-*

thoning. A phrase quite obviously borrowed from our running cousins, it technically refers to those races over 50-kilometers, the longest distance skied in classified competition.* Recently, various race organizers seem to have begun competing to see who can host the longest race. No doubt this trend will level off soon, dictated by reasonable human capabilities. But it is true that these long races hold some sort of mystical attraction for many recreational racers. Ski marathoners tend to be somewhat more serious than average citizen racers, but a bit less devoted than classified racers. But again there is considerable cross-pollination among these categories, with few skiers falling strictly into a particular group.

The focus of this piece is citizen and marathon ski racing. The subject matter will deal only with those aspects of cross-country skiing related to recreational skiing.

OFF-SEASON TRAINING

Several points in the area of off-season training deserve special mention for citizen racers. Improving your skiing technique is probably the most significant single factor linked to continued enjoyment of the sport. The vast majority of you are involved to varying degrees in other sports in the summer and fall. You can combine some form of ski-related exercise with your other activities, with a little imagination, therefore assisting yourself in improving your basic ski movements. This will help you become a more natural skier. Ultimately, you will waste less time getting used to the snow and your skis in the early winter.

There are the obvious choices, such as roller skiing, strength training, and hill bounding with poles (although these may not seem particularly interesting exercises in the summer months). Whether or not you choose these, there are some easily planned training tips to keep those skiing muscles in tune. When hiking, employ a long, "ski-walk" stride on the uphill. In biking, try to stand up when pedaling up long hills, and spin the "smaller" gears at a higher rpm. When running, cover cross-country-type

---

*Although the USSA has yet to define clearly the distance of a ski marathon, a ruling on this is forthcoming.

terrain, ski bounding or ski walking up the hills, much the same as you would on skis. When swimming, try to get in a lot of long-distance swims. If you are a tennis fanatic, set up some sort of simple arm exerciser, such as an Exer-genie or old bike inner tubes, to pull before or after the game. Most of these will add a dimension of variety to your normal off-season routine, as well.

SOME TIPS ON RACING TECHNIQUE

At least once a season you should make every effort to be videotaped while skiing. For most citizen racers I have dealt with, this has made a significant difference in the way those individuals perceive themselves as skiers. Self-image, or mental visual replay, is a tremendous force that is particularly important for older skiers who tend to lose perspective of their bodies in motion. After viewing a videotape of yourself, you will be able to visualize your motions. And with any degree of competent advice, you will be able to correct inefficient or poor technique.

One interesting by-product of skiing these long citizen and marathon races is that you don't ski too many of them before you begin to understand what efficient racing technique is all about. You simply cannot make repeated inefficient movements for 55 kilometers and feel very comfortable. I will not delve deeply into racing technique here, as it cannot be well instructed via the written word; a lot is lost in the translation.

The most common single technical flaw on the part of citizen racers, however, is skiing with the body positioned too far back. Correct, fast, and efficient cross-country skiing is done with the body up, forward, and riding with the gliding ski down the track. If this simple thought can be transposed to actual skiing movement, you will have most of your main competitors licked.

EQUIPMENT

The equipment needs of recreational racers are not significantly different from those of serious races. There are those who will never be happy with anything less than the latest and most exclusive equipment available. For these people, the psychological reassurance of having the "best" is probably far more important than any actual equipment differences. The best equipment advice that I can pass on to ski marathoners and citizen racers is to get skis and poles that are properly sized.

Though poles are easy to select, I am amazed how many racers are incorrectly fitted for poles. As a general rule, the pole should fall comfortably under the armpit, when the pole tip and your feet are on the same plane. If you are fairly strong in your upper body, you might consider a slightly longer pole, but only about 3 or 4 centimeters longer. Remember, on hilly terrain, longer poles are harder to manipulate, so select poles that will be practical for most of your racing.

More of a science is involved in selecting skis. Many citizen racers select skis of the correct length, but with the wrong camber, or stiffness, for the person's body weight. Skis that are too stiff require too much additional energy to compress the ski for proper kick. Skis that are too soft tend to be slower than other skis, since the kicking wax will be in contact with snow, even in the glide phase of the stride. A good way to avoid purchasing the wrong fiberglass skis for your build and needs is to recruit a racer whom you know has good skis and is about your same weight and build. Take that person with you to the ski shop, preferably along with his skis. Compare the camber of the racer's skis with the skis you plan to buy. If you can arrive at something fairly close, you probably won't be disappointed.

One other way of choosing skis, which perhaps is even more accurate, is to make your purchase at a shop that has access to a *ski deflection unit.* This apparatus, currently being developed and marketed by Inuit Ltd. of Minneapolis, is quite new, and for a while only a few shops will have them. These units test the stiffness of skis on the spot, giving you raw, objective data for comparing brands, models, and individual pairs. Citizen racers will benefit tremendously from these machines, since much of the field experience heretofore needed for choosing skis will be eliminated. Along with improved results, the skier's enjoyment of the sport will be greatly enhanced.

RACE PREPARATION

Since most citizen racers lack extensive experience in race preparation, this is an area where I can offer some insight. First, you should give some consideration to the number of races you want to tackle in a season and where they are located. Then, you should gear your training accordingly. Do not be too ambitious in mapping out your first few seasons. If, however, you have a couple of seasons behind you, and feel more confident about your abilities, then plan away. At that point, you should know what to expect from a season of training, racing, and traveling.

As you become more involved and caught up in cross-country training and racing, you will be drawn to some of the more established races in your area of the country. (See the list of major citizen races in the Appendix.) But also plan to participate in some smaller, shorter races before and between these larger races. If a lot of traveling is required to reach these races, allow yourself sufficient time to register and prepare before the race. If the race is well attended, try to arrive 3 to 4 hours prior to the start to allow time for dealing with crowds, parking, and other logistics. If you have not had the foresight to preregister for a big race, you should arrive at least one day in advance. But save yourself the aggravation, and register early in the season for races in which you want to compete.

Not only do many citizen racers participate in races throughout the country as part of their seasonal schedule, but many are beginning to travel to some of the major international events. There is already talk of a world league of the important citizen races, tentatively entitled the World Loppet. If this comes to pass, it will no doubt generate more interest in international citizen racing. This adds an element of romance to the sport, and provides a broad spectrum of participation and enjoyment in recreational cross-country racing.

If you are anticipating your first citizen race for the upcoming season, and need some guidance about the races available in your immediate area, you might start with your local ski shop. Some of their staff may be involved with racing or can direct you to persons or clubs associated with racing programs. The divisional offices of the USSA are generally the best sources on citizen races in each region. The various periodicals and publications that cover the sport in detail list races and events, as well.

Most citizen racers wonder what their training should consist of during the season, and before the big races. First, you should be doing a fair amount of distance skiing on a regular basis. But I would suggest incorporating alternating amounts of some type of speed work, such as *fartlek* or short, repeated intervals, during long-distance ski outings.* Generally speaking, you should build up distance skiing 2 to 3 weeks before your big races, and then gradually taper off distance and increase speed work. As the main races approach, be sure that you are well rested and sharp, not overtrained and fatigued.

OFF-SNOW TRAINING

If you are one of those unfortunate persons who loves to ski, but lives far from the snow, or if it has not yet arrived, you are probably wondering how to train and prepare for races with no snow. There's no question that you are in a less desirable position, but it is still possible to race and compete effectively without skiing every day. You must simply follow a regular routine of distance running and speed work, incorporating as many ski-related workouts as possible. Roller skiing is fine to a point, but toward the height of the season you should concentrate on a fair amount of hill intervals with ski poles rather than roller skiing. At this stage, you need to work on your tempo. Fast, powerful upper body work in conjunction with running, should help prepare you for the weekend racing.

Try to get the most from the snow, however. Arrive the day before and ski the course, or at least part of it: after the race, do some light skiing as well. This way, you will get the maximum ski training from your time on the snow. To a certain extent, it will carry you through the week of dry-land training.

THE PSYCHOLOGICAL EDGE

There is one facet of citizen racers that has always intrigued

---

Fartlek is Swedish for "speed-play." It involves skiing (or running) at various speeds over forest trails and through the countryside at will. It incorporates both aerobic and anaerobic training.

me. Due to their lack of competitive and skiing experience, most citizen racers approach competitions apprehensively, worried about their performance, equipment, and wax. But most of the older citizen racers are mature, experienced adults who seem to know their capabilities fairly well. This is a positive quality, which should enhance the enjoyment of the races. Experience will help recreational racers map out strategies for the upcoming events, such as focusing on beating a certain competitor, conquering a difficult section of the course, or merely concentrating on skiing well. If you feel intimidated either by the size or the level of a particular competition, avoid focusing on this. Rather, point toward more realistic and immediate objectives that will help you develop a positive attitude toward the race.

One's state of mind before a competition is a major factor in dictating actual performance. Sports psychologists have found that mental relaxation and confidence at race time, and subsequent competitive concentration, are the distinguishing factors between apparently equally trained and gifted athletes. Most citizen racers are able to keep their expectations well within their abilities, thus reducing frustration over not achieving set goals, as well as stress about competition.

Those persons who are not feeling confident at race time might try a few simple techniques to develop better prerace relaxation and concentration during the race. Refer to a previous race situation, and rehearse in your mind how that race went for you—its good and bad points. Concentrate on relaxing while you rehearse this event in your mind. Focus, in addition, on periods when you were either tense or not concentrating. If you are having difficulty with a particularly steep uphill, or a part of the course that bothers you, focus mentally on this area. Construct your approach positively in your mind, working out the way you would ski it under the best of circumstances. If you go through this type of mental rehearsal often enough before races, you will gradually become more relaxed and confident in competitive situations.

Some people perform better than others in certain types of snow conditions. If a particular condition, such as red klister-type snow for instance, is not your favorite, apply a bit of reverse psychology. If the conditions are bad, they are bad for all the racers. Use that knowledge to bolster your confidence in either your ability to apply the wax or to ski well in spite of it.

In the course of any season you will experience situations that seem to favor you in some way. Pay close attention to your feelings and the confidence that you develop from such circumstances; you can learn to apply the same state of mind to every race situation as you gain more experience. Similarly, if you consider yourself proficient in a certain aspect of your skiing, for instance, your double-poling or diagonal stride, use this as well to reinforce your mental confidence and therefore to improve your racing results.

THE RACE SITUATION

A common format for most citizen races and ski marathons is the mass start or wave start, where various categories of skiers start simultaneously. Few races follow the traditional racing format of timed interval starts. This is just the way citizen racing has evolved, and it offers another way of distinguishing between various forms of racing. Many people have a hard time remaining relaxed in the hubbub and tense atmosphere of several hundred people milling about in anticipation of the start. There is generally some confusion about the actual starting line. If there is one, it almost never remains a line, as people slowly edge their way in the direction of the race. False starts are common in smaller citizen races, but in the larger races, it is nearly impossible to call the crowd back. In the bigger races, be aware of this fact; know where and in what form the signal will come from and most important, watch the crowd. If people in front or in back of you are moving en masse, you had better do the same. It is hard to argue with a thousand other racers who have jumped the gun. Some races have been known to "thief start" as much as a half-hour early. So be there sufficiently early for this, should it happen. In cold weather, wear a warm-up top that can be discarded just before the start. Generally, the organizing committee will gather these fallen articles and transport them to a pickup point. It is good policy to dress warmly while waiting for the start. With the large numbers of people, it is usually hard to ski any distance to keep warm.

Once the race has begun, be aware of the people around you and what they are doing for the first few kilometers. Things tend to be fairly congested and a spill could cost you a lot of time in regaining your footing and battling the stampeding

Competitors in one of Europe's largest mass ski races, the 26-mile Engadin marathon in Switzerland. (Photo by Jerome McFadden)

racers. Broken equipment is not so much of a worry in these days of fiberglass skis and metal poles. (Carbon-fiber poles are not indestructible, however, so be a bit cautious if skiing with these in a large race.)

Try planting your poles out a bit farther from your body than usual, to establish both your territory and position in the race, as well as providing somewhat better stability. If one of your overzealous neighbors decides to borrow the track from you, a slight shove with a shoulder or elbow might be in order. During the hassle of the start, you may need to yell to people who are cutting you off to prevent potential problems. But do not try to *track* a person who has a solid line of skiers directly in front of him, he will not yield to you.* Only if there is a gap in front of a racer should you ask for track. But since many situations require split-second decisions, the best rule is do whatever you can that will not jeopardize another skier.

Once the race is underway, there are some things that you may tend to overlook, simply because there is a lot of company on the track. One is to let your mind wander, so you lose concentration on the race. Try to focus on the track about 20 feet ahead, watching for changes in the terrain or track conditions. This will improve your concentration on the race. Overtaking skiers frequently, within your established pace, is a great boost to your mental set. Of course, you will be passed by racers too. But focusing on those skiers' style or technique may help you maintain your concentration.

Inexperienced skiers tend to underestimate the value of feeding stations in a race, especially in marathon races. My best advice is to feed more and earlier in the race, since this is what you will be drawing on at the end. Sometimes it is hard to force yourself to consume two or three glasses of whatever is being served, while you are still eager and fresh. But you will pay for it later, when the lack of available muscle glycogen hits you. Then, it is too late to feed and have it do any real good. Avoid consuming fluids with large amounts of sugar, since

---

*To *track* another skier involves passing the skier in the same track. If a person calls out "track," the slower skier is expected to step aside momentarily so the person behind can pass.

they tend to "let you down" fairly soon after taking them. Race organizers should serve unsweetened juices, or the commercially available electrolyte replacement fluids at a lukewarm temperature, along with some easily digestible solid foods for less competitive skiers wishing to have a full snack.

AFTER THE RACE

Following any race, you should make a specific effort to calm down. Then, collect your equipment, and either head to a warm building or put on some warmer clothes. Before too much time passes, you should strip from the waist up and replace these wet clothes with dry ones. In the postrace excitement, many skiers overlook personal care. It is important to take steps to ensure that your body recovers as soon as possible to a normal state. Body resistance is lowest following a race, especially after a marathon. Without proper care, you are lowering your resistance to colds, flu, etcetera. Following a major event, be sure to get extra rest, make a special effort to replace fluids that have been lost, and take a recovery period of 2 or 3 days.

THE FUTURE

It's exciting to me picturing the hundreds of recreational racers skiing in various competitions across the country. The personal and physical challenge of skiing, and the potential fitness levels that skiers can reach give me great hope. I expect that the sport will continue to grow for many years to come, since cross-country skiing offers a wide range of individual challenge and freedom—from day tours to the excitement of racing.

APPENDIX

MINIMUM EQUIPMENT LIST

Day Tour
Personal Items

Skis, shoes, poles
Pants, shirt, sweater, hat,
  and socks (made of a
  material such as wool
  that retains warmth
  when wet)
Gaiters
Liter water bottle
Rain or storm shell
Pocket knife, can opener
Waterproof matches,
  candles, butane lighter
Sunglasses, sun cream

Day Tour
Community Items

Rucksack
Map and compass
Spare ski tip and spare basket
Flashlight
Wax
Space blanket
Lunches and emergency food
First-aid kit
Repair kit:
  screwdriver, pliers,
  wood screws, steel wool,
  strapping tape, five-minute
  epoxy, dot rivets, wire,
  nylon cord
Toilet paper

Parties traveling over avalanche terrain should carry avalanche beacons and snow shovels.

Additional Gear for Snow Camping

Personal
Soft pack with waist belt
PolarGuard or dacron parka
  and sleeping bag
Extra clothing; bandana, socks
Spoon, bowl, insulated cup
Toiletries
Foam sleeping pad

Community
Snow shovel
Tent
Stove, fuel, pots
Plastic splint
Food

Optional: wind shell, wind pants, PolarGuard booties, candle lantern, camera, books, chess set

WAXING TABLE

Snow Type	Temperature Range		EX-ELIT Sweden
	°C	°F	
FALLING AND NEW SNOW			
Very Cold (light powder)	−12° and below	10° and below	Black
Extremely Dry (falling powder)	−8° to 15°	5° to 18°	Black
Very Dry (powdery; blows easily)	−3° to −10°	14° to 27°	Green
Dry (blows with difficulty)	−1° to −5°	23° to 30°	Blue
Borderline Dry (barely blows)	0° to −1°	30° to 32°	Blue
Transition (clumps in gloved hand)	0° to −1°	32° to 34°	Violet/Red
Mushy (rolling snowballs dig in)	0° to +3°	32° to 37°	Gold
Wet (hand soaking wet after squeezing)	+2° to +6°	35° to 42°	Tö Kristall klister
SETTLED SNOW			
Very Cold (light powder)	−12° and below	10° and below	Black
Very Dry (small crystals will blow)	−8° to −15°	5° to 18°	Green
Dry (small crystals will form snowballs)	−1° to −10°	14° to 30°	Blue
Transition (large crystals, corns, or clumps)	−1° to +1°	30° to 34°	Violet/Red
Mushy (hand wet after squeezing)	0° to +3°	32° to 37°	Red/Tö klister
Wet (slushy)	+2° to +6°	35° to 42°	Tö klister
ALTERED SNOW			
"Skare"—Dry, Hard, Ice, Crust, etc.	−5° and below	21° and below	Skar klister
Crusty, but softer to mushy and wet	−6° to +1°	22° to 34°	Skar & Tö Kristall klisters mixed
Wet Slush	0° to +6°	32° to 42°	Tö klister med tjära

Note: Klisters are in tubes, and all other waxes are in cans. The listings given are only guidelines. Read the manufacturer's directions on the can or tube before you wax.

WAXING TABLE

FALL-LINE United States	REX Finland	RODE Italy	SWIX Norway	TOKO Switzerland
Light Green	Special 8571	Light Green	Polar	Green Special
Green	Light Green	Light Green	Special Green	Green Special
Green	Green	Green	Green	Green
Blue	Blue	Blue	Blue	Blue
Blue	Blue Special	Blue Super	Blue Extra	Violet
Purple	Violet	Violet	Violet, Red, Red Special	Red
Yellow	Yellow	Yellow	Yellow	Yellow
Red	Red klister	Red	Yellow klister	Yellow/Red klister
Light Green	Special 8571	Light Green	Polar	Green Special
Green	Light Green/ Green	Green	Special Green/ Green	Green/Special Green
Blue	Blue	Blue	Blue/Extra Blue	Blue
Purple	Violet/ Violet klister	Violet/ Violet klister	Extra Blue/ Violet	Violet
Red/Purple klister	Red/Red klister	Red/Red klister	Red/Red Special/ Violet klister	Yellow
Red klister	Red klister	Silver klister/ Red klister	Red klister	Red klister/ Violet klister
Blue klister	Blue klister	Blue klister	Blue klister	Blue klister
Purple klister	Silver klister	Violet klister	Violet klis- ter/Silver racing klister	Violet klister
Red klister	Silver klister	Silver klister	Red klister	Silver klister

Source: With slight modifications, from *Nordic Touring and Cross Country Skiing* by Michael Brady, 4th edition, 1977, Dreyers Forlag, by permission of the publisher.

SIMPLIFIED TWO-WAX SYSTEMS

SYSTEM	TYPE OF SNOW	TEMP. (F)	WAX
Swix Starter	Dry	up to 32°	Gold
	Wet	above 32°	Silver
Rex Universal	Dry	up to 32°	Minus
	Wet	above 32°	Plus*
Toko Touring	Dry	up to 32°	Minus
	Wet	above 32°	Plus
Jackrabbit**	Dry	up to 32°	Dry
	Wet	above 32°	Wet
Holley	Dry	up to 32°	Dry***
	Wet	above 32°	Wet

* *Rex "Plus" comes in a klister-type tube. (Most of the rest are in hard wax tins.)*
** *Jackrabbit wet and dry come in cake form.*
*** *Holley waxes are liquids, applied like liquid shoe polish.*

Note: Around freezing (32 degrees F), all two-wax systems are applied roughly if using the dry-condition wax, or smoothly if using the wet-condition wax.

WILDERNESS FIRST-AID KIT

Prepared by Gale Gregory

On every overnight trip you should carry along a fairly complete first-aid kit. Most kits sold in stores are not worth the bother to buy or carry. You can assemble a far better one yourself with a little help from your doctor. Completed, it will weigh less than a pound, and should handle any type of medical emergency until professional help can be reached. You can take this kit on camping trips all year around, but, of course, you won't need a snake-bite kit or poison oak lotion in winter.

Your winter first-aid kit should include the following:

- *Band-Aids*—10 of them, 1" wide, for blisters, scratches, etc.
- *Butterfly closures*—10, medium size, for cuts and lacerations that don't require sutures.
- *Sterile gauze pads*—6, 4"x 4", for dressing wounds and to use as compresses to stop bleeding.
- *Eye pads*—2, for eye injuries and snow blindness.
- *Roller gauze*—one package, 2" wide, for dressing wounds and holding splints.
- *Adhesive tape*—1" wide, at least 5 yards.
- *Ace bandage*—4" wide, for support, splints, sprains.
- *Aluminum finger splint*—Broken fingers are a fairly common outdoor occurrence.

- *Neosporin ointment*—One of the most common outdoor injuries in winter is the first- or second-degree burn. Fingers are always being poked too close to stoves and fires. The best treatment for small-area burns is plunging the injured part in ice water for a few minutes. In winter camping situations, however, frostbite is an ever-present danger, so do not overdo this treatment. Coat the burn with ointment, and bandage loosely.

- *Aspirin and codeine*—20 aspirin tablets and 10 ½-gram codeine tablets for relief of pain (stomach upsets, for instance, intensify with increasing altitude). Ask your doctor to prescribe the codeine separately, in case it must be given to someone with an aspirin sensitivity.

- *Antibiotics*—As prescribed by a physician, antibiotics can be used to combat infection. These drugs are not usually needed on overnight trips, but should be carried on longer journeys. It is important to know that any antibiotic should not be taken just once or twice. The course of treatment must be continued for at least 3 days so the infection does not recur.

- *Garamycin eye solution*—Useful for any eye injury or snow blindness. Use in affected eye 3 or 4 times daily and keep the eye bandaged.

Note: Some of these drugs require a doctor's prescription and should be used with his guidance.

273

MAJOR CITIZEN SKI RACES

EASTERN U.S.:   Paul Revere Cup   Concord, Mass.
                    Stowe Derby   Stowe, Vt.
                    Washington's
                        Birthday Race   Brattleboro, Vt.
                    American Marathon   Brandon, Vt.
                    The Fleischman Marathon Waterville Valley, N.H.

MIDWESTERN U.S.: Mora Vassa   Mora, Minn.
                    V.J.C. Tour   Minneapolis, Minn.
                    North American Vasa   Traverse City, Mich.
                    American Birkebeiner   Telemark, Wis.

WESTERN U.S.:   Frisco Gold Rush   Frisco, Colo.
                    Kongsberger Race   Seattle, Wash.
                    Rabbit Ears Classic   Steamboat Springs,
                                                  Colo.

                    Mammoth Mountain
                        Marathon   Mammoth, Calif.

INTERNATIONAL: Dolomitenlauf   Austria
                    Marcialonga   Italy
                    Konig Ludwigslauf   West Germany
                    Finlandia   Finland
                    Riviere Rouge   Canada
                    Canadian Ski Marathon   Canada
                    Vasaloppet   Sweden
                    Engadin   Switzerland
                    Norwegian Birkebeiner   Norway

Note: This is by no means a complete listing of all citizen races in the United States or the world. The list grows dramatically each year, and is hard to keep up with. The above races merely represent a few of the more traditional and established events. For a complete listing in your area, contact your local USSA divisional office, or you may contact:

Chairman
USSA National Citizen Race
Hickory Hollow
Dundee, IL 60118

CONTRIBUTORS

Ned Baldwin has been an avid cross-country skier and competitor for over 30 years. He led the Yale ski team in Nordic events and has twice been a member of the winning team in the 90-mile Canadian Ski Marathon. He lives in Toronto where he practices architecture. He has written books on cross-country skiing, of which his most recent is *Skiing Cross Country*.

Steve Barnett is the author of *Cross-Country Downhill*. His book details techniques for skiing the wide variety of snow conditions and slopes found when using Nordic skis for mountain travel.

David Beck is an avalanche consultant, veteran tourer, and unabashed lover of the winter wilderness. He has been director of Sequoia Touring in Sequoia National Park in California. He is the author of *Ski Tours in California*.

David R. Brower has been leading conservation battles and writing and editing books for over 40 years. From 1952-69, he served as executive director of the Sierra Club. He founded Friends of the Earth in 1969, and now serves as its president and general editor of books. His skiing and climbing have taken him all over the California high country.

Eric Burr is a professional ski patrolman, a Nordic ski instructor, and a part-time Nordic guide in California. His articles have appeared in *Nordic World*.

Peter Davis is director and coach at Telemark Academy in Cable, Wisconsin, which has one of the most highly regarded cross-country academic/ training programs in the U.S. He is currently Central Division regional coach for the U.S. Ski Team, and served as assistant coach at the 1978 World Nordic Ski Championships in Lahti, Finland, and as coach for the 1977 World Junior Championships in Ste. Croix, Switzerland. He was a member of the U.S. Ski Team for 6 years. He also directs two summer cross-country ski camps on each coast in the month of June. He is married and has two children.

Art Dickenson, M.D., is director of the Human Performance Laboratory at the University of Colorado in Boulder, and is head trainer for the U.S. Nordic Ski Team. His monthly column, "Nordic Medics," has appeared in *Nordic World*.

John Dostal lives in Stowe, Vermont, and teaches skiing at the Trapp Family Lodge.

275

CONTRIBUTORS

Sally and Daniel Ford are members of the Ski Touring Council and authors of *25 Ski Tours in the White Mountains* and *25 Ski Tours in the Green Mountains.* Sally edits books and Dan writes novels. They live in Durham, New Hampshire, with their daughter Kate, who if the truth be known prefers downhill skiing.

Ned Gillette, a former member of the U.S. Olympic Cross-Country Ski Team, is director of ski touring at the Trapp Family Lodge. He is a writer and photographer, and has been involved with several ski expeditions in Alaska. Formerly, he was winter director of the Yosemite Mountaineering School.

Bob Gray was a member of the U.S. Ski Team for 14 years, a two-time Olympian, and the number one ranked U.S. skier in the 1972-73 season. He currently runs the Green Mountain Touring Center, and has a farm in Hartland, Vermont.

Gale Gregory is an experienced cross-country skier, who has participated in several winter rescues. He has contributed to *Nordic World,* and wrote a chapter in *Snow Camping.*

John Hamburger is senior book editor at World Publications. Besides skiing, he has written in the areas of running, music, the environment, and fiction. He was a contributing author to *Politics as if Survival Mattered* and the *New Guide to Distance Running.* Previously, he was special editor for books at Friends of the Earth and was a freelance book editor for various publishers.

Trina Hosmer was one of the top competitors on the U.S. Ski Team from 1970-74. She combined skiing and running, and during 1971 was also a member of the U.S. National Cross-Country Team (running). In 1971, she qualified as a member of the U.S. Track Team in the 1,500 meters. She still enjoys citizen racing, and works as a computer programmer.

Bill Koch became the first American ever to win an Olympic medal in cross-country skiing, when he placed second in the 30 kilometers at the 1976 Winter Olympics. He began skiing at the age of two, and as he grew up skied to and from school every day. After a difficult year in 1977, in which he became discouraged about racing, Bill is returning to racing with renewed enthusiasm. His articles have appeared in *Nordic Skiing* magazine.

Wayne Merry is a mountaineer, a Nordic skier, and an author, who has spent many years in the north. He was formerly chief ranger at Mount McKinley National Park, and now is a wilderness trek guide in Atlin, British Columbia. He created Yosemite Mountaineering, with its extensive cross-country program, made the first ski crossing of Alaska's Brooks Range, and has done many extended treks on skis in Canada and Alaska.

Rob Schultheis, a contributing editor to *Outside* magazine and a staff writer for *Mountain Gazette,* has lived and skied in the Colorado Rockies for the past 14 years. He is currently completing a book, *Badlands*, about places of power in the American West, and resides in the Great Basin somewhere between Aspen and Bishop.

Richard M. Suinn, Ph.D., has written 4 books and more than 50 scholarly articles. He has worked as a psychologist with the U.S. Nordic Ski Team. Apart from his work with Olympic athletes, Suinn is professor and head of the Department of Psychology at Colorado State University.

Lito Tejada-Flores was born high in the Bolivian Andes, and raised in Southern California. A rock-climber since the age of thirteen, he started skiing at twenty-four, became a ski teacher, and later technical vice president of the Far West Ski Instructor's Association. With Allen Steck, he coauthored *Wilderness Skiing.* His second book, *Wildwater*, is a Sierra Club guide to kayaking and whitewater river running. He spends 3 seasons a year in Telluride, Colorado, and works in the winter as technical director of the Squaw Valley Ski School in California.

Steve Williams was special cross-country coach for the U.S. Ski Team. He has written articles on all aspects of cross-country racing. A former U.S. Ski Team member, he was a former editor of the U.S. Ski Team's *Coaches and Sports Medicine Journal.* He has been product manager for Trak, Inc., the past 2 years, and now serves as a product design consultant for Trak. He now practices law in Gilford, New Hampshire.

Bob Woodward began skiing at an early age in Colorado, and switched to cross-country skiing in the late 1960s. He has been a cross-country ski retailer (Sierra Designs), coach (University of California-Fischer summer cross-country camps), and director of a major touring center (Telemark). Bob lives in Bend, Oregon, and works as a freelance writer/photographer in the outdoor and sports fields.

Bill Yenne is a freelance illustrator, whose work has appeared in *Nordic World.* He works for a variety of publishers.

Kathleen Yoerg is an outdoors writer and author of *The Quiet Adventure Guide: to X-Country Ski Trails,* a guide to Midwest ski trails. She has recently moved to the Pacific Northwest. She brings the perspective of mountain skiing to this reflection on her extensive Midwest skiing experiences.

INDEX

A

Acadia National Park, 219
Aerobic metabolism, 79
Aerobic training, 87
Aging, and skiing, 86-87
Alaska, skiing in, ix, 145, 173, 224-41
Alpine skiing, 71, 118, 157, 158, 187, 197, 198, 202, 246
Altitude, effect of, 90-91
Altitude sickness, 202
American Birkebeiner Race, 213
Anaerobic efforts, 80
Ankle joint, injuries to, 97-98
Appalachian Mountain Club, 219, 221
Arctic, 224, 225, 227, 228-29, 239
Avalanche cord, 162
Avalanches, 139, 149, 155-62, 170, 184, 189, 194

B

Backpacks, 140-41, 169
Bicycling, for training, 75, 78, 84, 124, 244, 245, 246, 257
Bindings, ski, 18-20, 71, 138, 163, 200, 201, 237
Blood circulation, 80
Body temperature, 80, 81, 91-93, 140
Boots, ski, 16-18, 56, 138, 140, 172, 215
British Columbia, skiing in, 193-94
Brooks Range, 228, 229

C

Camber, ski, 25, 26, 27, 28, 68, 250, 259
Carbohydrate loading, 95-96
Carving around a turn, 53
Children, and skiing, 86-87, 250
Christianas, 66
Citizen racing, xv, 84, 89, 110, 256-66
Climbing over a fence on skis, 63, 65
Clothing for skiing, 33-35, 139-40, 155, 206-7, 215, 222
Cold, effect of. *See* Hypothermia
Compass reading. *See* Orientation
Conditioning. *See* Training
Corn-snow, skiing in, 66, 67, 70-71, 158, 179, 182, 185, 187, 189, 194
Costill, David, Ph.D., 96

D

Deep powder skiing, 54-65, 66-70
Depth hoar, 158, 194, 226, 230, 238, 239
Diagonal stride, 38-40, 116
Diet, 93-96
Dog teams, 225, 235-36
Donner Summit, 179-80, 183
Double-poling, 43-45, 78, 125, 129, 189, 200
Downhill technique, 45-53, 57, 60-62, 69-70, 187-89
Dry-land training. *See* Off-season training

**Other World Publications Books on
Cross-Country Skiing and Camping**

THE ORIENTEERING BOOK
Steve Andresen

ROCKY MOUNTAIN NATIONAL PARK TRAIL GUIDE
Erik Nilsson

SNOW CAMPING
by the editors of Nordic World *magazine*

TRAINING FOR NORDIC SKIING
edited by Dave Prokop

WINTER SAFETY HANDBOOK
by the editors of Nordic World *magazine*

World Publications
Box 366
Mountain View, CA 94042